A PERSONAL COUNTRY

A PERSONAL

A. C. Greene

COUNTRY

ILLUSTRATED BY

ANCEL NUNN

Foreword by LARRY L. KING

UNIVERSITY OF NORTH TEXAS PRESS
DENTON, TEXAS

Revised Edition
Manufactured in the United States of America

10 9 8 7 6 5 4 3 2 1

First Paperback Edition, 1998

Permissions
University of North Texas Press
P. O. Box 311336
Denton TX 76203
940-565-2142

The paper used in this book meets the minimum
requirements of the American National Standard for
Permanence of Paper for Printed Library materials, Z39.48.1984.

Library of Congress Cataloging-in-Publication Data

Greene, A. C. 1923–
A personal country.
Includes index.

1. Texas—Description and travel—1951– 2. Texas—Social life and
customs. 3. Greene, A. C., 1923– 4. Texas—Biography. I. Title.
F391.2G66 1979 976.4'06 79-7410
ISBN 1-57441-053-9

For

THE MOST IMPORTANT PERSON
IN MY LIFE

Contents

Foreword

THE "personal country" A. C. Greene writes about in this book also happens to be my own. We have shared not only a place—West Texas—and those paths and customs and myths indigenous to it, but also a common era. I was born thirty-two miles due east of his beloved Abilene, in the modest little village of Putnam, about the time he entered first grade. Herbert Hoover was president then and on the verge of sponsoring that Great Depression which the Greene and King families would keenly feel and never quite get over fearing. Our similarities do not end, but merely begin, with that time and place.

Each of us from childhood so loved books that we made early vows to write our own. Each served his writing apprenticeship for West Texas newspapers—he for the Abilene *Reporter News*, I for the Midland *Reporter-Telegram* and the Odessa *American*. It was great fun, even if our paltry salaries caused us to write with cheap cuts of meat weighing heavy in our bellies and with holes in our shoes. But I know of no way to better learn a place, and its people, than to attend its county fairs, courtroom disputes, football wars, civic gatherings, or other tribal rituals. We roamed the West Texas outback like gypsies, bucking its head winds and breathing its grit, seeing with adult eyes those places and events we had witnessed as children. Eventually we saw, heard, and observed enough to begin to fulfill the writer's lone duty—that of attempting to separate the myths from the realities.

I am confident that neither of us would have come to understand our roots half so well had we abandoned our shared native place earlier than we did, or had we failed to return periodically after our respective careers took us away—A. C. to Dallas and Austin, I to Washington and New York—so that we might make the necessary comparisons with a wider world. West Texas became our laboratory and our measuring stick, and in the heart's private country it always will remain our true home. It was the place where we first knew innocence. And the place where, as man must, we invariably began to shed it.

I read A. C. Greene's newspaper columns, book reviews, and editorials long before I met him. Indeed, it is something of a statistical quirk that we did not meet until the mid-1960's, so many were the shared friends and dreams. Once met, we discovered that we were neighbors of the spirit as well as of the map. Within minutes we learned that we had kin buried in the same cemeteries and that we sang the same hymns. I think we instantly recognized—as surely as two grizzled old West Texas ranchers would have recognized each other's cattle brands—that we had been forged, shaped, and marked by the same land, the same people, and even the same twangy accent. Many a night since have we shared the cup and midnight philosophies. We have shared—excuse me, Thomas Wolfe—"of time and a river" and much more. We have shared a personal country.

It is quite possible that we did fleetingly meet in our early, small world defined as "the Callahan Divide"—and simply did not know it. One of my earliest and most thrilling peregrinations occurred in 1937 when Putnam's second-graders were herded into family cars by teachers and mothers who had determined that our limited educational opportunities somehow might take a giant leap forward should we visit Abilene Airport. The excitement of the city (and Abilene *was* a huge city then, maybe 15,000 or even 20,000 people) proved too much. On the way back to my native village I disgraced the family name by upchucking when car sickness overwhelmed me during the dizzy rush down from the summit of Baird Hill. But maybe, before that low moment, as I ogled the tall buildings and street cars and the impressive single-engine flying machines of Abilene Airport, I saw A. C. Greene among those city sophisticates who at once impressed and alarmed me.

For the city meant Sin, make no mistake about it. Sodom and Gomorrah had received no less than had been coming to them, our preachers said, and my father, bred from generations of rural stock, reinforced the lesson at home. Even Putnam was too big for him, too crowded and too fraught with modernist meddlers—it containing upwards of 1,500 people in those long gone days and limiting a free man as to the number of milk cows or chickens he might legally keep within the "city" limits.

Quite without knowing it, A. C. and I witnessed the last of the horse culture in West Texas. As he writes in this book of thinking little or nothing about horses or mules pulling Abilene ice wagons and road graders, so I assumed nothing unusual in Putnam's farm-or-ranch based boys riding to school on horses they tied under mesquite trees on the school grounds and fed bundled roughage during the noon hour. My own father in times of inclement weather saddled up a fox-trotting paint horse, Old Prince, to deliver me to the schoolhouse door. It was a source of burning embarrassment that I was not permitted to mount a horse to school alone, as did numerous of my exact contemporaries. This was the price I paid for being born to a mother whose genes and temperament discerned disasters which my father—who at once worshipped her and was gently bullied by her—did not dare permit to happen because of blame certain to accrue solely to himself. Reading A. C. Greene's book, you will discover that my family held no monopoly on such strong, dark, and slyly Machiavellian women. I do not know what A. C. makes of this, but I personally think we owe them thanks for helping to make us crazy writers. Where else might we have so early learned those proper suspicions, guilts, and fears which are necessary both to the understanding of and to the making of drama?

The first twenty-five years of my life, except for a period of military service, were spent in West Texas; for another decade I was a part-time resident, dividing time between my home territory and the office of the West Texas congressman for whom I labored in Washington. When A. C. Greene writes of Crane, McCamey, Kermit, and other windy villages of the Texas desert, he brings me the sun, grit, and odors of the oilfields where I sweated during teenage summers. We had moved westward from my father's Old Home Place farm in Eastland County with the outbreak of World War II, following the oil boom and ultimately settling in Midland, so that my father might assist the war effort—and sagging family fortunes—by pissanting heavy objects in a pipeline crew. Though Midland was but a swift four-hour drive from the farm where he had been a boy, it never became "home" to the old man. Never mind that he spent the last twenty-seven of his almost eighty-three years there and died there; no, home was where the heart was. And he had left his heart behind on that October day in 1942 when we pulled up stakes and moved further west in unconscious imitation of the early pioneers.

I doubt whether such strong loyalties to a tiny piece

of ground exist in much of America today: after all, who can care that much about some bald, surburban plot in a housing sub-division of no history beyond that of the corporation formed to build it? One of the reasons *A Personal Country* strikes sparks and responses in me is because A. C. so obviously retains an old-fashioned love and respect for the land in which he was rooted and which first brought him to bloom. I know that he sometimes loves it, as I do, not because of, but despite, some of its darker sociopolitical preferences or parochial instincts or cultural neglects. Occasionally, when A. C. and I discuss the wonders and warps of our personal country over midnight grog, I get the notion we have much in common with Faulkner's young Quentin Compson, who tries, as a newcomer to Harvard circles, to articulate his love of his native South and suddenly finds himself blurting: "I *don't* hate it! I don't hate it, I *don't* . . ." Mr. Faulkner knew something of those tugs-of-war ever present in the human heart, yes, and of those frequent painful collisions between the heart and the head.

Every page in this book is a walk down memory lane for me. It brings back the language and the objects ("storm cellar . . . cut dog . . . tow-sacks . . . goobers") and the events (the Clyde tornado of 1938, Cisco's Santa Claus bank robbery) of another time, another place. It reminds me how uncompromisingly black is "country dark" with no street lights or neon signs to tint it, of old sights and smells long stored away in memory's attic-trunks, of old streams once waded and now dry. But you do not have to be a native of West Texas to share the basic emotions and experiences of this book. In recreating his special corner of America in a time when it was green to his eye, A. C. makes it and all special corners everywhere indelible in the memory of those who were there. He is writing of a universal theme—home, then and now—common to the universal experience. I believe that is a definition of literature, isn't it?

The world has changed; America has changed. Even Abilene. Putnam, too. Where Abilene is a going and growing entity of perhaps 100,000 now—and probably on the way to breeding the urban ills common to this era—Putnam has virtually been wiped out by a superhighway and now claims a population of a mere 203 souls, though I doubt you could round up even that many with an armed posse and search warrants.

A year or two ago, in the company of two of my three former children, I sought out the old concrete porch and steps which had sat snugly against the long-removed yellow house in which I had been born in Putnam. Gone, too, were the outbuildings and the small cow shed and rabbit hutches where my father had managed to preserve all that he could of his agrarian past. For a while I thought the old porch and steps had somehow disappeared. But, man's memory being fallible, I had looked for it in the wrong place and almost missed it. It was hidden in a tangle of mesquite trees, I remembered as bushes, tall winter grasses and hardy stubborn weeds, and it seemed only half its normal size. Nowhere could I find my barefoot baby footprint which, I was certain, had been impressed upon it during my diaper years. Little was in sight but wild growths and neglected old dirt streets slowly being reclaimed by them. I suppose, logically, it should have been a depressing experience. But as I stood on those old concrete steps, seeing in the mind's eye that which is not gone so much as merely used to be there, I felt a certain exhilaration and thought: *This is where it all began. This is my place.* I feel much the same when reading *A Personal Country.*

LARRY L. KING

Washington, D.C.

Some Words

I HAVE NOT SET OUT to write a history of West Texas, neither have I tried to do a guidebook. If this is a history, it is an emotional history of a boy and a man in a place, and part of that place in them.

Therefore, I have neglected vast corners of the tract because my path and my past went there for no significant occasions.

I haven't done a lot of research to discover new events. I haven't written about anything I wasn't moved to discover from private memory. Where there are facts related I have tried to relate them in as accurate a way as possible. When I have relied on hearsay or legend I have tried to remember to say so. Even so, I am sure some readers will recognize one or two of the stories herein as being among those universal classics of folk heritage. But in my relation of personal experiences, I have tried not to tell a single lie, unless Old Time has misguided my memory.

To describe my inheritance I have had to relate a lot of family secrets and other accumulata which come into one's life like salt and sauce come into one's food—not the nutrient but the taste of it. This means, of course, that a great deal of this book is autobiographical. This must be explained at once, for even my wife would be forced to deny me autobiographical necessity, although not so much as I myself would.

My West Texas is bounded by my experience, and is not so wide as it is deep. If I write of roads and of towns they are roads I have rutted by use; towns where I have kept an internal diary for the removal of individual bricks, the addition of a street light, or the demise of a hamburger stand.

But this does not imply, the reader will understand, that I have gained infallibility. I have only hoarded observation. There are a number of places and events which should go into a proper inventory of the region, and I have left them out. I have not spent many pages, for example, on cowboy and ranch life because, while always a paramount presence in West Texas, it was not strong in my emotional experience. Neither have I gone deeply into the economic story of oil in West Texas, even though it supplies an important peg on which to hang the area. Again the reason is experience.

No, the purpose of this book (and discussing purpose is a deadly pursuit for an author) is simply to find out, from one life in one region, if all of us are not gifted from the soil whence we sprang, seeded by the people, and watered by the times. And if I seem to spend too much time searching my own recollection, it is only to help the reader find the same identity.

A. C. GREENE

Paisano,

Austin, Texas

1968

A Debt

THERE ARE A DOZEN BOOKS concerning West Texas which have been so useful to me as to form new bones in my frame. I have tried to mention each in those parts of the text where I have relied on them but I want particularly to credit C. L. Sonnichsen's *I'll Die Before I'll Run* for helping straighten out the John Larn story for me, and J. Evetts Haley's *Charles Goodnight, Cowman and Plainsman.*

There are people, too, just as valuable as any source books, whose contributions I acknowledge with warm pride: Robert Nail, who went through heat and chill on my projects, and whose untimely death just before the manuscript was finished robbed me of much of the pleasure of writing it; Jake and Frances Mossiker, for giving me literary shelter; James H. Atkinson, a noble companion of my youth whose influence time has not severed; Raymond Thomason, Jr., generous with aid and humor, and Angus Cameron, the editor who first thought it might work.

This book was finished while I was a Dobie-Paisano Fellow, and the beauty and inspiration of the late J. Frank Dobie's Paisano, and the financial assistance and time afforded by the fellowship were instrumental in hastening the completion.

Finally, I humbly ask all my aunts and uncles, named or implied, that they forgive my misinterpretations and remember only my love.

A PERSONAL COUNTRY

1

A Place Called West Texas

GOING WEST, through Texas, you leave Fort Worth and come out suddenly onto a rolling, bare-hilled country that stretches away on every side. Without warning you have been set adrift on a billowy ocean of land.

Behind you have been pine forests and tangly river bottoms and blackland farms that crowded the highway. But here the plow has never been. This is ranching country. You notice windmills lonely in the long, sweeping pastures, and cattle, grazing on the far slopes, are like tiny figures set there to give some comprehensive scale to the landscape. There are no houses, no people, few roads, and scarcely any trees. The overwhelming sense is solitude, and you may begin to feel naked and defenseless, moving across so much openness.

But there is beauty here, the beauty of space and of freedom, and the beauty of the wind feeling its way along the brown, grassy swells and ruffling the yellow ridges. It is strong, stark beauty, having so few ornaments that each plane, each shadow and broken feature of the land, must play an intense part in the composition, subtly forcing the eye out to the horizon and up to the sky.

This stretch is the farthest eastern finger of another, broader, higher place; a place called West Texas. Its barren grandeur, which gives way within a half dozen miles to woods and creeks again, is a suitable preview of what lies west. The way you feel here, released by the openness or oppressed by so much space, is a premonition of the emotion that will overtake you when you reach that larger land.

It seems to me that this bit of West Texas Rolling Prairie (to give it its geological name) is thrown out as a hint or a warning to the traveler that he is approaching another kind of Texas from where he has been, a sub-Texas, unlike the rest of the state in landscape, in people, and in philosophy. It is a land for which the stranger should not be unprepared.

My spirit rises at the sight of this isolated prairie, as I know I am going toward home, even though this very piece of terrain once cost me an intended bride who, taking one bewildered look around her at the endless waves of land, fled back to New Jersey, promptly and forever. It

was a test, and she failed, through no fault of hers. But I am thankful that something so detached as a landscape could take an adequate measurement for me of so intimate a situation. People who do not like West Texas frequently cannot like West Texans. The land is too powerful in them and it is an excessive land.

I said I was going toward home when I headed toward West Texas, but the phrase is more symbolic than actual. I left West Texas several years ago, probably forever. I left it the way a wise son leaves his father and mother, and for a good many of the same reasons. It is an old story and millions of us can tell it.

But when I left West Texas it didn't leave me. Much of my adult life the people close to me have accused or excused what they considered my inexplicable actions with, "That's because he's from West Texas." I haven't always appreciated the differentiation but I accept the

general truth of it. I am a product of the place in ways obvious and ways intricate. It has stuck to me a great deal more than just by adding a nasal drawl to everything I speak and causing my tongue to say "piller" for "pillow," or "git" for "get." It has entered my values and judgments, given me many of my moral standards, and shaped (maybe warped) my ambitions.

Some of this grew from a childish ignorance, brought on by the cultural isolation of the place and its society, amusing to recount—but who knows how profound? For instance, I wanted to be an archaeologist, but I didn't know you could go to school and learn; I thought it was something passed along among families like royal blood. I might have been a librarian, except that in West Texas all librarians were female and I assumed the profession was restricted to women. My economic standards formed part of my situational ethics and when I was very young West Texas convinced me that the ultimate income a man needed was three dollars a day. This specific certainly enlarged, but it left shapes and traces of itself. All such things you outgrow—and I have—but you cannot scrub them from your blood—and I haven't. West Texas is too vigorous a soil to grow in.

This ability to identify so much with one's place of birth is becoming rare in American culture. I don't think my children have it and I have not tried to give it to them. They have lived in places that didn't strike up through the soles of their feet or assault their eyeballs. If there are fewer of us who retain our identity with a region there are fewer regions powerful enough to force an identity. In our mobility and our conformity, in our ability to shape our physical circumstances and adapt nature to our convenience, we are losing sectionalism, not just in its less desirable ways but in its meaningful sense.

All this lay undisturbed for years, this feeling for a

place, this realization of how deep the roots extended. In fact, for a good while I resented some of the interior proddings I felt and was annoyed when I thought my obsolete West Texas ethic was acting up. Then, in a rather short space of years, I lost most of the members of my family, and where I had grown up with an extraordinary circle of kin, I found myself having to reach halfway across the continent to find a relative.

Like leaving West Texas, this removal taught me something about myself. Separated from close relationship, I could recognize my inheritance without having to acknowledge it to anyone. The obligation was erased and suddenly the debt was increased. This, too, has happened to millions of us.

But in my own case I felt a double burden, because I knew, for the first time, how much the place and the past had created in my people what influenced me through them. I thought of the size and shape of the experiences that had made me and I wondered where and why it all began. How much of me was red dirt, was sand hills and mesquite under a hot, dry sun? How much was wind and long, empty plains? What was born of slow-spoken close-mindedness, gained from a frontier brush-arbor camp meeting, or what was begun in a dugout where a young girl looked in fright and hatred at the wilderness around her?

And I began to see something beyond the land and beyond my blood with the land in it. There were the others outside my blood who shaped me, for West Texas was, and is, as demanding a social environment as its natural elements are demanding. Its people were and are different from other people; sometimes delightfully, sometimes in frustrating manner. So I was bound to be different, too, for I had inherited some of all of it, even if involuntarily: the history, the suspicions, the tragedy and optimism, and (I am told) more than my share of the rigidity. Ah, our West Texas rigidity; preserving us, destroying us, driving us away emotionally or physically, or drawing us back. It drew me back.

So I BEGAN A JOURNEY, sometimes in the mind and in the memory, sometimes a literal journey to see it again. It was made for my own uses, and what I really wanted was to lead myself back to something concrete, to recover some ground which was indicative or might even have proved to be definitive. But it has not been altogether my journey alone. There is a universality to being born and growing up that does away with regions or even nations. If our lives are ever alike, it is at their beginnings. And so I say (for the final time) it is a story millions can tell.

2

The Boundaries of Its Life

YOU DO NOT HAVE TO REMOVE yourself very far from West Texas to have left it far behind. It is not duplicated in the regions immediately surrounding it.

Editors unfamiliar with the locality will occasionally change the term in a manuscript from "West Texas" to "west Texas," saying it is merely a geographical description. The west portion of Texas is certainly a great deal more than West Texas, but it is also somewhat less. The capital W reflects not just a direction but a set of the mind, a frame of outlook and expectation.

West Texas, for example, has nothing in common with Dallas (except to shop there), although Dallas lies not too many miles east of where West Texas begins. On the other hand, West Texas shares even less with El Paso, and that city is hundreds of miles farther west in Texas than is West Texas itself. So much of West Texas is an attitude brought on by the country and its natural forces, tempered by its history. In those adjoining regions, history was inherited slowly and differently and moral conditions have not been nearly so uniform. In West Texas most of the people think more alike.

So I would create a few boundaries for the place, defined more by instinct than the way it lies on a map. In the touring-car days of my boyhood my father would gear our way to the top of a steep climb known (for the nearby town) as Ranger Hill, and when he arrived at the top he would always announce (a man not given to profundity), "Well, we're back in West Texas." This was his personal boundary, and I give the incident more to stress this private kind of interpretation than to offer it as a line of demarcation. Just about everyone in West Texas has his own idea of where West Texas begins and ends. So do I.

I would begin it at the Brazos River, on the east, and extend it west for about four hundred miles to the Pecos River. (And this might be a good place to give the accepted West Texas pronunciation for those two rivers: *Brazz*-us and *Pay*-cus.) There are several particularly good reasons for starting West Texas at the Brazos. The first is history. "Beyond the Brazos" was the semiofficial description of the Texas frontier for several decades; too many decades and generations for the distinction not to have entered into the legends of the land. Legends can become attitudes, and in West Texas many of them have.

Nature, too, takes the Brazos for a dividing line. Several trees (the black gum, honey locust, and water oak among them) stop on the east bank.

Marking off West Texas from north to south is a little more difficult. The northern border is fairly exact along the Cap Rock, which is a tall abrupt escarpment rising two hundred or more feet from the rolling prairie. On top are the High Plains or Llano Estacado (Staked Plains), where you know very well you are in a different country. Then if you come east from the Cap Rock, along that tier of counties bordering the Red River, you have established a fairly workable north boundary—although some people in Lubbock (excluded by my line) might argue with you.

I hold to my separation because the nature of the land and the society support me.

Drawing a precise line along the south of West Texas is even less satisfactory. There are no sharp physical changes to make the division. Fortunately, the defining influences in West Texas seem to run east to west like its main highways, so the southern limits aren't so important. When the pre–Civil War settlers started coming up from the south toward West Texas it was something they were avoiding, not seeking, so they usually stopped at Brady or San Saba. But my purpose in defining West Texas isn't to quarrel over boundaries. It is to confine a few common points of view and ideas. The West Texas that produced me and still fascinates my social instincts is up to me to define.

Beyond these geographical lines, there is the matter of elevation which contributes to an identity. West Texas has an atmospheric similarity that comes mainly from the fact that it lies between one thousand and three thousand feet high. Much lower or much higher than these altitudes creates a different atmosphere. Below one thousand feet the humidity is high, the heat is sticky, and the south wind doesn't always cool things off. Above three thousand feet—as on the High Plains and beyond the Pecos—you find distinct changes in vegetation and in the way things are done with the land. And the winters get blizzardy. Above the Cap Rock is a tableland with some of the finest irrigated farming in the United States. In some places, along the escarpment's edge, these lush, green rows lie above but only a few hundred feet away from the roughest kind of West Texas dry ravine country, so dramatic is the change.

But to me West Texas is at least as well defined by its attitudes as by its statistics. That is why I place so much importance on the Brazos as a boundary. It lies not just between two regions but between two cultures, two societies. The Brazos was the old dare-line, where frontier life called you to taw.

Perhaps my reasoning is tinctured by the old voices I hear from my youth, speaking through yellow-white mustaches and beards, talking contemptuously of people "going back" to Sherman or Cleburne or Denton. "Back" was another place, not "here." "Going back" was defeat. It was giving up, selling out, letting something whip you instead of dying before you would admit you were whipped. And when they "went back" it caused them to creep away in the night, leaving an empty cabin or a string of unpaid bills. The old-timers were proud they had been able to hang on, regardless of what shape they were in, "here" where things were tough. Survival was their criterion.

I had a great-grandfather who let the drought of 1884 whip him in West Texas, just as it whipped a lot of good men (and continues to whip them). It drove him bankrupt, and it drove him "back." He didn't live long after that. It might have been the sound of rain falling on the sheet-iron roof of his little store "back there" that cut his remaining time short. I missed his death by thirty-five years, but I feel close to him. I, too, went back, although my reasons were toward a form of success rather than from failure. Even now you do not do it except with a taint of surrender. In West Texas the ability to stick confers a special kind of kinship on you. It also means native sons have a special place in West Texas when they stay, especially when they stay in the face of some talent or opportunity that should send them to other places. A great many of these native sons continue the line that grandfather brought to the frontier even if their own inclination is to get out. This leads to one of the special uses West Texas society can be put to; it forms a nicely controlled laboratory for studying history and the continuity of generations, for a great percentage of the history of the region has been witnessed by no more than three generations. There are thousands of persons in West Texas who have this special perspective, for, like me, they have heard the story of the land directly from the lips of the people who took it and subdued it. Until now this danger of worshipping the past has not been too obvious in West Texas because of the vigorous cycles of change which have picked the country up without letting it stagnate economically or culturally. The old Indian frontier culture died but was immediately succeeded by the excitement of the railroad culture with its opportunity to introduce civilization into a virgin land. This second phase of the frontier, when it closed, was replaced by an agricultural economy which was just putting to use new scientific and chemical discoveries with new implements and new tools to try out. When the new farming phase was ending—with some parts of West Texas recognized as being unfit for anything but grazing—then came oil to revitalize the lowering economic momentum. Except for some sagging during the Great Depression, oil swept West Texas along with a strong hand until the 1960's. After that the changes slowed, populations dropped, but the energy crisis introduced a new cycle. So, under the impetus of change, West Texas has not had time to sit at the feet of its monuments; the sons and grandsons were still competing with the memory of their ancestors, not bowing down to it.

There has been a great deal of movement within and into West Texas. It is an easy place for a newcomer to gain acceptance, and a lot of the country has been settled up or developed within the last three or four decades. This means that people get closely identified with communities or with certain ways of life or business and their fellow citizens take it for granted they have been there since (in old-timey usage) "who laid the chunk." Which reminds me of a matter of interpretation that arose one time when I was working on a West Texas newspaper. I became annoyed at the careless way some of the reporters were using words, and so I took an obituary to the editor to show him why. This piece of writing spoke of a man who had been born in Gatesville "but had been a native of Tuscola for the past thirty years." I said someone should instruct the staff what constituted a native. The editor agreed and passed a rule which baffled me at the time but which now seems like a workable West Texas decision. Henceforth, he decided, you could not call a man a native unless he had lived in a place at least forty years.

RAINFALL OR THE LACK OF IT, the thing that may have killed my great-grandfather, puts its mark on all West Texas life. Economy rides the seesaw from year to year, going up or falling down according to those few precious inches above or below normal rainfall. There are very few spots in the United States where the general population enjoys rain so much. Uninitiated radio and television weather experts will get called down by the natives (assumed or born) when they speak of "it's a beautiful day, not a cloud in the sky, the forecast calling for fair weather . . ." This may be pretty, in one sense, but not nearly so beautiful as a black, overcast day with the clouds threatening to shed tears at any minute, or a strong, wet south wind scudding the dark masses overhead. Then, with the crack of thunder and the silvery split of lightning, rain bursts over the land in a gully washer—and you have a truly beautiful day. Rain is scarcer in many parts of the world, but most of the time those places don't depend on it because they know it isn't coming. But West Texas lives right on the edge of its annual precipitation. Newspapers and television stations pay as much attention to the day-to-day moisture standings (so many inches above or below normal from this date last year, etc.) as Wall Street does to the Dow Jones stock averages.

Annual rainfall also forms a means of regional definition. One identification of West Texas is simply that it is dry. Dryness creates a way of life more demanding than the facts of heat or height or abnormal wetness. The too-dry region is hardest to accommodate by man because he is the thirstiest animal. Even when he is trying to adjust to dry living he consumes more water than he has any right to expect nature to supply. This is one of the ways in which rainfall influenced the history of West Texas. Up to the 1870's even the occasional scientific expert who wandered around it thought most of the area was uninhabitable. It was too dry for crops and humans. As one of the early Army officers reported, "This country will be unsuited to human use for a hundred years, if then anyone wants it."

What these investigators lacked was not information but imagination. They were basing their scorn on their experience of living on the eastern seaboard. (How often, decade after decade, has this old memory dogged West Texas, causing houses to be built against winter cold when they should have been built to alleviate summer heat, or causing farmers to stick with heartbreaking crops or fragile seeds because something in those who planted harked back too strongly.) But the old Anglo-Saxon greed for land, to own the very dirt, the rocks and the gravel, asserted itself, and the early settlers examined their hopes more than the experts' reports. They turned out to be more accurate than the geologists and biologists. There was more underground water than the scientists had guessed, it just took the mass-produced windmill to bring it to the surface. West Texans also discovered their soil to be quite fertile if there were sufficient water poured on it, and some kinds of crops even seemed to thrive on hotter, drier cultivation.

But the biggest single water fact West Texas learned was conservation. You had to catch and hold the water that fell and not depend on finding it. The hand-dug well was a possibility, but the cistern, which retained the rainstorms, was more realistic. Around the turn of the century West Texans began building dams to create lakes. With the development of modern earth-moving machinery, lake building became as important a municipal exercise as laying sewers or paving streets. West Texas is now wet with lakes and from an airplane looks as if someone had shattered an enormous mirror and flung the pieces. Water sports—boating, fishing, skiing—are the most popular pastimes in that broad country where, less than a century ago, on the same spot, cavalry troopers went mad from thirst or survived only by killing their horses and drinking the blood. (Before someone accuses me of quoting television drama as history, let me quote facts, that this occurred during Colonel Ranald Mackenzie's campaigns of the mid-1870's out near Lamesa and Colorado City where today the 6.6-billion-gallon Lake Thomas has been built.)

But to return to rainfall as a defining measurement of West Texas, we may say it is an area where no more than thirty and no less than twelve inches of moisture makes up the annual average precipitation. Palo Pinto, Parker,

Jack, Erath, and Comanche counties, along the eastern, or wet, side of West Texas, all catch thirty inches or so per year. Going west this figure decreases at a steady, and astonishing, rate of nearly three inches per county, which means that when you have reached the 100th meridian, only 125 miles from the Brazos, the rainfall is nearly ten inches less. On the far edge, along the Pecos, the catch is down to twelve inches annually.

This has a great deal to do with crops, agricultural pursuits, and money-making in general, as was said, but it also has had much to do with the ethics of society in West Texas. With adequate rainfall mankind may, in a manner of speaking, let some things wait, knowing nature will take care of them. Such a climate is generally forgiving. Society may spend extra moments thinking its own thoughts, not having to stand such constant watch against its natural foes.

On the other hand, with less than twelve inches of rain a year the land becomes a desert where man has little control over what it does for him. Everything belongs to the whim of a tyrant force which leaves no room for error. Sometimes in West Texas, of course, the moist margin of difference between "dry" and "desert" is so thin that men who have lived there all their lives begin wondering why they ever thought those early explorers were wrong about life not being meant for the place. I knew one rancher who would ride out in the middle of his pasture after nightfall and pray for rain.

"I just don't have the faith to do it under that damn dry sun," he explained.

THERE IS one other bit of physical unity inherent in my West Texas. It was once the bed of an ancient, inland sea, whose dry littoral, now hundreds or thousands of feet below the surface, is almost exactly where my boundaries run. This sea was there during the Permian period of the Paleozoic era, about 270 million years ago. A range of mountains ran along its eastern side, passing about where Fort Worth and Dallas are, cutting off any drainage so that a giant evaporation pan was formed. Here, in this Permian Basin, were laid down most of the natural resources of West Texas, the gypsum, salt, potash, and petroleum. Its final shrinking took place in a sort of sump which was beneath what are now Ector and Midland counties.

West Texas owes more, economically, to that Permian period than it does to any subsequent time, except those recent years which brought man to it. This old sea, in a sense, remains down there because sometimes you can still taste its saline waters if you are at an oil well which is drilling down to its bed. Although it is millions of years old and hundreds of feet down, I think the presence of this unifying subsurface relic has had the power to affect history. There is no doubt that once the drill bit cuts into its pockets and traps in the limestone and sandstone containers of oil, history has been made. But it seems to have had more than just an economic influence. What lies on the surface is a dim but powerful prediction of what rolls along below. According to geological description, West Texas writhes in ancient, frozen agony. Listen to the violent rhythm one scientist unconsciously achieves as he tells of the subsurface "folds, faults, intrusions, slips, slabs, and slides . . ."

A pocket of gas formed in the Pennsylvanian period, left asleep like a powerful beast in hibernation, comes roaring to the surface up the drill pipe thousands of feet through its man-made passageway, bursts free of its ancient sea bed, bursts free of time, and becomes a headline in today's newspaper—but how long ago did it take place, and of what age was it really important? That is why I like to believe that even when he didn't realize where he walked, the pioneer's outlook and optimism about West Texas were moved by what was down there, ancient history that was yet to be written, and in his hopefulness he felt it.

3

Some Arteries of Time

In West Texas "where you are" starts with a highway. House numbers don't count for much. The land is too big to be pinned down by a digit or two, so the significant numerals are on those black asphalt ribbons of road that tie the spaces together.

They are good highways, like most of the roads in the state. Building highways is one thing Texas does for the public in a superb fashion. I suppose no state does it better. The roadways are wide, well paved (only county roads are gravel), and marked with plenty of directional signs to keep the traveler oriented. And in West Texas there are certain highway signs a visitor may encounter for the first time—WARNING, LIVESTOCK ON ROAD; CATTLEGUARD; DEER CROSSING; CAUTION, STRONG WIND CURRENTS. The state highway department is always working on the roads, widening them, adding a litter-barrel turnout, or straightening the curves so that your automobile can have a surer footing at eighty-five and ninety miles per hour, which is about the speed at which a high percentage of West Texans drive. This fine system of roads carries this built-in attractive risk, of course, so it is not surprising that West Texas, despite a scarcity of population centers, contributes a brutally high proportion of Texas's annual highway slaughter, which generally is the worst in the nation.

Paved roadway glistens like water when you look far down it in a hot sun. This mirage effect grows especially disconcerting out around Sweetwater and Roscoe where there are long acres of irrigated fields which, in fact, do bring water almost to the highway itself and where there are also shallow-water lakes, after a rainy spell, which stand out on the horizon so that it looks as if the highway mirage is joining the real water on either side of it and will plunge you into some sudden and spectacularly unannounced lake—but the lake disappears then reappears farther ahead until you begin to doubt all water, or trees or hills.

A four-strand barb-wire fence, stapled to shaggy cedar posts every ten or twelve feet, stands guard between the highway world and the fields and pastures along nearly every mile of West Texas road. The grass of the bar ditch, sowed by the highway department, usually Bermuda or some bright-green kind of "civilized" growth, spreads in a thick carpet over the stray newspapers, beer cans, cracker boxes, and throwaway drink bottles. Inside the fence will be mostly native grasses, curly mesquite, buffalo, or side oats grama, growing in clumps rather than in a spreading cover.

The dirt of the pasture will often as not be red clay (fancifully called "chocolate loam" by the old-timers who were trying to sell the farming idea to immigrants in the time of the eighties and nineties), and it turns pinkish to orange on the surface, forming a crust or shell half an inch thick in the dry summer time, which you can lift off in pie-slice chunks.

To the unpracticed eye a West Texas pasture is bewilderingly brown, especially so to a visitor used to deep-green lushness. The typical pasture is dry-looking, except in spring, and the grass turns yellow or brown and stays that way most of the year, remaining green, if at all, only

down near the roots. But grass-eating animals love it and it puts flesh on them as cheaply as any combination of land, vegetation, climate, and investment cost in North America. What most people don't realize is that the brown grasses store sugars in their stalks and leaves, making them even more nutritious in the brown state than in the green. A long brown-grass pasture seems to be running away from the highway, carried over the slow curves and swells of the land in an almost voluptuous way. The old-timers who came to West Texas while the Indians and the buffalo were still claiming all of it said that in some valleys the native grasses grew high as the belly of a horse—that good old pioneer comparative which has almost lost its useful quality not merely from being overworked but because a lessening number of persons have the kind of acquaintance with the bellies of horses to know just how high off the ground one is.

These first-comers to West Texas were usually herdsmen and hunters, men to whom grass represented meat and meat riches; men who, in their excited minds, seeing it all, could imagine this grass being converted into beef merely by driving a few skinny cattle onto it. No wonder they pushed out to frontier without reckoning the dangers or the ethics of what they did. With longhorn cattle then to be had almost for the rounding-up, and free land with free grass lying out there a gift from God, it was the sudden vision of a new life, and one ordained (before long) in their motivation by the Almighty who gave them the grass and the ambition. This may have had something to do with the holiness with which the cattle business is still viewed by many West Texans. It was kind of God-ordained, but it also called for a vast amount of daring, shrewdness, bravery, and primitiveness. You worked hard, it was chancy, by all odds it was dangerous—but God was your partner. And it wasn't easy—as you might expect, God being your co-manager.

West Texas puts a moral question mark after success, especially if it comes easy. Cattle raising afforded a magnificent opportunity for those old land-grabbers to tower above their fellow settlers both in power and in money, but it was always sanctified by the demand for sweat that went with it. Later, when a huge number of the cattle ranches became oil fields, this partnership with God wouldn't work. One time I went up to Scurry County when the last great Texas oil boom was taking place there, and went out in the north part to talk to an old rancher named Pie. Dusk was falling in its beautiful purple shades over those rolling plains (the most beautiful time of a summer day in West Texas) as Pie and I sat out on the front gallery of his ranch house.

Across the horizon from one end of the arc to the other were the tall lines of electric lights on the drilling rigs, boring away into his land. There must have been two or three dozen visible from the front porch, and every one of them represented maybe a hundred thousand dollars of potential income to Pie.

But while we were talking the old rancher excused himself and went into the house for a moment. He came back out with a rifle and a box of shells. "You want to have some fun?" he asked me, and without waiting for me to accept or decline, he leveled down on one string of rig lights and began shooting. At first he fired carefully and with an accuracy one expects from a West Texas rancher who has carried a gun in his saddle holster for forty years, but then the marksmanship seemed to become secondary, and under the influence of our past and the bourbon we had consumed, his shooting became more desperate. Popping one or two bulbs on each rig, he worked his way across that horizon that was all his, and talked in a rambling, scornful way as he fired, "Sons of bitches . . . sons of bitches . . ." Pie's gesture had a kind of offhand nobility about it, a grand rejection.

I asked myself, was I reading too much symbolism into what he was doing? Earlier, as we talked about the oil boom, he had showed a certain amount of greed, telling me how much oil was being discovered under his land and gleefully comparing it to a lesser (but still staggering) amount being found on another Scurry County man's holdings. But Pie also hated what the oil companies were doing to his moral code. He hated the idea that none of this new wealth was his doing, as his cattle and his land deals had been, based on his own experiences and heartbreaks and skill. No, this oil company had just come in there offering him enormous sums of money for the mere privilege of drilling holes and didn't even ask his advice as to where he thought maybe the holes ought to go. They proceeded to put down so many holes they made him (and his heirs) worth millions, but they never asked a damn word of advice from him, nor his help nor his concession once they had his goddam signature on that piece of paper. Even God called on a man for more help than that, for more scary moments and more sleepless nights.

Later on I talked to one of the drilling company's officials and he laughed and said, yes, they all knew about Pie, and took his target practice into consideration on the rigs. Along with most of Scurry County, they laid it off to Pie's being just another ornery old character with enough money to get away with it.

But I say it was something else. I say that every time he stepped to that front door and saw those lights on his horizon he heard a voice saying, "Pie, it's sinful."

On the other hand, a bawling Hereford yearling would be singing his praises.

I never see a wide, clean meadow of brown West Texas grass but I think of God and Pie.

EVEN BEFORE THE TRAVELER has passed the Brazos he will have noticed a different kind of tree. Twisted and rather ugly, it never stands straight and seldom stands very high. Twenty feet is tall for it. In the summer it is a pale green, lightly tinted with yellow. The leaves are lacy, and when you pluck one you see the petals are tiny, narrow pieces running from both sides of a central spine like the backbone of a fish (bipinnately compound of two pairs of pinnae, in botanical terms).

This tree is the mesquite, and although it is found throughout South, Central, and West Texas it is most closely identified with the latter. The mesquite is a symbol of something West Texas has always admired—persistence. It is a creation made for surviving: the bark is rough, with shallow fissures and thick scales. The roots are deep and drought-resistant and the mesquite is not easily damaged by disease or insects.

At certain periods the tree oozes a gum which is similar to the brown mucilage we used in school, and in fact, my great-grandmother told me it was the only kind of glue, except for flour and water paste, she ever used as a girl. When I was a boy some of my companions used it as chewing gum, but I imagine that this native "chewing wax," like that produced from wheat and fresh tar, has been wiped out by affluence and bubble gum.

In the late summer the mesquite drops bushels of long, thin, hard, and smooth bean pods which have their seeds set in a sweet, spongy tissue. Cattle will eat these ripened pods, especially if the grass is thin and no other feed is provided, but they are even more attractive to quail, dove, squirrel, and even coyotes. Humans (my case, at least) find them distinctly bittersweet and unpalatable. Milch cows are never allowed to eat the beans except as a means of survival because they give milk a bitter taste which pasteurization does not remove. Some of the Indians used to prepare a ground meal called pinole from the beans and also used it as the main ingredient for an intoxicating drink.

My mother got hold of a recipe for mesquite-bean jelly which she used to make as a "surprise" for various friends. While it was a pleasant change from that artificial monotony of breakfast sweets one buys in the grocery store, it had a heavy kind of taste and ultimately a little went a long, long way. (I think there may still be a jar unopened, after all these years, in my cupboard.)

The mesquite tree is additionally provided with thorns, a fact for which it is probably most famed. These are from half an inch to two inches long, are not only needle-sharp—they are quite capable of penetrating a leather shoe sole—but they leave a painful, lingering, infecting substance once they puncuture the skin.

As a shade tree the mesquite is more symbol than substance, leaving a dancing pattern of sunlight over the ground. Nobody in his right mind, in West Texas at least (Frank Dobie did it down in the Texas Hill Country), cultivates the mesquite as a nursery tree or an ornamental, although it is tolerated as a yard plant. Even in West Texas, which is seldom well supplied with trees, homeowners tend to apologize about it if they have nothing but mesquites around their homes.

But despite this scorn, West Texans admire the mesquite. The ranchers go to extraordinary and expensive lengths to eradicate the trees from their pastures as water-depleting pests but it is a war never won. Whatever it is in a tree, in a man it would be heart. This ability to survive and re-emerge is botanically remarkable, for the mesquite is a relatively slow-growing tree, remaining a bush for years. Coal oil poured around the trunk will cause the tree to die, but as in the case of chopping one down, the stump sprouts readily. The commonest way to clear pasture of mesquite is with a bulldozer, which uproots trees and bushes and then piles them up for burning —but somewhere down in that deep, red soil a mesquite soul waits to be resurrected, somewhere in the plural stomachs of some cow a mesquite bean lies undigested, waiting to be expelled onto the soil and to take root again, provided with shelter, moisture, and fertilizer.

So the mesquite, instead of withdrawing, continues spreading over West Texas, and cleared fields have to be patrolled continually against reinfestation. In fact, the pioneers said there were few mesquites when they came to West Texas. They said the massive herds of buffalo kept the bushes cut down or grubbed out, buffalo, unlike cattle, grazing green things down to the very roots. Some say the mesquite was brought up from South Texas by the longhorn drives that trailed across West Texas on the way to Kansas. However, I find emphatic references to the prevalent presence of the mesquite (spelled half a dozen differing ways) in the writings of the earliest explorers, so the tree was never really scarce. This tenacity and rugged individualism causes admiration, even at the moment when a curse is being laid on the mesquite. It is the national flower of West Texas.

Mesquite makes good fence posts and has been used for some kinds of furniture (it is ghastly), but its prime virtue is as a fuel for barbecuing. It makes the finest cooking coals to be had, according to believers. The ranch cooks and professional barbecuers will use no other wood. Cabrito, that Mexican delicacy which involves a whole roast kid, is specifically prepared over mesquite coals.

A really ancient mesquite, warped by the wind, is quite a beautiful thing, and even the ranchers who hate them most will spare "an ol' big 'un" at a fence corner or along the row where it has grown for three generations. Some of these landmarks get to be ten feet or more in girth and have been associated with legends or legal descriptions of the land since the first surveyors came through ("thence to a muskeet southeast by 10 varas . . .").

Now and then some too-smart professor or dendrochronologist will arouse considerable combustion in one of the weekly newspapers of the territory by announcing that Grandpa Bullard's old mesquite out back of the Forked J Ranch headquarters (which Grandpa said was there when he come up through Buffalo Gap in 1875) couldn't possibly have been more than a bush before 1900.

The mesquite loves life and will grow almost anywhere. In fact, most West Texans think it prefers the dry red clay or the worst soil God has to offer. It has about its annual bloom a mysterious sense of danger in springing forth prematurely and it is traditional in West Texas that spring isn't safely abroad in the land until the mesquite acknowledges it. The late Frank Grimes, editor of the Abilene *Reporter-News*, made an annual affair of running his poem warning those who would disregard this prophet:

We see some signs of returning spring—
The redbird's back and the fie' larks sing,
The ground's plowed up and the creeks run clear,
The onions sprout and the rosebud's near;
And yet they's a point worth thinkin' about—

We note
  that the old
    mesquites
      ain't out!

If the mesquite asked too much of the land it could never have stayed in West Texas. If it had been too straight, too easily shaped or worked, it would have been victimized; without its thorns and rough bark it would have been a pretty, pampered import. So West Texans see in it a replica of themselves.

THERE IS ANOTHER natural signpost in West Texas which shares the pasture with the mesquite. It is the mountain cedar, or Mexican juniper, springing dark-green against the red earth, living greedily on thin, dry soil where even the mesquite cannot thrive. Cedars mark the brows of the deeper ravines and those places where the earth has been wounded too deeply for nature or man to repair. "Cedarbrakes," a certain rough, raw kind of land is called, and it is good for nothing but grazing.

Most of the cedar in West Texas is not tall and straight enough to be used as fence posts. Only on the hills west of Mineral Wells and Palo Pinto, through a long valley you enter at Metcalf Gap, do the cedar choppers still operate, cutting down and topping out the trees that are suitable for commercial use and filling the air with the delicious odor of burning cedar and a faint haze of blue smoke.

This is a marginal occupation that seems to attract loners and people of an isolated turn. The cedar choppers and their families stay to themselves and live in a tribal fashion, most of them handing on the trade to sons or sons-in-law. They work when they want or need to, cutting out a load of posts and hauling them into town to the post yard when they need money. It is hard, low-paying work whose rewards seem to be in the way of life it allows you to lead—although Texas writers have tended to be too romantic about the cedar choppers and their ways, confusing lack of contact with splendid solitude.

This piece of highway, which is hilly enough to be reminiscent of some parts of New England, used to be rather dangerous because it was so narrow and twisting. But it was a delight to drive in the days of open automobiles—or at least before the air conditioner closed the car into a sealed world of its own.

In those days there were clans of charcoal burners here, too, and once started, the fires could not be allowed to go out, so they burned day and night. Coming through the narrow valley, walled in by tall, steep hills and thick, low stars, one could sense the presence of others both from the heavy fragrance of the fires and from the winking light of a fire here and there, high up on the side of a hill. There was no electricity in this part of the world, and with whole families out tending the charcoal mounds you saw no other evidence of man's presence as you drove through at night.

Today the charcoal burners are gone from those Palo Pinto ridges and the cedar choppers operate with the gasoline-powered chain saw more than the ax. I cannot believe there will continue to be families devoted to this work. Surely the sons will not follow it. It is not only hard but it lacks that element of grandiose Americanism, that thing we call (most especially when speaking of a life work) "a future."

I often wonder who is going to do these minor, unacceptable, and unambitious jobs such as cedar chopping? There are a few hand industries still going in our nation—outside the purely artistic kinds like weaving, basketmaking, and jewelry creation—but can future generations be recruited to do them? Or will all future workers in these pursuits (which have no professional demands other than a quiet satisfaction at doing a certain grade of work) be the rejects and dregs of industry rather than the deliberately self-assertive men who have traditionally done them? West Texas has its share of these hand-work jobs—cowboying is the most prominent. It is very possible that despite the popularity of television programs and advertisements embellishing the life of the cowboy with adventure and reward there will be none within another generation. It is not a job for the ambitious, and what alive, conscientious American can afford to admit he lacks ambition? Only society's rejects—and rejects don't make good cowboys or even cedar choppers unless they can wrap their rejection in something stouter to live for.

UNTIL AFTER World War II, a good three quarters of West Texas used the native cedars and junipers for Christmas trees rather than buying the balsam imports which have taken over the seasonal market, even in West Texas.

Going to the country to cut the Christmas tree was a ritual and, in retrospect, seems to have been almost as important as the gift-giving ceremony. In Abilene, where I spent my boyhood, we drove south of town about fifteen miles to a line of hills that crossed the county going east and west and were covered with cedars—which farmers and ranchers regarded (and still do, of course) as pure and simple pests.

Finding an appropriate tree was a matter of judgment and engineering. Few of them, that far west, were straight and tall, so the first problem was selecting one least twisted and crooked. We would chop what we hoped was a tree small enough to get in the house—I secretly hoping each year we would get an enormous one but my women-kin continually cautioning against the deceptive quality of cedars on a mountainside as compared to cedars in a living room.

Once, when I was no more than five years old, this led to a chain of events which came near to breaking up my mother and father's marriage. My father was generous, impetuous, and adventuresome in those days and rather defiantly defensive of his judgments. Just the wrong sort of man to be continually argued with and second-guessed by a bunch of womenfolks, which he was.

We had gone almost to Buffalo Gap, then turned on the old Belle Plain wagon road to get to the Cedar Gap hills. As we had moved into a new house, my father declared this was the year to get a real tree and despite the clack and clatter of my mother, my grandmother, and my great-grandmother telling him each one he picked unthinkably huge, he finally cut down a full, round beauty, almost straight in its growth, and rather violently defended his choice.

"I guess I didn't come from three generations of carpenters not to be able to gauge how tall a tree is," he said.

"Well that one will never fit in the living room is all I'm sayin'," my great-grandmother responded. His own wife, my mother, never sided with him in his life, always taking the side of her mother and grandmother, so it was a necessity of his masculinity for my father to ever voice a firm opinion.

The ride back to town with the big cedar on the front fender (joining what was almost a caravan of other Christmas-tree gatherers as we entered the city limits) was cooler than even the December Sunday afforded. Even as we unloaded the tree off the car, there in the confines of residential lots, clipped hedges, and sidewalks, it was quite evident that we had gone well beyond the upper limits of our ceiling—or maybe even our roof.

We pulled the tree into the house and with all three of the women making constant pointed (and ultimately accurate) remarks about the impossibility of the size, we got the tree to the living room and set up somewhat in position. The top two feet or so of the tree were bent parallel to the cracked-ice ceiling.

"You'll have to cut it off and it will ruin the shape," my grandmother, in obvious tones, pointed out.

"We will not," my father said.

"I'd like to know how you think we can use that tree without cutting half of it off," my mother said.

"I'll show you," said father, and he went to the kitchen and brought back a big auger which he had inherited from one of those three generations of carpenters he talked about.

He knelt down and before the first of the women could scream, began boring a hole in the floor of the new house. When the uproar broke, seconds later, all three of the women were on him, awkwardly, uncoordinated—but effectively. My mother then fled from the room in wild tears, I huddled in a corner in fear and amazement, and my father, dodging away from the scene of his crime, ran from the house, drove off in the car, and, despite predictions that the marriage was finally wrecked and "he'll not come back," reappeared late that night carrying a large carton of salted peanuts which he claimed to have found lying "out in the middle of Sayles Boulevard." The too-tall tree, making a ninety-degree turn a couple of feet from its tip, took up half the room as well, but it was one of the finest Christmas trees I believe I have ever shared.

A CEDAR TREE has a delicious smell and although I have bowed to commercial expediency and no longer have one for Christmas, there is nothing more nostalgic to me in the season than the smell of cedar—whether it is present or remembered. I understand the use of a green tree to celebrate Christ's birth is pure pagan symbolism but it means more to me than any other tradition outside the music and carols. When I was a little boy one year someone lighted a small piece of the cedar and remarked they wished the whole house smelled this good. My grandmother and I got a pan from the kitchen and, with her warning me eight times a minute to be careful, carried a smoldering cedar branch throughout the house. This has become a tradition with my own family—the only tradition I can claim to have originated. Each Christmas (and by now we have ritualized it) we sit before the open fire and sing carols, then take a smoking twig of the tree around the house, carrying the Christmas smell to every room and continuing our songs as we go.

THROUGHOUT WEST TEXAS, on any road from freeway to ranch track, there will be few miles in which the path is not guarded by a barbwire fence. There is an art to going through such a fence and most West Texans learn it from childhood.

Most fences have four strands, rising about four feet high with the bottom strand about one foot from the ground. There is an etiquette of procedure used by two people going through a fence. One of them takes the next-to-top wire in his hand and pulls up while pushing down with his foot on the next-to-bottom strand. Once through, the first person does the same thing from the other side of the fence for the second passer. It is tricky. It requires a certain amount of experience, instinct, and the habit of years to lay the torso parallel to the deadly wires and slip the torso through without slicing coat, shirt, and skin in the movement. The modern two-spike barbs are machine-cut and slice like a razor. Older three- and four-pronged barbs are simply impossible to traverse.

Getting a woman through a barbwire fence is not so much a process as a performance. Each time it is done it turns out differently, successful or not. Needless to say, in the old days of long, full skirts and multitudes of petticoats, it was tried only in dire emergencies. Barbwire (or "bobwire," as West Texans always say it) seems to have a menacing if inanimate second sense for when a human passing through is nervous or uncertain. It almost cannot be fooled, and even the saggiest, oldest, mildest-appearing fence—even a rickety three-strand relic—will react savagely when approached by a woman. Of course, in contemporary female clothing, the going through a barbwire fence by a woman does offer certain visual prospects which seemingly shy, range-recluse cowboys have been known to take advantage of, for there is no more awkward or revealing posture for even the prettiest, most modest girl than the half-crouch, half-waddle employed, from sheer necessity, in manipulating through two not too widely separated strands of barbwire while wearing a tight skirt.

It is interesting, although not too historically important, to note that West Texas ranch women were among the last in the country to take up the wearing of men's pants.

THIS IS THE WORLD of the highway, and the cities, when they come, appear suddenly, and are gone as quickly. Between them is space and roads and scattered here and there a ranch house which forms its own world away from the highway.

Joining the highway, for a West Texan, becomes a social act. It is his river, his railroad station, his airport, and looking down it he can see what might have been or what may be of his fate. That is why most West Texans are so satisfied, so at home, when in their own car, driving on their own highway, no matter where it is taking them.

4

The Beginning of a Journey

I SAID I made a journey and that sometimes it was a literal journey. My road going back to West Texas begins then, in a literal way, at Weatherford, for I have always left and come back from the eastern side of the place.

Weatherford has not changed much since I have known it, or maybe since the Civil War when it was the jumping-off place for whatever there was of West Texas. Weatherford is an old city, as frontier history is written, a stone city, the façades of its buildings reflecting all the prevailing tides of fashionability of its times, but its alleys lined with the backsides of history: field stone, ashlar, old hand-molded brick, keystoned arches, and the masonry and carpentry of other times.

There is a lot of me in Weatherford, a little more, I suspect, than is left of the ordinary traveler who passes through a town. Weatherford has always been the swinging gate that opened up my personal country of West Texas.

Once on the courthouse lawn—when the courthouse had a lawn instead of being surrounded by ranks of parking meters—there was an immense man-made watermelon, some nine or ten feet in length, symbolizing Parker County's primary claim to agricultural fame. But the imitation watermelon is gone and the claim of Parker

County to melon supremacy no longer holds good, although just a block away there is a celebrated farmers' market where growers still bring their truck to sell: fruits, melons, squash, tomatoes, leafy vegetables, peanuts, eggs; home-canned goods (in Mason jars), their pickles, spiced peaches, chowchow (a hot or mild relish made from green tomatoes), watermelon rind preserves, and home-collected honey. It is a very individualistic place, not yet overcome by commercial considerations. Most of the stands are run by the actual people who grow the crops or can the foodstuffs, and some of the labels are in spidery script written by hands which spell laboriously, the calligraphy studied out in unsteady curlicues the way my great-grandmother wrote, showing little schooling but much style in the curves and dashes. Like the cedar choppers, these workers can't be with us long.

The courthouse, splitting two streams of furious traffic, dominates Weatherford in its tall, white Victorian aloofness. From the steps you can look around the square toward another day, at rows of buildings and store fronts draped in the splendid substance of frontier architecture; sad buildings with sad eyes, tall windows which have to be raised or lowered with a long hook-holding pole, shielded by wooden blinds or handmade shutters that would bring a fortune from the right sort of big-city mystique hunter. Above one entrance, that of a red brick building with mysterious initials emblazoned on it in the forgotten secrecy of an old lodge hall, stands a life-size knight in full, silvery armor, alert within a niche, looking brave but doubtful as he faces the world with a half-raised shield and a half-lowered sword. What did they have in mind, those builders of that particular age whose ideas seem to us more alien than those of the pharaoh who erected the Great Pyramid?

Weatherford, giving off the odor of history and the

aroma of the past, has been home to some oddly important names. Here lived a young Mary Martin running a dancing school and surely not capable of even dreaming where the stage would take her. John Huston, another entertainment personage, was here for a while with pausing parents—a pause created somehow by a race horse, Huston once wrote. Douglas Chandor, a court painter in England, chose Weatherford for his last years.

But my attachment to the town centers on its western edge where the highway splits into U.S. 80 and 180, forcing you to make a decision as to which route you will take through West Texas. And my emotions focus on a decision made there. To an eating place which sat in the Y of those diverging highways I brought a girl one rainy spring morning on my way west. Took her away from Dallas without her consent and without the knowledge of her family, and told her, once we were rolling west in the boxy old Hudson straight-eight coupe I drove, that we would not stop until we had made it to Abilene to be married. Wouldn't stop, that is, unless she relented and gave her Sacred Word that she wouldn't try to get away.

"I think you mean it," was all she said. For miles she held herself in pride and silence, withdrawing against the door on her side of the car, as if she were making ready to fling open the door and scream for rescue the first time I slowed down. And, for all I know, she was. (To this day I have not asked her because I am not sure of her answer.)

Until we had driven through Weatherford, then hunger or love got the better of her. "Aren't we going to eat?" she asked, as quietly as though we were long married and on a pleasure trip. Her question was her Word, and we had turned in at that eating place. I had helped her from the car, a cool, uncommitted "Thank you" for my

reward, and into the café and a booth and two glasses of tepid water and two menus and our orders given and the waitress departed and then, only then, did she look me full in the eyes and say, "Let me see my ring." A noble surrender.

Something of me in Weatherford, then. That night in Abilene we were married in the front room of a preacher she had never met before, who advised her that I was the sturdy oak and she the clinging vine. And I can still go into that café, sit at the counter drinking bad coffee, hope the juke box might still have the song on it we played that morning, and secretly deplore the sentimentality of doing it at all. But never fail to try.

THE DRIVE on Highway 80 from Weatherford to the Brazos River is interminable. The markers say it is fourteen miles, but the traveler who drives it from either direction becomes discouraged. His insides flag, his expectations flare, then droop, as he tops hill after hill, rise after rise, and still finds before him nothing remarkable at all. We have all found roads like this—stretches which belie their mileage by their effect on us as we drive. Once there was more individuality to this road between Weatherford and the river. When I was a boy, when my family was driving to Fort Worth or Dallas, we would stop at the fruit and vegetable stands along the roads near Weatherford and buy tree-fresh peaches or field-ripened watermelons or berries or tomatoes or a dozen other kinds of country produce, sold by the men or their womenfolks who had planted, tended, and harvested it all; men proud of their collaboration with nature in creating such firm, acidy tomatoes or fat, sweet, runny Elberta peaches. Their pride was expressed somewhat in the universal advertising custom of such stands in slicing a Senator Watson or a Rattlesnake watermelon and propping up the halves to the view of the passing public so the rich, red, firm meat could speak for itself.

But now a new car, rolling along a divided, limited-access highway, with radio and air conditioner going at their job of climate creation, is reluctant to stop and haggle over a crate of strawberries or a peck of Early Porter tomatoes. Fruit-stand proprietors today (they have not disappeared altogether) don't cut a four-inch plug out of their watermelons to prove how good and ripe they are. The plug of the family watermelon, for a small boy, corresponded to the dasher of the hand-cranked ice-cream freezer—by tradition it belonged to the youngest male. And he was allowed to eat off the red meat of the melon, saving the rind end to stop up the hole.

Down the road I eventually reach the Brazos River.

It is a mystic river for me, and crossing it is a mystic experience. I know why. Catclaw Creek, which flowed (after a heavy rain) between our house and the fairgrounds in Abilene, emptied into Elm Creek, which in turn joined the Clear Fork, a true waterway which emptied into the Brazos. So, as my grandmother used to tell me when I was a child and we footed our way from the end of the streetcar line over Catclaw bridge, I always had to cross the Brazos to get home. Or to leave home, either, and the process can be much more or less difficult according to where home lies, I suppose. A man never has but one true home, the rest being but extensions of that place, and the house at 3118 South Seventh was my true home.

The Brazos River is one of the two genuine rivers of West Texas, the other being the Colorado. The Spanish found them both and named them both, confusing the names somewhere in time so that for a couple of hundred years one would as likely be called the other. This is evidenced in the name of the Colorado, which means "red," although the Brazos is much more apt to carry red water. One might say of it, as an old emigrants' handbill said of the grass, that "brown is its natural state," that red is the Brazos's natural state and the natural state of most water in West Texas.

A friend of mine, John Graves, wrote a quietly beautiful and very personal book about the Brazos River right along where I cross to reach West Texas. The book, *Goodbye to a River*, relates some of the dark, bloody history of the Brazos valleys and its banks, history in those days being made along rivers like news, today, is made along highways. But John's book relates more than history. It puts the Brazos and all other familiar rivers in their place as landmarks of the spirit. That is why any time I cross the Brazos on that Highway 80 bridge I look downstream to see if there are ghosts fording Emigrants Crossing a couple of hundred yards below, the ghosts of the Forty-niners who headed across West Texas for California and gold—or, as often, death. Anyone in those times who set foot beyond the Brazos knew he had violated the unwritten agreement between white man and Indian which made the Brazos the wall of protection for the red man and his buffalo chattel.

But that was long before my day, of course, and history, while it lays the foundation, seldom bothers to keep the house. To me the Brazos begins with the later memory of a spidery iron bridge and a hump in the middle

span, the heavy timbers of its floor rattling and rumbling beneath the wooden-spoked wheels of our touring car, and the water a scary sight, swirling around the stonework piers in a red flood. The Brazos was a terrible river for flooding before the Corps of Engineers built Possum Kingdom Lake and controlled the seasonal spills of water from down off the High Plains where the river begins, and out of the little hills and breaks where it surged in spring and late summer, unconfined by banks which are low and wide apart.

Creeping over the high bridge in our car at night, we could look down on the dark waters of the swollen Brazos, menacing and more angry-looking in the offside flicker of our headlights, and my father would begin telling of cars swept off bridges into rivers, or ferry slips overshot and whole families never seen again . . . bridges "like this one here" that were originally made for wagons and collapsed under the double harassment of floodwaters at their feet and automobiles on their back, dropping carloads of people into the whirlpools and quicksands of the flooded night. Or my favorite image brought on by one of his terror stories about roads which invited your speed as they curved up a wooded rise, then without warning ended over an abutment where once was a span, now swept away, so that you soared off in unnatural flight, plunging frightfully into a watery grave, never even realizing until all four wheels were in the air that you were doomed. My father talked continually of death on the highway; joking, familiar talk from a man who never gave death the proper kind of due, and then one day he and my mother met it on the highway, but not in my childhood, so his early talk is still amusing and remote, something to remember because it was so much a part of every journey we took. "Carl, look where you're driving . . . you'll kill us all."

When I hear it echoing from those Brazos River days it is still a jest that small boys like because it is pitting adult bravado against adult fear.

At another period, later, by then being somewhat the master of my own destiny, the Greyhound and All-American buses I rode used to stop at one of the two "catfish cafés" that competed with each other across the highway on the eastern end of the Brazos River bridge. I never realized how much bus riding in those days was like stagecoach trips of the nineteenth century until I read the historical account of Waterman Ormsby, which tells of his transcontinental journey on the first Butterfield stage through West Texas—an account we shall pay closer attention to later.

In West Texas the bus stops were made at each town, although sometimes the village might be so small the driver would only slow down and sound his horn, looking to see if anyone would flag him down. But the sounding bus horn served more than just to alert a potential customer. It was reassurance given to the little town that life was still remembering it. The Butterfield stage drivers carried brass bugles which were blown lustily as the stage approached a station, primarily to alert the stationkeepers but, in a sense, also to reassure the station that nothing worse than civilization was coming.

Riding the bus in my youth was closer to exploration than traveling with its superhighway successors is today. Emergency stops were more frequent; I have been on buses destined for the West Coast which ran out of gasoline, thus sending the driver, who wore puttees and flared, blue whipcord riding britches, walking or hitchhiking to the nearest fueling spot. I have even been a passenger on a bus when the driver got lost and had to stop and ask directions. It was not uncommon for the driver to stop the vehicle and let one of the passengers off to answer a call of nature, it being a great distance between restrooms in that era. The rest of us would sit patiently or not, as it were; there always seeming to be one Midwestern woman aboard who kept asking out loud, "What in the world are we waiting for? What's that man doing?" (Don't ask me why I thought she was a Midwesterner; the accent I suppose, or perhaps I thought no West Texan could so overlook the obvious.)

That is partly what the Brazos River bridge cafés bring back to me. They are still in business, advertising catfish dinners, caught from the river that runs a few yards away. There are years of hearing the air brakes hiss, remembering the suitcases and other baggage strapped to the top carriers and covered with a tarp, for these buses were not the tall, flat-nosed monsters of modern times but were boxy and had an honest motor out front and a dishonest ornamental observation platform built on the rear.

I suppose that each year thousands of people pass over the Brazos bridge and never mark the passage. It may even be that at night not only the bridge is passed but all the West Texas that lies beyond it, so that when dawn reveals the landscape to the driver he cannot recognize the fact that he has gone through a separate place. No part of the world is very important, I suppose, unless it is part of you.

Driving west up from that wide Brazos valley you are climbing all the time until you have come to a special place, wider, almost barren, where the hills have been cleared. Topping one last, nude hill you see a needle in the sky that turns out to be a tall smokestack. At its feet are three or four brick buildings and all around are foundations, just managing to top the weeds.

This is Thurber, and to West Texans who drive through it Thurber is an awesome place, not only because it is a ghost town with all the desolation and loneliness inherent in the term, but because it reminds them, even today, that Thurber was never a West Texas town like any of the others. It had a kind of dangerous pretension. It was built of brick and it scorned cotton and cattle for its wealth. Thurber was a mining town, an industrial city, and a true city, while most of the rest of West Texas burned cow chips for fuel and gathered buffalo bones to

sell to survive the droughts. While other towns in West Texas considered the buckboard and the buggy the ultimate in transportation, Thurber had a siding for the Pullman Palace cars and private sleepers which were set off the mainline Texas & Pacific Railway at Mingus for the short ramble down to Thurber's station on the town square.

Thurber was owned entirely by the railroad, through its subsidiary, the T&P Coal Company. It was built all of a sudden in the 1880's when the low hills were discovered to be full of bituminous coal—the largest supply of railroad fuel in Texas. At the same time vitreous clay was found and a big brick-making industry was created. All the buildings in Thurber and most of the houses, even the small ones for the miners, were made of brick. All its streets and sidewalks, its smokestack and pumphouse, the bandstand on the square, railroad abutments, bridges, and watering troughs—all were of brick.

Thurber was not only a ready-made city, it was peopled by strange races, immigrant miners who spoke strange tongues and had impossible names: Italians, Welsh, Poles. Even the supervisory personnel were outlandish. They were Yankee New Englanders and Pennsylvanians.

It became a large city with a population of ten thousand at its prime around the turn of the century. The first bicycles in West Texas were brought to Thurber—possibly because it was the only city with enough paving to make bicycles functionable. Thurber had an opera house which drew truly great performers and, despite the fact it was company-owned and company-controlled, had the biggest horseshoe bar between Forth Worth and Los Angeles where cowboys were not allowed.

Company big shots lived around and on a knob called New York Hill (the very name a sneer at the surrounding country), and there were fancy eating places and pastry bakeries in the town. All of this the other West Texans found at once awe-inspiring and annoying. This unreal quality hovered over Thurber the way legend hints at Lost Atlantises heaving up from the foam on wild, unheralded occasions, only to disappear again. From the first, Thurber's story was not that of West Texas.

Thurber had been built all at once, its population had come all at once, and everything it did it did all at once. When labor troubles threatened in 1900 it became totally unionized all at once—becoming the only one-hundred-per-cent union town in the world. And as things turned out, it died all at once. First, the T&P locomotives stopped burning coal, so there was only half a market for the product of Seam No. 1. Thurber turned to paving brick and supplied hundreds of miles of its purple pavers (which weigh twice what an ordinary brick does) for main streets and highways throughout the Southwest, but then came concrete and asphalt roads with quicker, cheaper construction.

For a while it seemed that oil might save the town. Thurber's general manager was the man who discovered oil at Ranger, and pretty soon the T&P Coal Company had become the T&P Coal and Oil Company and Thurber's biggest building was its headquarters (it pioneered the use of gasoline credit cards). But by the late 1920's my father could note the decline of the place and as we drove through he could not refrain from remarking in West Texas self-righteousness that pretty soon Thurber would dry up and blow away.

One morning in 1933 the company announced the city was being abandoned. The utility poles came down and their wire was salvaged; the water and gas mains were ripped out of the ground. Supplies on the shelves of the company stores were sold at cost and the windows boarded up—in prescribed company manner. (And are still so boarded.)

The rails of the T&P branch were reclaimed, the oil-company records were shipped to a new headquarters in Fort Worth—and Thurber ceased to exist even more rapidly than it had been born.

The last thing I can recall as having shown portents of new life in Thurber was a small sign that appeared beside the highway one day that read TEXAS SOUL CLINIC and waved a hand-painted arrow in a southerly direction. After a year of seeing it, one trip, passing through, I went down that indicated road and came finally to a four-strand, new, tight, barbwire fence erected squarely across the road.

What is the name for the sin of disregarding your surroundings?

5

How the Oil Came

THE VALLEY in which Thurber's miners pitched for coal looks as if a strain of giant, prehistoric digger ants had sometime before man reared immense hills of bare, black dirt. But it isn't many miles west until the last brick foundation is lost in the underbrush and the last mine spur-rail dump has meandered to the final location, and you are climbing.

This is Ranger Hill, my father's landmark. An easy passage today—long and pretty, but neither very steep nor very hard—for fifty years it was considered the ultimate test of draft animals and automotive machinery. Making it up Ranger Hill "with high gear tied down," as the hot drivers put it, was the only acceptable brag an automobile owner could make in those parts.

But even at seventy miles an hour, or a more legal speed, you notice that topping Ranger Hill changes the landscape. The change is toward the flat, dry, wide, and high.

The road into Ranger is red Thurber brick, down under the numerous asphalt coatings. Eastland County, where you are driving, being near Thurber and hitting sudden wealth (as will be explained), put in one of the earliest paved highways in West Texas—brick, of course.

Before the Civil War, Eastland County was sufficiently far from the buffalo prairies and the Comanche

War Trail to draw a few inhabitants, and the 1860 census of the unorganized county shows a population of ninety-nine. This figure was pretty good for a section so far west, especially if we consider the strong possibility that there were a few cowboys nobody bothered to count, a few people who weren't interested in being counted, and possibly some aboriginal or foreign sorts who weren't weighed worthy of being counted.

Eastland County got its name from the "Black Bean" incident when 176 captured Texan invaders were forced, by Mexican officials, to draw beans from a pot—the 159 white beans meaning life, 17 black ones meaning the firing squad. William Mosby Eastland drew the first black bean.

The Texas & Pacific Railway was built through the upper part of the country in 1880 and pulled loose the little pioneer settlements; Ranger Camp Valley, named for an old site of the Texas Rangers, shifted two miles westward to the rails and became simply Ranger. Red Gap, twenty miles farther down the line, carted its belongings over to the steel and renamed itself Cisco.

The most important man in Eastland County history didn't even live there. He was William K. Gordon, the coal company's superintendent at Thurber, who rode around the countryside a lot on his horse and became convinced there was petroleum under Eastland County. This was fairly farsighted on Gordon's part because geological reports had denied there was oil in the area and some drilling in nearby parts of West Texas had been all dry holes.

By 1915, Gordon had some 300,000 acres under lease for the T&P Coal Company, and when a long drought pinched the country in 1916 and 1917 a group of Ranger businessmen took the local over to see Gordon at Thurber, begging him to drill for oil. He asked for 15,000 acres of leases and in a mass meeting Ranger signed up for 25,000.

The first try was on Nannie Walker's farm, where enough gas was hit to make anybody wealthy today, but then, without pipelines, there was no market for natural gas outside a few big cities. Gordon moved the drilling rig a few miles south to the J. H. McClesky farm and got down to 3,000 feet, dry hole, when the New York office wired him to pull out the drill and plug the hole. Three thousand feet was very deep for an oil well. But Gordon had nearly twenty-five years of curiosity to satisfy, so he disregarded the telegram. On October 21, 1917, the No. 1 McClesky roared in with 1,700 barrels of crude oil a day. It was also an unusually high grade of crude, bringing (then) $2.80 a barrel, so that one well figured out at a third of a million dollars a week. It didn't take the rest of the world long to find Ranger.

RANGER TAUGHT US the definition of "boom town." There were oil booms before and booms were to come, but the Ranger boom was the classic, the standard against which the others are measured. By the end of December other oil companies had land men crawling all over the territory signing up mineral rights. As a portent, the old well at Nannie Walker's farm came to life and waked the whole town early New Year's Day, 1918, with an awesome roar as it started blowing millions of cubic feet of gas, then belched strongly a few weeks later and gushed up oil. Before 1918 was out other wells had flowed 7,000, then 8,000 barrels a day, and finally one hit 11,000.

The effect on the countryside was spectacular. Ranger, which had 800 persons when the McClesky was drilled, was roiling with 30,000 a year later and more

arriving on the special trains the T&P ran from Fort Worth five times a day. (The railroad's receipts are a good yardstick: $94,000 worth of business in Ranger in 1917 and eighteen months later, $8,146,000 annually.)

Right outside Ranger, along today's Interstate 20, was a gate with a metal sign over it, MERRIMAN CEMETERY. This was the site of the old town of Merriman, Eastland County's first county seat. By the time oil came Merriman had been reduced to a Baptist church and a cemetery. The church turned out to be sitting right over a pool of petroleum and the congregation was offered a goodly sum for the drilling rights on its two acres. But the Baptists formed a drilling company of their own, hit three good wells, and voted to give the Lord eighty-five per cent of the money and spend fifteen per cent on a new church house.

The Merriman Cemetery made legend. It was reported that the cemetery association had been offered one million dollars for rights to the graveyard but the members had turned it down because it would disturb their dead. Some semipro bard immediately burst into print in an oil journal with a poem which began, "There's a churchyard down in Ranger . . ." and ending, ". . . standing guard above the gravestones in a lot that's not for sale." (I must have heard the poem given a dozen times in declamation contests during my school days.) Years later the legend was trimmed somewhat more to size when the head of the cemetery group admitted the land had been deeded for burial uses only and reverted to the donors if put to any other purpose.

THE TOWN of Ranger became impossible to get to, impossible to walk in, impossible to eat or sleep in. Any kind of flimsy shack was run up and titled a hotel. At least one major West Texas fortune was made when a sharp young country boy from Stephens County listened through the canvas room partition in the hotel where he was staying and overheard a group of investors talking about a big lease killing they were going to bring off next day. He buggied out at dawn (being a farm boy and understanding when a farmer has the most time for business) and sewed the deal up before the outside investors arrived.

Those were the days before oil fields used motor equipment to any extent. Mules and oxen pulled the pipe, cable reels, and boilers. They made loblolly of the streets when it rained. There were men in hip boots at every intersection in Ranger who got two bits a trip for carrying passengers piggyback through the mud. (It cost two dollars a night to sleep in a barber chair.)

Oil, of course, made money, and sin was its invariable companion. Whiskey palaces, gambling halls, and cabarets blazed through the night, waiting to accommodate the oilmen no matter which tower (the oil-field term for a shift) they worked. The names of the cabarets were colorful: Blue Mouse, Palm Island, Grizzly Bear, Old Oklahoma. In one twenty-four-hour period there were five murders in Ranger.

But the lawlessness got to be too much even for roaring Ranger. The Texas Rangers sneaked into town by the back roads one night (the gamblers kept watch at such points as Eastland and Cisco) and captured ninety gamblers and their equipment. A few months later the town's morals got a final jolt from, of all unlikely agencies, the Rotary Club. These gentlemen, joined by the police (who may have had mixed emotions about doing so, since the pay-off was rumored to be astronomical), went down the streets joint by joint, hauling out the wheels, dice tables and boards and smashing the bottles and kegs of outlawed (by prohibition) liquor. By the end of that day the sinners had given up on Ranger.

WITHIN A YEAR the Ranger pool had been proved to stretch from the north end of Stephens County to the south end of Eastland—nearly sixty miles. One field, Breckenridge, was as big as the original and almost as rowdy.

This was a petroleum frontier, an industrial new country in which greed offered the motives which fair play lacked. There was no thought given to conservation. The mechanical and technical equipment was about the same as had been used at Spindletop in 1901—cable-tool drilling rigs that strained to get below 3,000 feet; wooden derricks, some as tall as an eight-story building, which had to be constructed by hand; steam boilers for power, fired with wood or by piping crude natural gas directly from the well. The few trucks of a size to haul the cumbersome equipment were less useful than oxen because there were no roads, except dirt tracks, outside the towns.

The main difference between the oil booms of that time and a later day, however, was not so much in the technicians or the equipment they used as in what we might call the philosophy of drilling. Everyone wanted to get rich quick and looked on the chance to do so as one for which he was accountable only to his opportunity and skill. The average oilman of the period, while often, out of ignorance, nevertheless was totally irresponsible.

Oil lies in huge pools or reservoirs, and until such a pool has been drilled to its edges, no one can be sure how far it stretches. When a well hits it, the well taps the entire pool, in effect, and not just the oil that lies directly under one lease. So a frenzy developed when one well hit oil. There was no thought of cooperation because no one understood what it meant in those circumstances—just drill as quickly and as frequently as you could and get as much oil to the surface as you could. Sometimes this led to ridiculous situations, such as in Kilgore, in the heart of the East Texas field, where on one single-acre tract twenty-four wells were drilled, the legs of the derricks so interlaced that it was impossible to walk among them except on special paths.

This unrestricted drilling led to a rapid depletion of the reservoir pressure—that pocket of natural gas which accompanies crude petroleum and pushes it to the surface from out of its limestone or sandstone layer. Every time a new well was drilled it blew off a vast excess of that gas. Most oil men at Ranger didn't realize it was so precious, not just as a commodity in itself but as the cheapest and best agent for lifting oil to the surface. Promoters, in fact, liked to let a well "gush" for as long as it would because the spectacular sight of oil roaring up a hundred feet into the air stirred investors like nothing else could.

Today massive drill collars and valves keep this waste of gas and crude from taking place, and stringent regulations concerning well spacing and production days per month are set by the Texas Railroad Commission (which controls the petroleum production industry).

OF THE OTHER BOOMS around Ranger, one achieved a legendary status of its own. The field was named for the little village it surrounded, Desdemona, but throughout the oil world it was called Hogtown, because it centered on a marshy trickle known as Hog Creek.

Hogtown, for sheer bad manners, was the worst oil boom in Texas history, according to those myth-making experts who followed the booms. The original city of Desdemona had obtained a post office in 1870 under the name "Desdemonia"—a brave attempt to honor Shakespeare's "white ewe" of Othello. For some reason the post-office department didn't get around to changing it to the literary spelling until 1901. Desdemona, fifteen miles south of Ranger, played a hunch. In 1914 all its one hundred citizens met at the Hog Creek school and formed the Hog Creek Oil Company. They felt sure they were sitting on oil. The water wells gave off a substance called damp gas and it smelled exactly like the shallow oil wells at Strawn, according to some citizens who had traveled up there to take a sniff. For another thing, Hog Creek had an oil scum form on its quiet waters now and then. And to top it off, some local scientist had taken a map and drawn a straight line down from Petrolia, the hottest oil site in Oklahoma at the time, through Strawn (whose wells turned out to be minor), and found it extended right through Hogtown. How could nature go against all these signs? (The points were given in a letter a local enthusiast sent to his kinfolks.)

But this faith in signs took a bruising in the next four years. The first well, on a lease owned by the village barber, ran out of funds twice, then was a dry hole at 1,500 feet. An Oklahoman was persuaded to bring in his spudder (a drilling rig) but he too ran out of money without any oil on his bits. Fortunately for Hogtown's history, a third attempt got W. E. Wrather (who later became director of the United States Geological Survey) down from Wichita Falls and while exploring a fork of Hog Creek he found an anticline—an upfold of rock which sometimes traps oil. He said it looked promising, so a new Hog Creek Oil Company was formed and a third site picked for drilling. On the night of September 2, 1918, Hogtown finally got oil. The well promptly caught fire from the tool dresser's forge and it took three days of high-pressure steam from four boilers to put out the flames, but it became a 2,000-barrel-a-day producer. That tilted Eastland County a bit and drained several thousand of the Ranger crowd down to Desdemona-Hogtown.

From the beginning it was a mean, sinful place. Years later I talked to a man who lived through the whole boom, and he mentioned one well-known West Texan who had run a shanty café in Hogtown's palmy days.

"I don't know what happened to us," the man told me. "It seemed like nothing much mattered but 'get that oil out of the ground.' We lost our civilizing. We did things I don't expect anybody anywhere else did and I still can't tell you why. Like Charlie B——. I saw him get so mad once at a big guy who was sleeping with Charlie's girl that he got right down on the ground on the main street and rolled around eating dirt. There must have been a couple hundred people looking. Stuffing his mouth full of dirt and shaking his head and growling like a dog, out in front of that old tent where he run his café. This big guy just stood there watching Charlie eat dirt, laughing at him with an arm around this girl they were sharing."

The women who came in with the Hogtown oil boom were mostly like the one Charlie ate dirt over. They matched the town's nickname. They were brazen like few prostitutes have been in petroleum history, stopping men on the streets at noon to solicit trade and, according to the man who was there, "selling quite a bit of it in broad daylight on the back seat of a Model T touring car."

Squads of the professional ladies would drive out to the wells and offer the crews door-to-door service, day and night. Maybe this sort of thing happened because Hogtown was away from the beaten track, without railroads or nearby cities to civilize it. Maybe the local population was just too small to control the tide of sinful humanity that swept in, and so simply drowned in it.

The Desdemona-Hogtown field was one where the little operator had a chance. In Ranger the major companies controlled most of the producing leases—Humble Oil, then a smaller firm, was bought by Standard so that the big firm could get production in Ranger. But in Desdemona the majors hadn't taken the trouble to lease up the countryside and the Hog Creek Company only had 5,000 acres. Many of the other leases, handled by individuals who plunged the family savings into the only size tracts they could afford, were tiny. One lease was for a hundredth of an acre—about the size of a master bedroom. After the Hogtown field had been defined by drill-

ing it could be seen that had either of those first two dry holes been drilled as little as one hundred yards farther north they would have hit oil.

By January 1919, hundreds of wells had been drilled in the compact field, including a famous hole known as the Payne gasser which blew off 40 million cubic feet of gas a day and whose roar could be heard twenty-five miles away. Only a mile from the discovery well the Hogg well flowed 15,000 barrels a day to lead the field in production. There just weren't enough pipes, tank wagons, and storage containers to take care of the gushers, and earthen tanks and dirt reservoirs thrown up to catch the overflow were themselves overflowed. Dams were thrown across creeks and gullies, and lakes of crude oil formed behind them. At one time traffic on the road between Hogtown and De Leon (the nearest railroad) was blocked by a river of oil flowing three feet deep over the highway.

The townsite turned out to be the best part of the field and houses, shacks and tents sat amongst the derricks and confusion of the well sites. Lawlessness of the highjacking and extortion kind became a problem. The "protection" racket was so blatant that men were coming around to the derricks daily to collect from the workers, and some collectors were so cocksure they gave credit between paydays.

But the thug element moved on rather speedily from Hogtown-Desdemona. The Rangers had to come in, but that wasn't the only reason. The field showed its size quickly. It ran only about three miles by three miles and it didn't take long to drill this up. The boom had no place to go, so it left. "Live fast, die young, and make a beautiful corpse" is an old West Texas honky-tonkism, and (aside from the morbid beauty part) that's the way it was with Desdemona. The field output hit 7,375,000 barrels in 1919, dropped to 2,767,000 barrels in 1920 and was making only one tenth of that by the time the decade was out. Desdemona, from its frantic thousands, settled down to about 150 persons. But, for what that final nicety is worth, it's not called Hogtown any more.

RANGER'S PEAK PRODUCTION YEAR was 1919 when the field averaged 73,000 barrels of oil per day. Then the free-flowing gushers, the unrestrained drilling, took their toll and the field "blew its top," which means it lost its gas pressure. It has been estimated that less than one third of the oil below Ranger and Desdemona was actually recovered. A multimillion-dollar fortune awaits the invention of an exhaustive recovery system for petroleum. Dozens of schemes have been used, some successful if instituted early enough, but most all marginally successful at best. This waste, because it became economically evident, sobered up some elements of the oil-production business, and common sense, as well as new control machinery, was introduced. Ranger taught the oil world self-control, although it was a decade in coming, and even then the business fought hard against its own best interests. (It was not until the 1950's, for example, that West Texas oil fields quit flaring gas—that is, letting it simply burn off into the air.)

Ranger today has plenty of empty buildings which have grown accustomed to being empty, and people who have grown accustomed to seeing the town's population steadily dwindle. But the romantic aura (and the literal odor) of oil hung over the town for nearly twenty years, and when we traveled through, in the late 1920's, long strings of tank cars were continually lining the T&P. Even in the mid-thirties you drove to Ranger through a modest forest of derricks and pumps.

Maybe someday some engineer will discover a way to go back down into the rock and bring out the rest of Ranger's inheritance and restore history, and life, to the place.

6

A Town Fame Dislikes

WEST AGAIN. Out of Ranger the road rolls over low hills to Eastland where a mummified lizard lies in state in the lobby of the county courthouse. Old Rip is his name and he is a horned toad, or "horny frog" as Texans call these fierce-looking, but harmless, little prehistoric reptiles.

The story is that Old Rip was originally sealed in the cornerstone of the courthouse when it was laid in 1898. Then, in 1927 when a new courthouse was being built and the old cornerstone was opened, Rip crawled out, stretched, shot out his tongue, and lived again. Boyce House, one of the chroniclers of Ranger's oil boom, had by this time moved to Eastland and he spread Old Rip's story over the world until the horned toad became a celebrity. Rip traveled the nation, even meeting President Coolidge, and spent two good years of living before he died again. His four-inch body was preserved and laid in a velvet-lined casket for public display. Many Eastlanders think it not unlikely that Old Rip will come back a second time. As for Old Rip's first resurrection, there have always been doubters, but they have seldom lived in Eastland. The only local resident I ever heard question the toad's long sleep was a judge (now dead) who told me, privately, he was present when Old Rip was secreted inside the cornerstone the night before to await the next day's official opening ceremony. But the hoax, if such it was, evidently was too successful to be killed or too embarrassing.

Eastland has depended on the fading memory of Old Rip for most of the sparkle to her name. I thought at the time he told me of its inception that I detected something in the old judge which envied Old Rip and the hoax. Whatever the first facts might have been, the final facts are, in West Texas Old Rip is immortal.

TEN MILES WEST of Eastland is Cisco, and entering town I pass that shabby little motel where we spent our wedding night. We arrived after midnight, tired but wildly talkative and excited, and were so thankful to observe the motel walls were apparently thick and soundproof because not a stir was heard from around us. We were awakened the next morning, alas, by coughing, conversation, and other normal activities from the rooms on either side of ours. The walls, far from being soundproof, were thin and leaked noise. The occupants of the adjoining cabins had merely been staying quiet, listening to the newlyweds.

Cisco is a city which once claimed to be famous for having the largest hollow concrete dam in the world, the largest outdoor concrete swimming pool in the world, and the largest fish hatchery in Texas. Some of these are no longer valid, I understand, although of later years Cisco has found a new claim—one closer to the heart of commercial America—that it was the place where Conrad Hilton, the international hotel operator, opened his first hotel.

But something in history, or fame, doesn't care for Cisco. The cost of building the world's largest hollow concrete dam threw the city into bankruptcy during the

Great Depression, the state closed the fish hatchery in 1950, and Conrad Hilton's first hotel long ago lost all connection financially with Conrad Hilton and even flopped as an old folks home. For that matter, I have not spent another night in Cisco since that wedding night myself.

Cisco was also the scene of a West Texas legend—one unquestionably true. This was the Santa Claus bank robbery. It occurred in 1927 during the Christmas holidays, as one might suppose, and was a comedy of errors—except for the lengthy tragedy of death which followed in its unfolding.

The mastermind of the crime, for some unfathomable reason, thought that a Santa Claus suit would make an inconspicuous disguise when he and three others went to hold up the First National Bank. It only drew attention of the children on the Christmas-crowded streets, and one little girl even followed the criminal Santa into the bank and tried to talk to him while he was holding a pistol on the officials.

Then when some of the hostages inside the bank began leaping out the back door and alerted the whole town to what was taking place, the bandits killed a policeman and fled in their car, careening along the main street of town, everyone, including Santa, firing wildly from the windows of the car. (A blind, sidewalk musician, caught in the exchange of shots, fiddled feverishly out of fear the whole time.) After driving a few blocks someone in the car discovered the vehicle was practically out of gas. In preparing the getaway, filling the tank had been overlooked. At the south edge of town the bandits (one dying) commandeered another automobile, piling their wounded companion and the loot in the back seat. But the fourteen-year-old boy who had been driving the highjacked car calmly stood by and refused to show them how to operate the patented gearshift lever which had locked into place. When the pursuers appeared a block away the robbers ran back to their original car and drove off again, leaving the dying man and the stolen money behind.

They were eventually captured, tried, and convicted. One of the trio of survivors was executed in the electric chair and Santa Claus was lynched by an Eastland mob after he had killed a popular jailer in an escape attempt. Six men had died from the Santa Claus bank robbery before it was over, and the finale was as ironic as the untoward events that marked its performance. The body of the lynched Santa Claus was taken to Fort Worth for a family funeral, and as the service was beginning it was interrupted by a parade outside; a parade signaling the beginning of another Christmas season. A parade led by Santa Claus.

BUT THERE IS yet another part of me in Cisco, a memory of a time during the deepest days of the Great Depression when my father allowed me to accompany him on a weekly trip to that city with a truck load of Pepsi-Cola. His commission (and only pay) was two cents a case, and the truck held two hundred cases. This meant that with a day of driving (we took a looping, long-distance way to get there) and a good deal of sweat he could make as much as four dollars. Which he seldom did.

We waited to reach Cisco to eat lunch because in Cisco we could get hamburgers for five cents each and ice cream for nine cents a pint. Thus, with swapping two hot drinks off the truck for two cold ones from a customer's icebox, we could have a fine meal for only seven per cent of the gross income. (Is it the memory of the food or of the Depression that makes me remember the exact prices?)

Sometimes along the highway to Cisco I could spot enough empty soft-drink bottles thrown into the bar ditch to pay for our meal. (I wasn't allowed to pick up beer bottles.) It always was an amazement to me that there existed persons in our society so affluent as to be able to blithely toss out so valuable an item as a two-cent refundable bottle. Drunks, my mother always believed them to be. The sight of an empty bottle along the highway even today causes me to spend an involuntary instant touching my brake pedal.

However, Cisco represented a crisis in morals which still disturbs something in me to recall. One of the brands my father carried on his little soft-drink truck was Orange Crush. To stimulate sales, this company had a contest within each of its franchised territories—a simple contest in which prizes were offered to the persons collecting the most Orange Crush bottle caps, or crowns, as they are called in the industry. The first prize was a Silver King bicycle, with other prizes in descending order of importance, but to me the Silver King was so overwhelmingly paramount to anything else offered that I didn't even think about second or third prize. The Silver King was an all-aluminum bicycle which had come on the market a year or two before and it automatically established all its riders as holding magnifico status. I have forgotten the exact cost of a Silver King but it was something like ten dollars more than most good wheels and double the cost of some chain-store products. My hopes of ever owning a Silver King had been somewhat less than nil, but I wanted one more than honor, fame, or wisdom.

There was one awesome catch to this contest, for me. The rules stated flatly that employees of the bottling company and their families were not eligible. This posed a dilemma: if I didn't turn a hand to pick up some of the hundreds of Orange Crush caps I saw each week then there was implied a lack of industry and ambition on my part. If, however, I did pick them up I was clearly violating the rules. My mother gave me an answer rather too quickly for my uses. There was no choice there, she said. I must abstain. And not only abstain, but not help some other boy.

The only thing about her pronouncement which didn't beat the very marrow of my soul was the devilish thought that Daddy hadn't been there to hear it.

With childish hypocrisy and equal deceit, I put it on the poor man in such a way as to relieve him of moral overtones. I suggested that a cousin named D. L. be given

what amounted to a power of attorney and that D.L. accompany us on those days when we went on our long out-of-town route. Let him pick up caps as he would. My father, a man of fine moral conviction but of uncertain stamina when it came to letting others persuade him, thought about it and somewhat reluctantly agreed. "Family" didn't cover cousins.

As we were heading for Cisco early in the morning on the next trip—still dark, although it was summer—my conscience came on for its first twinge. The truck was a short-bed Model B Ford with two I-beams sticking out the back, and with three occupants the cab was too crowded for the driver to shift gears. To compensate for my (hidden) sins, I volunteered to ride on one of the projecting I-beams of the chassis when we were in a town delivering from store to store.

The first place we delivered to was a honky-tonk called Big Alex's which sat on Nine Mile Hill, southwest of Albany. My father was going through a religious renascence at the time and didn't approve of drinking, and his business calls to Big Alex's and such places were conducted with quick, crisp, and (for him) unaccustomed brevity of conversation—for my father loved to talk as much as any human being I have ever encountered in my life, unless it was his mother. But he didn't linger around the honky-tonks, not even for repartee with the frowzy but often pretty waitresses—women being a weakness he did have, under ordinary circumstances.

At any rate, we stopped at Big Alex's place and it was an experience I can recall with little trouble even now—walking into a honky-tonk at eight o'clock in the morning, just before the mess of the night before was cleaned up. The smell of the place was one that shot to the depths of a young prude's soul (which mine undoubtedly was): a combination of stale beer, tobacco smoke, human sweat, and some mysteriously elusive odor layered through the rest, which I can only call sex and leave to the imagination of the reader, for it was compounded of human and artificial odors initiated for the purpose—partly the cheap face powder and perfume of the girls who hung around these places, and partly that characteristic stench which the male animal gives off when he is inflamed to rut.

But moving through the smell of sin such as invested Big Alex's, I proceeded across the vacant barn of a dance hall, and out the back. There I found an Eldorado of Orange Crush caps strewn about the ground, glittering up at me like Sutter's gold. D.L. and I plunged into the collecting process as one does in those dreams in which there first appears one coin in the sand, then another and another until at last you wake from the sheer exhilaration of the impossibility of gathering them all.

D.L. had no moral uneasiness about places like Big Alex's, for his father (my father's brother Roy) was a more lenient, less rigid man who had fought in France during World War I and therefore had seen the world. So the same bolt of conviction didn't hit D.L. that hit me midway in our gathering of our gold. Suddenly a voice, like the one that wakened Samuel in the Bible, seemed to be asking, what was I doing? I managed some pale excuse in myself and left D.L. to collect the rest of the crowns while I went out to the truck and climbed weakly into the cab, afraid to turn my eyes to heaven for fear God really would commune with me.

Throughout the rest of the trip the effect remained. I was literally hurting from the position in which I found myself, wanting with all my greedy, lustful little heart to find acres and acres of discarded Orange Crush caps but thinking always of the strict injunction that "ye are in the world but not of the world . . ." which I heard almost every Sunday. Finally we came to Cisco and I did not have to undergo this double burden, at least, for Cisco had no such places as Big Alex's. Alas, there were also few Orange Crush caps to be found there, but this acted as a kind of recess for my conscience. The sheer sinfulness of finding a great many of the crowns operated on me in such a way that I was almost happy to come to a spot where there was less temptation.

My cousin didn't win the Silver King bicycle, although I have often wondered just who could have found more lids than the son of a delivery man? I suspect my father never did turn in the crowns we collected. He did bring home a baseball glove which was supposedly a prize at some minor level, but I am sure it was one he bought, or persuaded out of someone, my father being a great persuader. At first my disappointment at not winning the Silver King was so great that the glove represented only the bitterness of failure to me and I refused to use it. Later, my puritanical soul began grieving at the means by which the glove had come to me and I developed a deep moral distaste for it. Ultimately the glove simply disappeared. Poor D.L., now in his grave for many years, got, for his part in the shameful episode, a silver dollar, which was all my father could afford. On the other hand, D.L.'s reward, in contrast to my own, may have been a clean heart, for he was one of those blessed people who never saw the bad in others, so he may never have seen how deceitful my proposal was to begin with.

7

The Ominous Journey

THE ROAD between Cisco and Abilene is only forty-five miles in length, but when I think of automobile travel this bit of highway makes the first flash of recognition across my mind. We always seemed to have to pass that way no matter what our destination.

Travel was never just a process of getting from one place to another, with my family. Each trip was epochal, a reference point in the tribal annals for events wholly separate from the journey itself.

"When did Stub lose his eye?" someone would ask, referring to an uncle's injury in an industrial accident.

"Let's see . . . wasn't it the year we made the trip to Beaumont . . . when we went through Hico?"

A pause. "I thought it was the time A.C. got sick on chocolate peanuts."

"No, no. He got sick on chocolate peanuts that night we stayed with Mrs. Herman. When the car broke down in Fort Worth."

This brings a frown. "Then it must have been the time Mama wouldn't drink the Dr. Pepper." (My great-grandmother thought this Texas soft drink contained dope.)

"That's right. At Waco. And it made Carl so mad he tried to run into the interurban."

And on and on, the highways and detours reaching like pages in a diary back to what happened.

Part of the passionate quality of travel with us came from the fact that my father was usually the only adult male among three suspicious, strong-minded women of his wife's family—my mother, my grandmother, and my great-grandmother.

My memory of those journeys always begins in the dark. Something would awaken me—the stir in the house or an intensity within my body—and warn me I was missing excitement. (Young boys are the only people I know of who are capable of this kind of alarm.)

I would come awake quickly, in the manner of the young, and there would be soft light coming down the hall from the kitchen. Voices would be speaking, too low to understand but with recognizable tones—my grandmother's soft remonstrance, my mother's higher, younger sound, urging her to do this or not to do that, the negatives transmitted themselves better than the positives. Then the scratchy old-woman's complaint of my great-grandmother, forming a kind of female bass to the arguments about food preparation, the gathering of supplies, and the necessities of the trip.

Soon my father's stronger voice would be heard, after he had come in from packing the car (as it was put) and this would have me fully aroused to the realization that we were about to set out for Fort Worth, Beaumont, San Antonio, or Colorado City—places in the family atlas of Important Destinations.

The start of a journey was never quite early enough for my mother and always a bit too early for my grandmother, even though my mother was the late riser of the two. They lived in almost constant opposition all their lives; without hate, but seldom in agreement. I cannot say whether or not it was a natural mother-daughter resentment. My experience of watching my own daughter and her mother, my wife, is too narrow, too tinctured with closeness to be valid in judgment.

For my grandmother a journey was an act of deliberate peril. Everything contributed to fear. The clouds that came up from nowhere to darken the land were but the face of some disparate god of personal spite. This unlifted threat of disaster was bequeathed me by all three female generations that nursed me to manhood. They reminded me by word and act that man is never alone in his choices. As soon as God leaves his side, or he leaves God's, in rushes the Devil. Hard work and self-effacement were the only ways to thwart Beelzebub; sweat was the holy water of purification. If you dare stand up to be seen, or leave your house to perform some challenging act like moving across the face of the earth, then you are inviting divine testing—you are assuring yourself of it. So we seemed to undertake our departures by figurative candlelight so as to escape notice, for that short period of dawn grayness at least, of the moral responsibility which came from asserting our existence.

On the road we drove waiting for the next disaster, having escaped evil only from one mile to the next, never for good. The thanks we gave were more often for what we had missed than for what we had been given. My family could always find reasons to view a gift as a potential ticket to despair or dissolution.

Our vehicle, in the earliest days, was some kind of open touring model, but I can never recall the top being let down. It had side curtains with heavy glass panes sewn into the artificial leather fabric. Inside, with the curtains up, was dark and scary. The seats were firm and cold, and the rain was always coming down, making a drumhead of the fabric top stretched over the wooden bows—although this is plainly a specific memory of mine rather than any general condition because there is never that much rain in West Texas.

Luggage was carried wherever it could be tied, strapped, or sat on. One of my father's jobs was to locate, then attach, the expanding metal luggage carrier which fitted to the running boards. But even with this (you could only use one side of the car because these racks blocked the doors) there was not enough space, so I was usually given the honor of straddling an old brown leather suitcase belonging to an uncle but being used by my grandmother. Luggage was scarce and precious in our family and ownership was not so important as the circumstance of who was using it at any one time. Sometimes a particularly voluminous, costly piece of gear would be passed around from one journey to the next for a matter of years before its true owner broke the circle to reclaim its use.

My father always did the driving, although not without help from the various nondrivers such as my grandmother, who only learned how to operate an automobile after she was well into her fifties, and my great-grandmother who died at age eighty-four without ever understanding the basic usage of such items as brakes, steering wheel, horn, or gearshift. There is a family legend that my grandfather on my mother's side, a red-haired gentleman named Ambrose who had a notoriously short-fused temper, tried to give Granny a driving lesson in an EMF automobile back in the green years of personal motor ownership. But she was inclined to try and control the auto as one did a horse, and ended up almost immediately in a ditch, tugging at the steering wheel and shouting "Whoa!" This brought on a blast of polite obscenity from her son-in-law which alienated Granny from the auto forever. (The alienation from the son-in-law had preceded this by several years.) Nevertheless, when riding as a passenger she knew what her eyes told her, and she had an imperious kind of comment which verged on command when she espied a traffic danger that my father, the driver, was apt to overlook or not sufficiently to acknowledge in advance.

THUS IN THE DARKENED MORNING we left our house, the air of old dismay closing in on a home empty of life. The rest of us waited in the car while my grandmother prowled from room to room, in fear some seed of doom had been planted behind, by carelessness, to flower in the hideous subsequence of our departure—a gas jet left cracked, secret water faucets giving out a trickle that would gain a roar once we were past the city limits, and above all, the terrible certainty of fire. An electric iron was always smoldering on the sheet-covered board; a hot-water heater, innocent of thermostat or other automatic controls, was sure to be boiling dry and the galvanized metal of the tank collapsing in a deadly lava, eating its fiery way through floor, joists, and foundation beams, consuming the interior of the house until, by the time the outside world saw evidence of it, alarm was too late. These were the inevitabilities my grandmother patrolled against, never failing to find something of potential death or ruin.

Getting into the car at last: "Did you find anything?" from my mother.

A sniff: "Certainly."

My father: "Had you left the hot-water tank on?"

"There was gas escaping in the front bedroom." It was a statement which amounted to an accusation because my mother and father shared that room.

Mother: "Where?"

"The petcock under the highboy."

A snort from the driver. "That hasn't been turned on since last winter." (This being July.)

"I smelled it when I walked in the room."

The dialogue is diffuse and scattered at that point, going in several possible directions, becoming a round of accusations and counterclaims.

Once on the road, my father faced other problems of travel. The matter of rivers and bridges was a severe one. My grandmother didn't want to cross any bridge when the creek or river was full because she had a theory that so much water was bound to be secretly eating away the supports. One might think, therefore, that in dry weather a bridge would be no obstacle. But this is overlooking the problem of quicksand.

I have never encountered quicksand and I am not sure my grandmother had, but she was an expert on it. Quicksand need not be wet to be deadly. Quicksand was quick sand. The name told everything. It was quick in the sense that it worked rapidly, engulfing a man (or woman) so swiftly that he (or she) hadn't time to extract a foot, much less an entire leg. And those unfortunate enough to sink to the waist were doomed, even though whole squads of would-be rescuers were standing nearby with all the standard quicksand rescue apparatus. It was the weight of the sand itself that gave it its awful sucking power, creating of the innocent natural element a beast with a cunning mind and lightning tongue. I could imagine it creeping up alongside some low bridge and pouncing hungrily on the first high-pressure tire that came within licking distance, pulling car and contents under.

So you were never safe around rivers. Floods were self-evident menace, known and understood to be instruments of judgment (and a flood, in my grandmother's nomenclature, was any running water). Despite the fact she spent a great many years in East Texas where deep rivers and springs are the normal rather than the unusual, her girlhood had cast her among people whose lives had been spent on the frontier where tanks and ponds were the only natural water, therefore running water was invariably dangerous, for the sudden downpours, the wet northers, the cloudbursts were great things for showing you how disastrously you had located your cabin, dugout, or stock pen.

For this reason, among a host of others, she also despised night travel. Her fear was not from collision with another vehicle (in fact, she welcomed the sight of another car because it showed her that someone else besides her son-in-law was foolish enough to be taking this forlorn route) but from the ever-present danger of unknowingly driving off the end of a demolished bridge—finding yourself and vehicle suddenly suspended in mid air, thoroughly conscious that in a twinkling of an eye you and yours would be plunged into eternity in the dark waters of the flood beneath you. (And about that time, as luck would have it, Thornton Wilder's novel *The Bridge of San Luis Rey* came out, a story which centers on the catastrophe of a bridge giving way, and my grandmother, who was a librarian, thrilled to have such high-level corroboration of something she had anticipated all her life.)

The bridges along the road were almost all narrow, spidery, and rattly, originally constructed for passage by wagon and buggy, laid with timber floors which rattled like bones or rumbled like kettledrums when any weight moved over them. In most cases, crossing was restricted to one vehicle at a time on account of width or fragility or both.

The main bridge over the Brazos, on the route we used, was located at the forgotten town of Brazos. It was a swinging bridge, a frightful span swung from cables about three inches thick, suspended between two pairs of towers and reaching across an impressive width of river. The bridge site was about a mile from the little town. You drove down a muddy lane, made a sharp turn around a hill, and just like that, the bridge was there. It had a remarkable tendency to sway, and the planking was not bolted down solid but was laid in flexibly so that the bridge could twist and turn without cracking. It was scary in broad daylight, and in the dark, or during a rain or flood, it could be hair-raising.

My grandmother refused to ride in a car across this devil, as she called it. She walked over, and did that only after the bridge was cleared of vehicles. As it was a rather

long bridge, walking created its own traffic problem. Later, years later, a massive steel and concrete bridge was constructed over the Brazos a few miles south of that swinging one, but the first time she came to the new one she walked over it, too, just to be sure. It was so solid it seemed to have changed her whole outlook on bridges, and I never heard her voice her bridge fears again. But I must add, in her memory, that the swinging bridge over the Brazos eventually did collapse, dropping a bakery truck into the river which was at low water so that the driver was able to wade out, undrowned by the flood and unclaimed by the quicksand.

AROUND CISCO, east or west, the road could be a twisting, hidden thing, going through plowed fields and barn-

yards, cutting around farmhouses and, in one instance, running between the kitchen door and the privy. Trying to progress over it at night was unwise and to do so in a hard rain was foolish. You could not go many miles until there was before you what looked like a river in flood, spread out over the dirt road. Then you backed up and there was nothing for it but to arouse someone at the nearest farmhouse and get advice on alternate routes.

Remembering, I am amazed at how willing people were to be awakened and asked foolish questions by foolish motorists. I think, at that time in West Texas (most of the rest of the nation being somewhat better marked and paved), cross-country motoring still had some of its taint of adventuring, and persons who undertook it were granted a form of indulgence, were tolerated in a way that the ordinariness of motor travel today denies those who need help. From the car I could hear rural voices directing my father back to the first left-hand road, go about two miles to a cattle guard, then veer right along the turn row to where a gate will let you through to a pasture, follow along the fence to a shallow ford on the creek that's supposed to be rock-bottomed if too much dirt ain't washed down, and then get back on the main road.

Driving those directions was risky in itself, and at night a sheer matter of chance—going through strange fields along paths or trails, easing the front wheels of the car into what looked like a rushing river and never knowing if you have the precise rock bottom the farmer promised, but knowing the public highway had been so washed out it would be a week before cars could use it. These were the alternatives: to drive with danger or turn around and go back.

Sometimes we would drive, slowly, without knowing where we were or whither headed, pulling through mud, holding our breath while we eased off into unplumbed chug-holes full of water, until it would seem like hours and hours since we had seen a light or met another car. And if, in those times, we did encounter another car there would be a conference in the middle of the road, or one car pulled over as far to the right as possible to let the other pass. When they met, the drivers opened their curtains, calling to each other across the stormy night.

"Which way've you come from?"

"We come by Palo Pinto. How's the road back of you?"

And the exchange was made—advice to avoid a certain place, or a certain stretch, to not let a specific farmer pull you out with his mules if you got stuck because he charged three bucks or five bucks instead of the customary two. Or sometimes it turned out that both cars were lost and maybe even would turn around and return the way they had come, discovering there was nothing ahead but greater grief.

COMING WEST to Cisco the highway, for many years, led through Strawn, past a huge warehouse which displayed a prominent sign, EXPLOSIVES (or it might have been DYNAMITE). I suppose that because of coal mining activity around there this firm was a distributor of high explosives. But little did the owners know of the havoc and spiritual unrest they were creating with that sign. My grandmother began worrying about Strawn a good twenty miles before we reached the town. She had recollections of entire cities wiped off the map by untoward disturbance of dynamite stores. Her distress increased as we neared Strawn, the state of the roads seldom contributing to anyone's peace of mind, and I can admit at this remove that her fear was contagious. I sensed a kind of thrilling terror myself, half hoping, half fearing it would be our privilege to discover nothing but a vast hole in the earth where Strawn had been, yet feeling vicious and guilty that I had these unnatural desires. I repeated this process a few years later when the American Airlines started flying their Ford tri-motors over West Texas, coming in loudly and low with the dusk. What a thrill it would be if one could fall in our front yard, but not hurt anyone aboard. (Yet I knew that if no one was hurt the event would lack the compelling fascination and importance of dire death.) And have I even yet managed to shake the guilt I feel at such times as I secretly look forward to something of like nature, too civilized now that I am a man to really want calamity, but isn't that what it amounts to?

Rain was a little more common, or seemed to be, over around Cisco, and the entryway to that city survives in my mind as a continual series of bog-holes and detours. Reaching Cisco one dark and stormy night we stopped to arouse a gasoline seller and discovered in the process that some high-center bit of detour coming into town had skewed off the plug to the oil pan. My grandmother wasn't along on the trip, and I wish she could have been, for the circumstances were perfect for doom. In the first place, my father and my Uncle Grady (my mother's only brother) had flouted fate and left for home entirely too late, with mother and her sister-in-law, Pat, warning them that they shouldn't travel at night and casting about in their female minds for some remembered mechanical breakdown to predict—neither having the slightest knowledge of how an automobile was put together. They were delighted, I am sure, when the oil-plug wreckage was found.

The hour must have been midnight because I had been asleep for hours with my head in mother's lap. I rose up in the dark, hearing mysterious muffled voices and thunder growling all around. My father and uncle were discussing the situation with the gasoline seller whom they had aroused. My uncle was mad, I could tell, not only from his tone of voice but instinctively, he having inherited his red-haired father's celebrated volatility. Having to stop at this hour (an admission they had left too late) and get an unhappy man out of bed to sell a few gallons of gasoline, then to discover that the oil plug had been ruined, this would raise my uncle's internal processes to the demolition point. Unlike my father, Uncle Grady would blast off an oath with little provocation.

I heard him, unseen in the dark: "Well, goddammit, I don't care how, I want it fixed." Some muttered comment from out of the night, then another oath from Grady.

"Now, Brother . . ." my mother called from the car, trying to pour oil on the troubled waters, or avert trouble which Uncle Grady didn't mind in the least accumulating. His wife, a new wife at the time, hesitated to exercise her rights, but laid a cautioning hand on my mother's arm, "Now Marie, you know your brother well enough to realize you can't stop him once he gets started."

A blacksmith was finally gotten out of bed, somehow, and he emerged, in traditionally huge size, carrying a kerosene lantern to confront the broken-down car and the people who had caused this inconvenience.

"Run it up on the curb here and I'll take a look at it," the smithy said. (This was a customary way to elevate the underside of a car in an emergency.) But my uncle refused to start the motor with the oil low and for a while it looked as if we would sit there all night. Finally my father, who was uncharacteristically quiet in the presence of that particular uncle, asked why we couldn't push it.

The blacksmith, by then sensing he would get little

gratitude for getting out of bed to help these travelers, suddenly darted behind the machine and began heaving, while my mother began exclaiming for him to wait. The blacksmith thought she was concerned about our weight being in the car and he yelled for her to keep her seat. But it did matter because what she was exclaiming about was not our weight but the fact that the car was in gear and she was leaning over the front seats to disengage it. As she did, however, the Samson at our rear gave an infuriated heave and the car raced across the brick pavement heading for the curb and my mother somersaulted over into the front seat, her flapper-length skirt dropping down over her head and her pretty bloomers (step-ins were sinful) with their legs tied in fetching bows, completely exposed amid the kicking and screaming. With a jolt that kept her pinned on the front floorboard, the car mounted the curb and bashed itself to a stop against a light pole. It fell to the lot of the blacksmith, now chastened by the events he had set in train, to come running with his lantern and rescue my mother who was not injured at all but so mortified by her exposure that she wouldn't answer the poor man's questions or look him in the face because, as the women put it, he had seen "everything she had."

By the light of his lantern the blacksmith crawled under the car and found the sheared-off plug. He backed it out of the pan and proceeded to open his little shop, find a piece of metal the right diameter, and cut a new plug. The men had gotten quiet by now and I got out of the car and stood in the night, just inside the blacksmith shop, while the rain began to come down with an earnest thrust and the women stayed inside the car, my mother, of course, refusing to come into the lighted place where the innocent but condemned blacksmith was. When it came time to replace the new plug, the smith found that the gutter where the car was reared up on the curb had filled with flowing water, but he crawled under anyway, taking his lantern as far under with him as he could, and although the picture may be false, I see in my mind the chiaroscuro surrounding the car, him partially under it, the lantern protected so the hot glass wouldn't break in the rain, the other men peering down under the car, only their faces visible in the yellow lantern light, my uncle holding the lantern, turning it one way or another as the blacksmith directed. And when the plug did fit, the break repaired, the conference of the men around the lantern, an exchange of bills (hesitantly he charged five dollars for the job), putting more oil in the crankcase, oil drawn a quart at a time from the hand pump of the gasoline man (who had gone back to bed leaving his friend the blacksmith to settle up). By the time the car was started, backed down from the curb, and the blacksmith congratulated on his handiwork, we were good friends, the two traveling couples and the workman. The rain continued. It was all done by lantern light, and as we drove away from the place we saw him slouching back, a big man certainly weary, to close his shop and get a little more sleep before dawn.

They are all gone, my mother and father, Uncle Grady and Aunt Pat, all of whom were so young then (my mother barely twenty-two), and I am sure the blacksmith is also gone. His shop, at least, disappeared decades ago. The night around the lantern, in the rain, the waiting, is all mine now.

FROM CISCO to Baird is a twenty-five-mile stretch in which there was (and is) little habitation. For years the highway went by way of a T&P siding named Dothan where a monument informed you this was the route of the first military telegraph line into West Texas. Then the road passed the site where the grandiose city of Vigo had been planned at the turn of the century, went around an oil company tank farm which was almost a town in itself, and into Putnam, which had already faded badly from its brief days as a health resort (the mineral baths in the basement of the Mission Hotel now lie under twenty feet of Interstate Highway 20).

West of Putnam was the beginning of what I call the "Carl, stop" section. The filling stations of that day were mostly a single pump in front of a hardware store or some other masculine establishment. It was considered unladylike, in our family, for a woman to approach a man and ask where she could go to use the bathroom.

Baird, fifteen miles along the way, had one place which the women had spotted through experience, a simple two-holer of the period but marked LADIES so that no embarrassing questions were necessary. The fact that any female seen going off across the pasture in that direction caused all male eyes to "see where she was heading" was bad enough, but tolerable in comparison to a badly expanded bladder, which seemed to be an inherited weakness among the Coles and Dockrays (or Dockerys) of my mother's line.

But Baird was far, and Putnam had an unfortunate reputation among our women, so as soon as the highway was empty of other cars, the cry went up, "Carl, stop." Usually it was Mother or my grandmother, but now and then it would be Granny, the tough old great-grandmother who had learned better control in the days of frontier travel. She could be even more insistent than the younger women, and she was not above cutting loose in the back seat of the car, attempting to use her snuff spit can for a receptacle. (With her layers of skirts and petticoats it amounted to a hidden undertaking, so far as delicacy was

concerned, although not necessarily always a successful one.)

So a stop was made, the car pulled over to the side of the road, a great deal of nervous looking around was done, to be sure no oncoming motorist would spot the inconvenienced women as they squatted behind mesquite bushes or in oak clumps, or would not see them crawling through the barbwire fence and know why they were heading for the bushes.

My father's idea of the best of all jokes was to honk the klaxon at what he had timed as the most inappropriate moment, bringing the women flocking in from the field in degrees of disarray. He would take on a serious look and apologize for having "accidentally hit the horn button," or say, solemnly, that he had seen a snake crawling across the road toward their roosting place. These occasions were the only ones on which I ever knew my mother to indulge in an indelicacy. "You caused us to wet all over ourselves with your honking," she would accuse him.

The breaking of the journey to accommodate the women plagued my father into modern times. Even with superhighways and super-service stations he would have to stop at least once on a trip to let my grandmother go outdoors because she claimed she had found all the commercial restrooms in a condition she called "filthy." This term, in her usage, defied definition. I think maybe she just liked nature.

NEARING BAIRD, the highway became a winding trail around the sides of an elevation called "Baird Hill." There were really two Baird Hills, the one used by motorists, the other a famous feature on the T&P Railway at that point. In fact, for years there was a tiny community named Chautauqua at the beginning of the west-bound grade where a helper-engine waited to boost freight trains up Baird Hill.

The Baird Hill of the autos was just across a narrow valley from the railroad and afforded a motorist one of his best chances in West Texas to outrun a passenger train. The automobile benefited greatly in acceleration from the incline into the valley, whereas the train on the adjacent tracks remained elevated on a dump to a degree. If the automobile driver had enough nerve, in those days before pavement, to brave the slippery gravel and dirt of the sharp curves, he could have his machine flying along at a speed well in excess of the train's. It was out of the question, of course, for my father to indulge in such dangerous and unchristian games of chance with his family in the car. I secretly longed for the brakes to "go out" (a common affliction of cars in those days) and send us careening and glorying down toward death but arriving safe, eventually, on the dusty, straight road that carried on at the foot of Baird Hill.

A few years later when the Texas Highway Department built a solid rock wall along the canyon edge and banked the turns, it became the fashion to approach the top of Baird Hill at about sixty miles per hour (the *ne plus ultra* of speed then) and "throw 'er out of gear," allowing the car to drift through the curves at an ever-increasing rate of speed, the driver putting on the brakes only when it was apparent he must decelerate or die.

Not a few did die, and the patched wall, breached despite its thickness, attests even today to how easily it happened—if you care to walk over about a mile of private property to see the wall (or Baird Hill), the highway at that place having been abandoned in the fifties.

BAIRD IS a red brick town, the main street lined with buildings that are rapidly assuming an antique air and identity. The highway has entered and departed Baird in so many different routes that it is a waste of time to recall them, finally missing the town altogether in a recent project of the interstate system. It has always seemed ironic that these busy six- and eight-lane highways will be painstakingly looped around a village the size of Baird but will plunge directly into some seething traffic caldron like Fort Worth or Dallas. In West Texas the shifting of a busy road will almost always kill a little town, for most of them that are still alive after the changing agricultural and economic dislocation of the passing of the frontier and the agrarian society survive off the traffic of the highway passing through them.

West Texas is now a land dotted with sad, abandoned farmhouses and little towns which have expired so quietly as to ruffle few of history's pages. Mechanization has made farming in West Texas a business that requires a certain vastness, and the farm-to-market road system of the state, which has paved almost every county byroad and pathway, has combined with the automobile to draw anyone living on the land or in the little places off to the bigger cities.

Baird, being the county seat and located on a major national street, has remained alive, but all around it are the ghosts of cities of the past whose future at one time was taken to be secure. Belle Plain, some six miles south, was the first county seat of Callahan County when the formal machinery of politics was set in motion in 1877. (Belle Plain considered its real rival to be a place called Callahan City, of which a local editor reported contemptuously in 1878, "its days are numbered.") Belle Plain had a courthouse, banks, printing offices, and even a well-established school of higher learning, Belle Plain College. All roads led to Belle Plain, and thus today the trace going east out of Buffalo Gap, some thirty miles away over in Taylor County, is called the Belle Plain Road, even though it has been at least half a century since any vehicle was able to actually go direct from Buffalo Gap to Belle Plain over this road.

The old pioneers had a naïve belief in possession—being at a place or holding something worthwhile—which asserted itself in an attitude of, "if they want us, let them come here." This worked very well with springs and watering places, or trading posts established at strategic passes through the hills. But the railroad was all these things in itself, and it didn't beg, it accepted pleas. The T&P, being pushed through West Texas in 1880 and 1881, was in the hands of as tough a crew of robber barons as the nineteenth century afforded—the men who surrounded Jay Gould—and it went straight through on its surveys. Where a city such as Belle Plain or Buffalo Gap was already laid out and thriving, the railroad simply stopped long enough to plat its own rival, swing its vast propaganda machinery in motion, and continue on, secure in the realization that its city would almost certainly siphon off the life or completely kill the off-track competitor. So Belle Plain, which the railroad missed in 1880, is today a heap of old, dressed stone out in a pasture, guarded by a barbwire fence. The truth of the matter is, the railroad of the seventies and eighties didn't want to go through the small towns it found out through its virgin territory. It wanted to create its own cities so it could make money selling town lots. And that is exactly what happened in West Texas. Virtually every city of any size or importance was established by the railroads and sold by their land departments, while the few that were already there were either accidentally on the line of the railroad (like Colorado City) or they pulled up and moved over to get on the line, as Ranger and Cisco did. Otherwise, they mostly disappeared.

However, a few years after the rail building had cooled off from the high pitch of civic heat the promoters drove it to, some small market centers got dreams and aspirations which were to be dashed just as inconsiderately by the paved roads and the automobiles of the forthcoming twentieth century. Scranton, just over the line in Eastland County, had its hopeful years, with Scranton Academy fielding a football team around the turn of the century. But Scranton has become a tiny one-room post office now and five empty store buildings, with the flapping of the post-office flag the main, single, continuing activity in town. Cottonwood, just down the road, gave American letters a fairly important contributor, Southwest historian Lewis Nordyke, but today the city directory consists of a pole with two dozen name-signs attached.

There was a need for all of them once, when a community could be contained and sustained in a bend of a creek or a box canyon, when isolated farms and remote ranches meant going to town only once a month. Then you could call two stores, a cotton gin, and a Baptist and a Methodist church a city. You could give it a good solid name and get a U.S. post office the way Abbie in Jones County and Mt. Moro in Taylor County did. When the buckboard and the mudwagon took all day to get to Merkel from Nubia, when the mail hack was the only wheeled vehicle you would see coming down the county road for a week at a time, then Ovalo, Bradshaw, Shep, Potosi, could not only survive but feel ambitious, look outward toward a future as a city. How did the honorary colonels and majors whose grave pronouncements were taken as gospel by their awed lower classes know that something called asphalt and a thing named truck and automobile would destroy remoteness forever, and that their rivals were not Abilene and San Angelo and Weatherford—but Dallas, St. Louis, and New York? (The shrinking world continues to shrink, and now towns like Abilene find their proud population figures of 100,000 or more mean nothing when it comes to jet plane travel because they are too close to hugeness by only lying two hundred miles from Dallas.)

So for a time at every five or ten miles these little trade centers sprang up and grew ambitious. Thrived, at least, and I can remember setting off into the country for a Sunday afternoon drive with places like Hamby and Sambo for destination—where today there is only a suburb for something bigger. Now they are names on a roll call of meaninglessness—Admiral, Oplin, Nimrod, Eolian, Morton Valley, Okra, Romney, Wayland, Necessity. About all that is left in some of them is an empty-eyed, unused schoolhouse, the last structure left in the community after consolidation had moved the pupils themselves (in fleets of big yellow school buses which flood out over West Texas mornings and nights) miles away to what had been, at one time, distant rival cities.

Coleman County, which lies directly south of Callahan County, has the prettiest sounding town names of any county I know about. It is surely a matter of pure chance, for Coleman County is older than some of its neighbors and its cities were not planted and brought to life overnight, as were those of the railroad counties to the north.

Hear this list: Goldsboro, Novice, Silver Valley, Glen Cove, Talpa, Valera, Santa Anna, Leaday (pronounced *Lee*-day) Gouldbusk, Voss, Mozelle, Rockwood, Whon (like Don Juan), Trickham, Shields. And we might add the names of a pair of watercourses, Jim Ned Creek, named for a famous Delaware Indian guide, and Pecan Bayou, which is the last creek or river westward from Louisiana that I can discover to carry this Frenchified designation.

The names remain to charm us, but the cities, in so

many cases, are only something the mapmakers have left in print from either nostalgia or ignorance.

IN THE FINAL YEAR of the twenties a highway building and paving program reached West Texas and the route carried the pretentious title of "the Bankhead Highway, the Broadway of America." It was named for Senator John Hollis Bankhead of Alabama, who was famous for his legislative support for a national highway program. It didn't occur to me until years later that the Bankhead Highway began on the East Coast and stretched all the way to the West. I had assumed it to be purely a West Texas phenomenon, going no farther east than Fort Worth and reaching west certainly not past El Paso. In fact, for a couple of years, when the local newspapers were ballyhooing the coming of pavement, I had the idea it was restricted to that Cisco-Abilene section.

Therefore, I associated both Senator Bankhead and his granddaughter, the actress Tallulah, in a kind of natural way with West Texas. Here again I paid for my mistaken assumption when, during World War II, I was introduced to Miss Bankhead and mentioned West Texas in the tone of one native to another. The result, of course, was a completely blank shrug from this famous Alabaman, and I was hurt that she would treat somebody that way who had lived such a powerful part of his life on the Bankhead Highway. The term as the name for a road, for cafés, motels, and other businesses continued in West Texas up until that war and long after the national highway number system had replaced the naming system. It has been a while, in West Texas at least, since I have heard anyone refer to the Bankhead Highway and, for that matter, most of the old Bankhead route has slowly been swerved, abandoned, or put to secondary use.

BETWEEN BAIRD and Clyde the scenery takes on a benign, rural air, in a way almost satisfactory to a native of New England. Especially the old road which is lined away from the highway in symmetrical orchards, neat little truck-garden plots, chicken hatcheries, and vegetable-growing. Clyde is really an island of fertile sand in the sea of West Texas red dirt and for a long time was known as "the California of Texas" and had this painted on the municipal water tower. Peaches, apricots, berries, grapes, pears, melons—these were the rich harvest which was displayed along the Bankhead Highway in family-run fruit stands. Peanuts were a big fall item on the Clyde stop, and many a tow sack of Spanish goobers rode between my feet on the family floorboard. My father, who had too many quaint concepts to list them all in one place, insisted that raw Spanish peanuts were good for the stomach, and used this remedy on those rare occasions when he had that complaint. To my taste raw peanuts were (and are) rather sickening, although I can eat a pound or more of them parched. Our tow sack of Clyde goobers used to sit by the kitchen stove throughout the winter, even during the Depression days—such a sack could be purchased full for fifty cents or less, as I remember. There was nothing better than putting a pan of them (spread evenly and thinly) in the oven to roast. Catching them still warm but not hot (they are soggy while still hot) was the trick, and I preferred them slightly too brown. The sandy grit which clung to some of the shells remains a taste of Clyde in my memory.

Clyde was famous for its tornadoes, even then, although its two major disasters were still to come. (In 1938 a storm killed fourteen persons and wiped out half the town; in 1950 a similar blow took five lives and struck

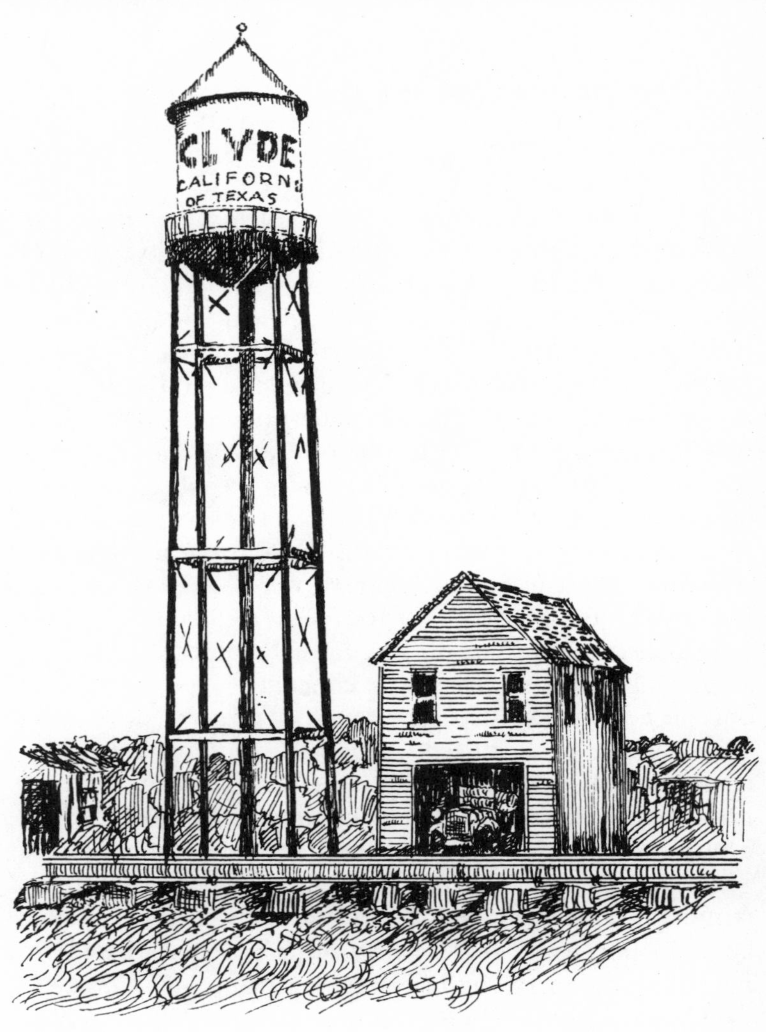

the other side of the town.) But this reputation as a "cyclone alley" furnished good grounds for my grandmother to grow uneasy when we motored toward, through, or near Clyde. Cyclones, at that time (I do not recall hearing them called tornadoes), were thought to follow some mysterious earth formation which led them to strike the same areas over and over. Abilene, only nine or ten miles from Clyde, has had one tornado that I can remember while Clyde has not only suffered major catastrophes but almost any spring reports sighting funnels or feels the lash of winds nearby. I know it is as unscientific as water-witching, but I can't erase the possibility of this from my mind. Who knows, of course, where the mysterious earth formations begin? Up in some secret gate of the Rocky Mountains, or the Montana Bitterroots?

A cousin of my grandmother's moved to Clyde to become a peach farmer and we spent a good many Sunday afternoons visiting there but not without staying in easy dogtrot of a storm cellar.

If I leave the impression that all my grandmother's cautions were foolish or consistently groundless, then I am creating an unfair idea. Her sin was not in her wariness but in her fear which kept her from ever taking the gamble, no matter whether the odds were for her or against her. She was an overbender. Her foibles and fears only endeared her to me, and although he mumbled about her forever, she and her son-in-law, my father, became as close as their extreme relationship would allow. The fact simply couldn't be overcome or overlooked that where he was broad she was narrow, and where responsibility rested on his soul like a feather, it weighed on her like a marble slab. As a matter of history, her fears were not groundless, they were just too damned prevalent. I have mentioned the case of the Brazos bridge which eventually collapsed. Clyde also bore out her alarms. The very farm—the very house—where the cousin lived, where she kept an eye peeled to the north for dark funnels and the other edged toward the cellar, was hit in 1938. Was, in fact, devastated, leveled, wiped off the earth stick by stick and brick by brick. The cousin and his family were saved only by getting the alarm in time for them to fall into a storm cellar and there to crouch and pray while the tornado whipped away even the fence posts and the well-curbings.

THE HIGHWAY WEST from Clyde today is a wide, double affair which bypasses the little town completely. The old road, which ran south of the T&P tracks (still the paramount man-made feature of West Texas in those days), was much more picturesque. It passed several natural lakes and even a swamp of cattails and a form of water lily that didn't bloom. Approaching Abilene it came to the crossroads village of Elmdale and, closely following the T&P tracks, made a half circle around the grave of the Lone Cowboy.

Local legend accumulated around this solitary burial which for years was marked by four cedar posts stuck upright at the corners of the grave. Someone later informed me it was the grave of a railroad construction worker, killed on the job or by somebody in the off-duty hours and laid to rest just off the right-of-way back in 1881 when there were no cemeteries about and few inhabitants to bother about positioning dead men. This sounds reasonable, but in my youth it was said to be the grave of the cowboy who, in the famous folk song, begs "low and mournfully" that they bury him not "on the lone prairie." While this may not be the grave, the song collectors do say the original dying cowboy met his fate on a ranch near Abilene, and so that narrow grave, just six by three (I am quoting the finale), is possibly nearby.

At any rate, the grave of the Elmdale Lone Cowboy intrigued me as a boyish traveler and I wanted to know more about it. However, my father was not of a historic bent, to say the least, and he replied that this grave was, in fact, that of a well-known local citizen named Henry and that if one approached the grave and asked in a loud voice, "What are you doing down there, Henry?" you would hear in reply nothing at all.

This is the kind of joke that is impossible to put in print but the import, verbally, was that Henry would say, "Nothing at all." It took me a good many years to come to an exact realization of what my father was trying to pull. And now when I think about those early morning departures when we were skirting Henry's grave, I still find myself wondering if, when approached with that question of what was going on underground, one wouldn't hear a sepulchral voice whisper back wearily, "Nothing at all."

MY BEGINNING in West Texas is just over a hill.

Physically it is Abilene, a town with a certain bracing beauty in its prairie openness, but particularly when approached at night from the highway, for it can be glimpsed from miles away, its lights dancing a thin line from north to south, making it seem to be an enormous city, much larger than it really is.

You are born someplace and most of the time it becomes, if nothing else, a statistic you can't escape. I was born in Abilene. But geography cannot work alone, so I do not give much mystic significance to that fact. You are also born some time which you become part of, and you are born of blood from a source which, even when unrecognized, plays with your future. But all this came at a point in time and a place on earth so that the intersection was unique.

A man cannot help but feel something compelling in his soul when he can look around and tell himself, even in strange, lost, or forgotten surroundings, "This is where I began." For most of us it is a more notable spot, by and large, than the spot where it might be said, "This is where he ended."

8

The Source and Since

I WAS BORN at noon one Sunday in a thing called the Abilene Emergency Hospital, which was nothing but a big, two-story frame house being used until the Baptists could finish building their new hospital over on the north side of town. I am not sure why, in view of their financial condition, my parents thought it necessary to go to the hospital for my birth. They were living in an apartment house and there may have been rules against having babies on the premises.

Births were considered a semipublic affair at the time. Besides the attending physician and nurses, mine was witnessed by my father, my grandmother Cole, a young medical intern who wanted to observe, and a man with a broken neck who was a patient. My mother was only seventeen and my father twenty-one, so I don't suppose it occurred to either of them that they had the right to demand privacy.

It was probably a good thing there were others present. My mother had grown quite fat for her size (she was a small woman) and the delivery was a difficult one. I still have trenches in my scalp where the forceps gouged me. It was not altogether my mother's fault. Most doctors wanted a pregnant woman to gain weight. The bigger the baby the better. I weighed over eleven pounds.

In the battle to save my mother's life, I was discarded. The doctor took a hasty look at my bloody, blackened little body and pronounced me incompetent to survive. He added that if I did I would be a hopeless idiot. A nurse, not unkindly but in professional haste to get back to the mother, pitched me over in a corner to die. Family tradition says it was atop a pile of newspapers, although I can't imagine a pile of newspapers being in the delivery room of even the Abilene Emergency Hospital.

My grandmother Cole, who was to make the difference so many other times in my life, got into a physical tussle with a nurse for possession of my carcass—the nurse insisting I was already dead. My grandmother Cole won the tug of war and she and my grandmother Green (my father's family spelled the name with and without the final *e*) spent the rest of Sunday holding me and protecting me from whatever it was that wanted me to die. Eventually the weary doctor, having brought my mother through the valley of the shadow, came over to see how I was doing and rescinded his prediction of idiocy. But he never got on a friendly footing with either of my grandmothers again, who considered him a heartless butcher.

The old hospital building stood at the corner of South Fourth and Sycamore streets for years and years, being converted to a middle-class apartment house as soon as the Baptists opened their new sanitarium. Some time in those after-years the old building burned, leaving nothing but the sidewalks, the concrete steps, and some foundation stones to mark the place. Nothing else was erected and in my own fortieth year I made a pilgrimage to the spot, never having stopped there in all the years I had passed it time and again.

I was stirring around in the dirt with a stick, looking for a square nail or some shard which might enlighten me as to the origin or age of my birthplace. An old man came by on the sidewalk and, as old men will who have nothing in the way of future plans to distract them, stopped to watch. Because there was no one else around and because one feels that old people should understand sentimentality, I told him this was the place where I was born, here where the Abilene Emergency had been.

"I remember that old hospital," he said. "The police chief used to drive the ambulance. It come right up alongside the building, right about there."

He hadn't happened to have ever been in the hospital with a broken neck, maybe? No, he'd never been in no hospital a-tall. Not yet, at least. But he remembered this one same as if he'd a-been in it because he was borned in that house next door on Sycamore and he was still living there now and he figured he'd die in about the same house, except his kids would probably take him off to some other hospital to die, which was all hospitals was good for, far as he's concerned.

The road back, only across a fifty-foot piece of concrete sidewalk to the front steps of an old gray house, for him. I started to say, as a joke, that he hadn't come very far in life but I decided he wouldn't see the humor in it. Besides, he had lost interest and started on down the walk toward town.

But there was a little boy standing there whom I hadn't noticed before. He was watching me with round, dark eyes and he had a runny nose. When I smiled and winked at him (that painful adult attempt to assure children we understand) he solemnly asked me what I was looking for. I said, oh, another little boy, maybe. I asked him where he lived and he said, "Here," without pointing to any of the houses around us, so I decided to leave it at that. I smiled again, said good-by, got in my car (which was pulled up at the curb where the ambulance drive had been) and left.

ABILENE WAS LAID OUT by the Texas & Pacific Railway as it built west. The town-lot sale was held March 15, 1881, and the first one auctioned off was at the corner of North Second and Pine streets. It was a good investment because the intersection remained the best commercial location in town for the next seventy years. Abilene was an instant success. A large crowd of land-hungry buyers had been living on the site in tents, waiting for the opening day, and by the time the sun went down the brand-new city had a permanent population of 1,500 or more. That will still get you a fair place on the West Texas municipal ladder.

There was no compelling reason for Abilene to be built where it was, between Cedar and Catclaw creeks. The railroad land agents went down the line locating town sites about every twenty miles. The railroad had originally intended building its city somewhat to the west, about where a little suburb named Tye now stands—a place it designated Tebo Switch, for some forgotten official. (When I was a boy Abilenians used to refer to Tye as "Tebo Tye, Taylor County, Texas.") I can't envision a modern city making it past the 100,000 mark, as Abilene has, laboring under the name Tebo Switch. Abilene is bad enough—a pretty-sounding name but one strangers have a devil of a time making up their minds about, some wanting to call it "*Abe*-line," others "A-*bile*-ene" and spelling it "Abulene," "Abeline," or "Abalene."

The plans to locate the town at Tebo Switch were changed by a couple of enterprising Belle Plain merchants named John and Clabe Merchant, who owned a big chunk of land along the Catclaw. They drove over to Colonel Simpson's Hashknife Ranch (which covered about half of where Abilene now stands) and persuaded the owner that town building rather than cattle raising was the coming thing in West Texas. The Merchants and Colonel Simpson then got together with the T&P's land developer, a Kentucky newspaperman named J. Stoddard Johnston, and between them gave birth to Abilene.

J. Stoddard Johnston came near to being unique in his calling, being an honest land promoter. He seemed to work on the premise that with as much land at its disposal as the T&P had (being one of the railroads which got huge land grants from the Texas legislature) there was no use lying about it. So when the land he had to sell was poor, he said so, and when he really believed in it (as he did in Abilene country) he was cautious to point out the pitfalls of pioneering, regardless of the land. In a wonderful broadside he wrote shortly after Abilene had been established, J. Stoddard Johnston noted that the prospective Abilenians must not confuse West Texas with the tropical parts of Texas then being promoted in the Rio Grande Valley where oranges, bananas, and sugar cane were possible.

"And as for those store-front loafers and soapbox whittlers who think that a fortune may be had for the taking on the frontier, they will soon find themselves pushing a broom in some boardinghouse for their meals, or herding sheep at twelve dollars per month."

The country didn't need any more lawyers, either, he pointed out, and common labor was a commodity in too full a supply. What Abilene really needed, he said, was an energetic young man with enough capital to put in a brick hotel.

Abilene was named for Abilene, Kansas, which had been the town at the end of so many successful cattle drives for the ranchers, who hoped the Texas town would emulate its Kansas namesake. Abilene, Kansas, had been named for a place mentioned in the Bible, so for Abilene, Texas, it was inevitable that business and religion both accepted the dedication of the town. Abilene, Texas, long ago overtook Abilene, Kansas, in size and economic importance, although not in colorful, romantic history or fame, and Abilene, Texas, today has the reputation among Texas cities of being the most puritanical and fundamental of any. Let us not belabor either point, but let us not overlook them.

WHEN I WAS BORN Abilene was still a young city. It had matured quickly, not going through the historical process of the frontier which the non-railroad cities had to survive. By 1886 Abilene had telephones and a water system (using hollow cedar logs for pipes). By 1891 it had electric lights and the most modern hotel between Fort Worth and El Paso. By 1892 a college had been established which, unlike other West Texas schools, is thriving today—Hardin-Simmons University. By 1900 it was a brick city (a phrase which had a more meaningful application at that time than it might now), and by 1908 it had built itself a streetcar line, two more railroads, and was shopping around for a motorized fire truck. It even had (and has) the same newspaper it had started with in 1881, the Abilene *Reporter*.

But it remained a frontier town because its gods were frontiersmen. I was not born on the frontier, neither was I given the kind of rural upbringing that might have preserved a frontier way of life past its day. But I was frontier-bred and frontier-reared, for the heroes around me, the legendary figures who stalked across my landscape, were from that time. The six-gun, already corrupted by Hollywood into a toy by the time I was born, kept its life-giving or life-taking position with those old ones. The soil was where everything came from and where everything went back to, they said. There was a class system which had only one basic requirement: survival.

The old ones were past their prime by then, but they ran the town. Not just the town as a place to do business or enforce municipal law, but as a community of beliefs, of expectation, of moral outlook. They had seen something we could never see, and we knew it. Not just a boy, hearing in awe of some old-days feat, but their sons, their daughters, their grandchildren. The young men who had come out to West Texas before the railroad got there, who had slaughtered the buffalo and trailed cattle for a thousand miles north, were old men now; confused and frequently lost when forced to make a public choice between a good road for the automobiles and a wagon yard in town for their horses. The paved roads and the parking lots won, of course, but there were wagon yards in town when I was a boy. And there were also old men who had been cattle barons. The Merchants, who had swapped out land with the T&P so that Abilene could be where it was and called what it was, were still watching in wonder what they had wrought. And Chief of Police J. J. Clinton had been marshal of Dodge City and had fought the Indians at the Battle of the Waterhole which Frederic Remington made famous with a painting that shows Clinton, gaunt and fearful, but defiant, looking over the sights of a rifle at some unseen red foe. Most of the old heroes were still being called colonel or major or, if modest, captain. I never knew them to look back very much. I don't think they could have been looking forward either. They were, I suppose, baffled at where they were.

I used to deliver the morning paper, just at dawn in the summer-time, to an old ex-trail driver who had been a state politician (only with a good deal more education and wisdom than either of those pursuits implied) and was called Senator Bryan. He would be out in his yard, watering his flowers, when I rode up on my bicycle and we sometimes would pass a few words. One day I asked him about some particular happening or piece of landscape thereabouts, and the old man gave me a concise but accurate account. I made comment to the effect that I would like to reconstruct it—whatever it was we had talked about—or wished it could have been preserved as it was so that I could have known it, too. But he shook his head in a kind of sad denial.

"No," he said, "you just should have been here."

9

Village of My Heart

EVERY MAN HAS a village in his heart, whether he comes from abounding Manhattan or the prairies of West Texas. It may be a crossroads town where every face was a daily familiarity, it may be one certain block within a metropolis, but there is a village he has kept. The village is what he refers to when he is making his life decisions. When he cannot go back to the village and display his prizes, in pride or in scorn, he finds less satisfaction in achievement. He does not always love the village but he can never destroy it, for it is himself in it that makes it his village.

Abilene is my village. It is the place I know best, the spot I have kept against change, although the town that made my village is very different, and so am I.

What does it mean to say you know a place? Must you remember the streetcars running through a cotton patch to get to McMurry College, or the big sign shaped like a tube of toothpaste that stood in front of Sloan's drug? Or what about Raymond Choate, the plumber, driving a Dodge truck painted and decorated to look like a fire engine, or knowing that Old Mrs. Gorsuch's Detroit sedan was the last electric in town?

Does knowing a place have anything to do with being evacuated during the night in a rowboat named *Miss Christine* when Catclaw Creek flooded in 1932, or remembering the black porters sitting in cane-bottom chairs on the sidewalks in front of the South Side hotels but not understanding what a whorehouse was when your uncle said that was what those places were?

Is having a village being there the night Al Shapiro brought a team down from Stamford and introduced the windmill pitch to the Abilene softball, and the umpire stopping play for thirty minutes while the rule book was being searched to see if it was legal? Or, at age five, calling Dixie Blanton, the professional flagpole sitter, who stayed on top the new Hilton Hotel for two weeks?

And can there be understanding of the things a town says unless you are able to hear the voices that go with the lost names, the ones whose flame was bright but whose candle was short: Freeman Holly, with me at that interrupted ball game; Arnold Pruitt, who lived on Sunset just across South Seventh from us; Parramore Sellers, born the same time I was; and Earl Proctor, the roughest, meanest boy I ever knew, but my friend.

And Jack Perry, whose dad ran a little grocery store on Grape Street, the father always answering the phone in a weary kind of voice, drawing out, "Perry Foood . . ." and we would wait a second, on the other end of the line, suppressing our laughter, and say with exaggerated concern, "He did?"

That list is long with them: Alfo Baker, R. L. Berry, Guy Kemper, Billy Pennington, R. V. Rucker. Kept forever young by being offered in a war that consumed them before they were twenty-five. How much of your remembering is not what they were but what you think they would have been? Those who seemed gifted toward some prescribed use? William Smith, of dour loyalty; Chuck Francis, the fairness in him already recognized by us as unusual; Delmon Rice, with a watchmaker's scrutiny of things.

Are our villages but the extension and expansion of human ego, or the last possible Eden where reality can retreat to innocence? I would rather think not. To me a village is where, for the last time, everything around you seemed made for your use and measurement. The beauty or drama of the locality may be as unimportant as whether or not the clock face, across which the time was measured, was beautiful.

Never again, after we leave this village, do we have such reliable references with which to frame our judgments and measure our importance. All we knew, in that brief time, was ourself. Thus, if we try to go back, our yardsticks look unfamiliar, their scales and markings wiped smooth. We can't remember what we were measuring against the deep-scored, beveled-edged bricks of the Elks Hall, or the significance of the steepness of the steps going up to the old City Hall's east doors, the length of the no-longer-used passenger platform at the T&P station. The only place where they can still tell you something about yourself is in the village of your heart.

THE COUNTRY around Abilene is a belt of change: farm lands to the east, harsher prairies immediately to the west. Taylor County, where Abilene is the seat, is harder to characterize because it is fertile loam along the wide Elm Creek valley, flat along its northern edge, rough breaks on the south and west sides.

Across the center of West Texas there is a low range of hills which extends for one hundred and fifty miles or so east and west through five or six counties. People living near them call these hills "the mountains" though they do not qualify in the least for the title, seldom standing more than five hundred feet above the surrounding country. But they furnish an experience for the eye and a pretty purple, gray, or green backdrop to that part of the country, depending on what time of day or which season you view them. They are the horizon, visible for many miles and from many angles, for there is little to interfere with your sight of them.

Now they represent only a slight barrier to movement or passage—here and there along their reach an extra-tall steel tower will soar above some ranch house, feeling for the invisible rays of television and radio which the hills would cut off. The highways that weave their way through at various points scarcely cause the foot of the automobile driver to increase its pressure by a toe's weight.

Still, they are a distinct break with the land; they are something unexpected and, in the geographical context, noteworthy for a contrasting kind of beauty. They keep their part of West Texas from being only prairie and plain; they lend the land a frame, make a boundary for the eyes, and they separate the inhabitants who live on either slope in a subtle but effective way.

These hills are called by a confusing system of names, when you ask about them from the people nearby. Geologists and cartographers generally refer to them as the Callahan Divide, Callahan County being approximately the easternmost point of their origin (and civilization, coming into West Texas mostly from the east, tended to name its features eastmost-first).

Directly south of Abilene this divide is sometimes called the Tonkawa Hills and sometimes the Steamboat Mountains. Here they reach a height of 2,500 feet or so, lifting from a plain which lies at 1,700 to 2,000 feet. In the early days, when the buffalo came down into this part of Texas for the winter grass, the beasts had to find a way through these hills and they used one big pass, or gap, coming and going on their migrations, so that when the settlers pushed up from San Saba and Brownwood after the Civil War they followed the herds through and the first town created thereabouts was named Buffalo Gap. All along the range in Taylor County these passes were named, because they assumed an importance then that modern roads and vehicles deny them now: Lytle Gap, Pecan Gap, Cedar Gap, Lemmon Gap, Coon Hollow, and on west through Nolan, Mitchell, and Howard counties in a roll call of similar designations.

Things in West Texas were named in a hurry and usually on the first and maybe last trip. Those first riders who came across the country, naming as they went, were apt to be more optimistic and a good deal more romantic than later acquaintance justified. Old maps of West Texas are glorious with Honey Creeks and Clear Forks, Turkey, Deep, and Bear Creeks; Silver Valleys and Water Valleys or Red Springs. Happy sites, all of which titles range from the misappropriated to the downright deceitful.

We sentimentalize pretty badly, affixing motives and integrity to our ancestors. We keep trying to out-guess them, with our own outlook and our peculiar problems as standards for our defense or interpretation of their personal hows and whys. We add stature to traits and habits they either stood short of or felt no particular use in developing. They had their own goals.

The old-timers were always bad about the quality of their recollection of West Texas, remembering one green valley they had ridden through and spreading it over an entire region; thinking of a wonderful life-giving spring they had ridden up on in the midst of a rocky, lost stretch and calling the whole world well watered. They saw something we can't see when we look today. They saw their hopes, which had to be good because there were no others.

The womenkind, who followed along at the urgency

of their men's letters, were inclined to be more truthful, or less hopeful. They seldom indulged in visions of grass belly-high on the horses or clear, pure water leaping from the living rock. The women lived out of the saddle and down next to the earth where there were stinging scorpions with horrible hooked tails curled over their backs, and brown, arrow-headed snakes whose bite was death. And sand burrs that got under skin and festered until the kids grew a black rind of embedded thorns around their soles from going barefoot. And the women knew that once a garment or a face or hand or foot had had the powdery red soil ground into it, not even the lye compounds they made themselves would dislodge it, except (in the case of the human body) to peel away a layer of skin.

But there was something else working, and the old-timers never tried to describe it, would have rejected the idea as sentimentality had you put it into words, and the womenfolks would have snorted and flung a brown, crumpled-paper hand in denial against the horizon, asking, "This?" There was something about the enormous wildness, and being first. "You just should have been here." Something that pulls the eyes across the land, sweeping the vision gently upward (even today), sending it to the horizon with the low blue and purple hills, lifting it to a pile of high cumulus clouds, into the thin, blue sky that seems to draw everything beneath it upward—man and moisture alike—taking man out of himself toward something more vital and bigger than his comparison with other men.

It surrounds him and isolates him in West Texas, making him alone, his own watchman and his own enemy. It makes him want to reach out and touch untouchable things, this wildness; to travel down a corridor of clouds that will reach some ultimate door in the horizon—and this is no pretty metaphor, for in the open country the clouds hang high and flat before you, achieving a three-dimensional synthesis with the horizon until, to a man on the ground, they are forming the ceiling of an immense passageway to that point in perspective where they meet the land.

So many of the first ones were idealists, selfish idealists, if there can be such a thing, but seeking to find a freedom in firstness that would allow them to wrestle with something more than other men. I found a letter one time, discarded in a trash heap when an old ranch house was being torn down. It was written in the seventies, before Abilene and the cities of the T&P had been established. It is a hateful letter, yet one that explains something no pioneer remembered having felt in the civilized years that came after.

It was written to a young lawyer who had come out to Belle Plain, by some friend whom the lawyer had left behind, probably an older man. It ran:

> We have had some little showers but not in time to benefit our corn at all. The cotton notwithstanding is looking very well. I am at a loss to know what to do. It is useless to make any sort of effort to sell now, as most everyone is disheartened, and if I venture to leave my place in charge of tenants it will go to destruction. Nevertheless, I want to do something with it in order that I may look out for some other spot.
>
> Have you ever been in Taylor County, and if not I wish you would see someone who has and get a full description of it; the streams, timber, soil, etc., how wide and how long the valley is in which Buffalo Gap is situated and whether a stream runs through this. Also ascertain the value of this valley land and whether a tract of, say, 1,000 acres or more could be bought to locate a ranch, and if then there would be enough

undesirable land in the rear to keep anyone from settling same in order that such would serve as an outlet.

I did want to get off and go see that country this summer but if I leave home everything I have got would be stolen. If I do leave here I want to go to some good, watered portion of country where I can obtain a good body of valley land at a low price and then have an immense range in the rear of such land as would be likely to remain uninhabited until the next Centennial. Also ascertain if all this sort of land in Taylor County is settled, if any unlocated, and what such is held at by those who had first pick.

How is Tom Green compared to Taylor County? And what about Eastland? You are in a condition to find out all about this thing for me and do it and write me all the particulars concerning same, as I would like to know the respective differences, etc.

If I could sell my place at a reasonable price I would like to travel about six months and in my travel would like to find a beautiful valley of lands with ever-running water through it, said valley to contain about a league of land and I could buy it for about $4 an acre.

But this is not all. I would then like for this valley to be surrounded by the roughest land imaginable, such as brakes, hollows, rough timber, etc., and fit for nothing but grazing purposes, with no water upon it, and to extend for several miles each way. Then if I could buy such a place and had enough money to buy me a small stock of cattle, I would be fixed as far as I could during my life and fix it so that it would be a comfortable place for my children. And I could be off to myself where human beings "as they are called" would not have the pleasure of forming so many opinions and where they know more of other people's business than they do of their own, as has been my experience with the majority of said animals.

> In fact, I have become so disgusted with the things that I am almost tempted to go to the "Exodus" and disown the white race and become a negro [*sic*]. Doing this, I believe I could get a few good neighbors and as it is, all that is desired by a white man is to pull down and browbeat his neighbor, or anybody else, until the oldest and most overbearing ones can outdo the others, then all is well. A man, to live in any peace with his children growing up, must go where he can obtain a place to keep them from such observation and when they are old enough they can be educated in the true principles of life. Whereas, as it is, God Almighty himself could not do it where they come in contact with such brutes as I have had the misfortune to be with during much of my life, and I would rather see both my boys . . .

THE WEST TEXAS FRONTIER was never a democracy, it was an aristocracy. Not of blood, but of deeds. What a man could do was what a man could become. "He didn't amount to nothing" is still a phrase of ethical comment more bemeaning than "He failed."

The town meeting, the secret ballot, the two-party system were not born and did not flourish on the West Texas frontier. There it was strength against strength, and when one party in contention grew strong enough to devour or contain the other, it did so. Strength was the democratic principle involved. Dying for a weak cause was foolishness, dying for a stubborn will was heroic.

But this adherence to a social philosophy of primitive strength did not breed a cruel society, as one might suppose, or a Spartan one where denial itself became the life-form. Christianity made the difference. For all its fundamentalistic, Calvinistic moral attitudes, West Texas society is so established as to cause the individual to bow to certain personal rules of responsibility and conduct, a Christian code of ethics which stops well before rugged individualism turns it into brutality. Hypocrisy, that occupational disease of humanity, follows in many cases, but seldom meanness.

If there is one instantly recognizable characteristic of West Texans it is their friendliness. It is almost impossible to overstate this trait. The newcomer, whether traveling through or settling down, finds constant and often overwhelming welcome, even in the larger cities like Abilene, Midland, Odessa, and San Angelo. If he so desires he becomes an immediate member of whatever group he wishes.

Helpfulness is so ingrained in common affairs—especially at times of visible emergency—that other West Texans take such acts as being pulled from the ditch, driven somewhere out of the way for gasoline, or offered physical assistance in many forms almost for granted.

It is a land where the casual acquaintanceship is not only tolerated but demanded. You seldom enter one of the numerous highway cafés without getting engaged in conversation by some of the other customers or the waitresses. And most times when you do not open your mouth you will still be included in whatever general conversation is taking place. Someone at the counter will address himself to the room at large, ending his declaration, perhaps, in a rhetorical question which is uttered directly at you, the stranger. The speaker may not expect an answer but he is never displeased to get one, or a silent but agreeing nod.

And in such matters as asking for directions, for help, for the time of day, for anything, one is as likely as not to get positively embarrassed at the quality and quantity of response. Motorists halted by the road—particularly elderly people and women—almost without exception can count on someone stopping to ask, "You folks need any help?" The pickup truck (which has long since taken the place of the horse as common carrier) will pull off the highway onto the shoulder. A wind-tanned face will appear from a rolled-down window and ask if he can do something, or if something is already being done, to see if you have all the tools you can use.

This is genuine, this phenomenon of friendship. It is not through conscious civic effort or part of an image-building undertaking by a chamber of commerce. It comes from many sources. History, certainly, goes back to a day in West Texas when every human owed every other human the responsibility of mutual survival. And West Texans, being predominantly Anglo-Saxon, may have inherited from this tree some of its legendary regard for the guest, a tradition which says even one's enemies must be taken in and aided if they come hurt and appealing.

I think it also comes with the country and the nature of the land. Distance has something to do with it, and the traveler is always more of an adventurer than a commuter. In such a wide land you move across it with purpose and destination in mind, seldom casually. There is also the feeling that most of the people you find in need of help will be strangers, persons not knowing where they are or what they must do—the innocent presumption that a native would have known better than to get into trouble in the first place.

Added to all this is the fact that in a lonely place most people get lonesome, and even the chance, brief encounter along the highway can fill a day with the sweet flavor of human companionship it so often will lack. So simple curiosity motivates some of this. (I have never found the old frontier code that one does not ask questions of strangers to be applicable to modern West Texas. The opposite obtains, and on occasion a West Texan will seem to be prying your life story out of you and, getting it or not, will be telling you his in as intimate detail as you wish to hear it.) There is a detachment possible to living in a large city which, along with obvious circumstances, obviates casual involvement in others' affairs. If you have spent your life in a small town or a scattered rural community (as have most West Texans) you do not know this, and when someone from outside moves in, the new neighbors will seem to be nosy.

Yet there are areas of privacy which are denied in the big city that West Texans will not enter. In a cafeteria, for example, you do not seat yourself at a table with a stranger unless the stranger invites you to. In parks and public places, individuals and groups keep a respectful distance apart, though space is at a premium. And New Yorkers, in particular, cannot get over the fact that West Texas pedestrians, no matter if there is not a car coming for blocks, will stand on the curb waiting for a red light to turn green.

WEST TEXAS has always had a certain number of realistic persons who saw the futility of trying to keep down one race for the benefit of another. Slavery, which had come only to the far eastern edges of West Texas, did not leave its dead roots for each generation to disinter or stumble over, and although the black population there was denied the kind of freedom the rest of West Texas took for granted, there has never been the brooding and oppressive night of hate that overhung so much of the South and some eastern parts of Texas. I cannot recall a Negro lynching having taken place in West Texas.

Most of the discrimination against the Latins in West Texas was on the economic level. Several children from Latin-American families were in every school I attended throughout my education in Abilene, and the girls, from my male standpoint, were quite popular among the Anglo boys. It is hard to practice social discrimination against someone you desire or admire. As for the Jewish inhabitants, they were (in my youth, at least) under almost no implied or direct social or business restraints, being active in civic undertakings and social clubs with little consideration for their religion or traditional inheritance. (I was in high school before it fully came to me that my friends, the Cohen and Goltz children, were of the same lineage that Hitler was driving out of Europe.)

So, while no racial Utopia by any means (the Southern tradition was too strong), it never became impossible to dissent in racial matters and it never became necessary, or popular, to use White Supremacy as a political rallying cry in West Texas. Not every Southerner was raised to believe the South should have won the war, and set out from the sick heritage of the Southern aristocracy and away from the female social network that perpetuated it, a number of West Texans were given a kind of fair racial outlook by Southern family members who would have found their teachings unacceptable in the rest of the South.

I think that paramount to any historical, tribal, or geographical influence, the friendship and tolerance of West Texas comes from the simple premise that one is supposed to do good for others. The Christian ethic, whether as religious code or as social conditioning, is at the bottom of most of this thinking.

Paradoxically, but not surprisingly, religion is the least tolerant area in West Texas society. God is too important to be left to whimsical personal concept. There is *a* way, each denomination believes, and you either seek it or are forced to acknowledge its existence. Church houses are scattered in overabundance on city corners and at crossroads hamlets. In the backwater alcoves, where all other forms of social practice have disappeared with the cotton gin, the bank, and the village post office, the white-frame church stays.

Signs along the roads warn you that God is both seeking and rejecting you. You are urged to find Him through a variety of spiritual stimuli. (FOLLOW THE CROWDS TO THE FIRST BAPTIST CHURCH, a sign near Breckenridge says.) Little churches and big ones offer timetables, erected in the front yard, with precise hours for

when their particular Almighty can be approached within.

"Church" is one thing—open and understandable—but God is another; mystery, and personal; love, but dangerous. So when we look at God in West Texas, we must do so in a parabolic tone, separating Him from those church buildings where men gather in His name, then separating those churches from Him.

10

God in West Texas

SUMMER HEAT in West Texas has a glittering, shimmering quality about it which makes anything viewed from afar look like a mirage, and you can never be quite sure until you are on it.

The sun burns hard. It burns the color out of cloth and paint, it burns the moisture from the soil. It burns the sin out of people because sin is a moist, soft thing, tinted pretty colors.

About a month after the spring rains, if there have been any, the ground starts cracking open beneath the summer sun. The red clay earth turns to brick and the grass becomes a brown blanket tufted with clumps of yellow straw. Pretty yard plants die without water from a hose or can. But the goathead sticker sends out tendrils two yards long, and it survives. The mesquite, with only needle slivers for leaves, finds enough water through its deep roots, and it persists. The prickly pear, which holds its deep green through any kind of drought, seems to want neither water nor soil to expand. It is a spiritual lesson, the kind of parable the West Texan can apply to his own life.

West Texas is like the Biblical lands, a hot, dry desert country with low, blue hills along its horizons which are nothing but hot rocks when you reach them. Perhaps it is this kinship with the land of the Bible which causes it to hold to the fundamentalist religions, to cling to dry, feverish beliefs which demand more of a man than he is capable of offering even God; beliefs which promise him nothing on earth but sweat, frustration, and retribution for error. Which pledges him to loneliness while raising before him a golden City of God in the hereafter wherein he will find the Garden of Eden and Adam restored, the music of harps and gates of precious stone and a street of gold which cannot be dimmed.

Perhaps it is the belief that this earth will be devoured by fire, man's works and monuments licked clean by flame, which causes the people of West Texas to feel that in the desert, theirs is an especial warning from God. Like the Muslims, they defend and evangelize with the sword, love and emotion being intellectual terms which God rebukes as frail footings for faith.

The loneliness of the high sky makes men see God. But he is seen in the fiery sunlight and not the cool moonlight which bathes the countryside in a supernatural coating so wonderful and confusing that men draw indoors to avoid it. Uneasy, they look out from the shadows and predict pagan infections from being under it, remembering, perhaps, how it has made them sad, times past, for something they could not perceive in the absence of sunlight.

Therefore, God says the greatest virtue is to work hard, for work leaves you no time to question Him. If, through work, God should bless you with an abundance of His riches, then it is a sign of acceptance and favor, for God loves the strong, the shrewd, the sure just as He despises the weak, the lukewarm, the uncertain.

God still comes down and watches what men do in West Texas. He goes to the plain, cream-brick churches on Sunday mornings for Sunday school and the sermon, but He is back for evening worship and Wednesday night's prayer meeting. He wears suits from J. C. Penney's, if He wears a suit, making note of who is not faithful in attendance, who remains steadfast to The Doctrine, and who has faltered.

But beneath the dry skin of West Texas and behind the washed-out looking eyes which are accustomed to being focused on vastness, there is expectation to match the distance. Someday they will see Him. And He will proclaim, in that day, that all their years of denial and colorlessness will become a flaming banner for the unbelieving world to see, and for those in error to acknowledge as they plunge over the lip of hell.

There is the vast expectation that He can be found, that He is waiting to explain why life is like it is and why He demands it be that way. For they love God with the only kind of love they can truly understand as not being sinful somehow. They love God and they keep His commandments the way they were given and the way the land will let them be kept.

And above all else they want to do what God wants them to do. Since He speaks to few of them clearly and aloud, they sense that He wants their lives to be lived cautiously and slow. What is done to them they accept as His will or their sin. Sometimes it is the drought, the hail, the cyclone; sometimes it is the inability to go to school, or to marry for love, or to work for themselves instead of a boss—the ultimate creed of personal happiness. God doesn't like for His people to pick and pry, to seek answers beyond the Sacred Page, to say aloud or in their hearts, "I wonder . . ." God chastises those who think they know too much, who taunt Him with their knowledge, who refuse to accept their lives as His will.

Nothing can change that, for there the sun is, His eye, and it is so brassy it seems to be a mirror, following you with a blinding shaft no matter which way you turn.

But there are things and thoughts which lie like the low, blue mesas on the horizon or high like the distant clouds, remote but pleasant: things which never are exposed because if you do not let yourself know they are there they can be kept hidden, and when God moves away to look a moment at some other place, when the searing sun is removed from the sky, as it is on a summer evening and suddenly the moonlight rolls up from the earth, these soft, hidden things can be taken out and held tightly in the palms, the eyes denying their presence, the lips never speaking their names, but the heart feeling them lovingly. For a moment it is safe to love, under the lovely, soft shadow of the moon-time.

My old granny used to say that if you didn't wear a handful of green leaves in your hat when you went out on a summer day, the sun would cook your brain by pulling out all the moisture and cool from your body. And you would surely die.

GOD IS THE BIGGEST INDUSTRY in West Texas and serving Him is the largest profession. He enjoys the highest social standing, controlling not just the way men and their families go about their lives but having a hand in the larger destiny of cities, the moral and political orientation of the whole region. God counts heavily in a public way.

Mostly He is represented by churches. Cities vanish but the lonely, little white-frame churches, left over from the turn of the century, are still sitting where there used to be towns. Now there is nothing but twin lanes of asphalt and perhaps a weathered sign that says BOYD'S CHAPEL or UNION RIDGE CHURCH—the "Union" coming not from political affiliations in the Civil War but from the frontier practice of one church house being used by several denominations.

Or His presence is witnessed by massively ugly First Baptist churches in towns like Ranger, Breckenridge, and Sweetwater, Colorado City, and Anson; of red brick or (worse still) brownish-purple, their tall doors reached by high front steps. Most of these were built in the 1920's, many times with new oil money where the booms hit, leaving enormous buildings for half an audience when the boom rolled away. Sometimes the town's biggest church will be a memorial erected with beef money which came after some ranch family discovered that it was, by God, going to be rich in spite of the way Mamma and Papa had had to struggle and starve in those early West Texas years.

The big First Baptists are usually matched in size and ugliness by the First Methodist churches, some of them still having the letters "M. E. C. S." carved somewhere about the building, unchanged from the days when the denomination was the Methodist Episcopal Church, South, the slavery-inspired division within Wesley's sect which was not healed until late in the 1930's. These, like the First Baptist churches, will, most of the time, be near the downtown business districts, holding the spot where they began worship during the city's infancy.

Situated in new parts of town, because it generally came too late to inherit one of those frontier locations, will be seen a newer, brisker kind of God's house, stripped of all forms of ornateness, having not even a cross to top it, or stained-glass windows showing Christ the Good Shepherd. This will be the Church of Christ, never called "First," like the Baptist, or "St. Paul" or "Westminster" like the Methodist, but only a place name such as Highland, North Side, College, or Riverside. Looking as cool and unemotional as a Sears, Roebuck branch store or a suburban bank; Jesus without a beard, rawer, more aggressive, more attuned, perhaps, to West Texas. Challenging those other, bigger Baptist or Methodist temples across town in both numbers and influence.

These are the three most familiar faces of God in West Texas. There are others, but like fresh-water streams running into the sea, they seldom change the taste. The socially best people, and some who would like to be considered the socially best people, often go to the Episcopal churches, scattered like precious jewels through the land and seldom found outside the more heavily inhabited and wealthier urban places. They give milk-punch parties after Sunday school and seldom light the church on Wednesday nights for prayer meeting (the test of the True Believer). And some congregations, even in West Texas, have gone so High Church as to call their preachers "Father."

The Presbyterians are also found mostly in the cities, and in West Texas, at least, are a bewildered sect, pulled between the slave-owning memory of the Southern branch membership and the modern-day liberalism of the Northern branch, whose hold on John Calvin has loosened entirely too fast for some members. But the Presbyterians came early to West Texas (the first church to meet in Abilene was a Southern Presbyterian congregation, as a plaque in T&P Park in the middle of town points out), and today have on their rolls a high proportion of family doctors, lawyers, and the quieter professions which enables the group, as a denomination, to serve as unofficial religious arbitrators for the community when the extremes of fundamentalism cause public strife as attempts are made to apply them politically. Dancing in the high schools, wet-dry elections, even Sunday store openings have created public rifts along religious lines in most West Texas towns at one time or another, with the Presbyterians going to both sides (sinful and virtuous) to apply reasonable compromise.

Roman Catholics are in West Texas, too, and in larger numbers than the frequency of their edifices gives evidence, although now and then, springing toward the sky, is a giant and unexpected cathedral in some otherwise God-forsaken little farm community like Hermleigh, in Scurry County, or Rhineland, in Knox County, where German or Czech settlers brought their bleeding statues and mysterious rituals into this place of sun-brazed purgatory for the soul. West Texans still hold the Catholics to be foreign, the church where uncommunicative Latins traditionally go, where priests smoke cigars in public and have cocktails with the better-class parishioners, where imported Northern accountants and oil company executives attend Mass and hear bells ring through clouds of incense, and the choir doesn't ever sing "Love Lifted Me." Still, there is a kind of social prestige associated with Catholic Church membership in West Texas, if you can keep your Catholicism strictly to yourself. The very foreignness of the Roman Church gives it an attractive aura.

THERE ARE the usual dozen or more remaining denominations. Some are small, but rich and growing, like the Lutherans and the Mormons, the Sunday seats filled with middle-class merchants, managers, and store owners. Sometimes, however, the smaller denominations are just holding on in a certain area, hoping a death will be balanced by a birth which will remain in the faith of its father.

Religion now is a serious business, and done as a business in many cases, for business in West Texas (as in all America) demands that it be taken seriously at all times. Religion is not a frolicking, emotional binge, such as afflicts the hillbilly snake handlers, the banjo plunkers, and the all-night shouting matches of the Holy Rollers or those wild-eyed, hoarse radio preachers down along the Rio Grande who pant and rave as they get their breath or lose it in pursuit of God Almighty's almighty dollar.

The frontier, they say, was different when it came to religion. The brush-arbor meetings in the summer were full of loud fervor. The Methodists had the mourners' bench where sins were wrestled to the sod, and the Baptists, especially the Hardshells and Primitives, who have almost disappeared, broke into hallelujahs at the peak of their fiery sermons. I have even, in my own time, heard the boom of the loud "Amen!" volley through a Church of Christ congregation, and the preacher stopping his sermon to say "Thank you, brother."

The personal evangelist, owning no denomination, once had a good thing going in West Texas, and the older people still refer to famous preachers who practiced their faith with the power and separation of a cultist. During the Depression, a time when zeal was the only occupation available, men like Johnny Lovell built huge frame churches the size of gymnasiums (looking very much like them, too) in the bigger towns and took up the Sunday collection in No. 2 wash tubs, with Brother Lovell up front, pacing the platform and shouting to his crowds, "Keep it light, breth'ren . . . keep it light," meaning: put folding money in the tub and not silver. And they had choirs of 150 voices singing his theme song, "Gimme That Old-Time Religion," accompanied by a band which looked like something John Philip Sousa should direct. But those exhibitions were mostly in the days when money was scarce and fundamental sin-fear was the only recreation the poor folks had. Money aims toward dignity, and today the larger of even the most fundamental churches in West Texas have a quiet quality of wealth to match the Oldsmobiles, Buicks, and Cadillacs parked on the church-house lot.

MY MOTHER'S SIDE of the family was all (as West Texas says) Church of Christ. This is a severely fundamentalistic and plain-worshipping church with autonomous congregations. It denies it is a denomination, does not allow the use of instrumental music (except pitch-pipes, used by the congregational song leader) or choirs in its services, and holds itself singularly and literally to the Holy Bible for practices and beliefs. (NO BOOK BUT THE BIBLE; NO CREED BUT CHRIST will be seen on bumper stickers borne by members' vehicles from time to time.) Other churches sometimes call members "Campbellites" in derision, because of the historical connection with the nineteenth-century evangelist Alexander Campbell—although the mass of Church of Christ members claim direct and connected historical relationship with Jesus Christ as the founder. This brings up the interesting aside that in West Texas a few Baptist old-timers refer to the conversion of John the Baptist as the beginning of their church.

But calling Church of Christ members "Campbellites" in public causes them to get their feelings hurt—and arouses wrath. In fact, the word cannot even be used jokingly around them. No public figure or newspaper columnist in West Texas would dare do it because the Church of Christ is a powerful, and growing, social and economic force and, of recent years, has become potent politically. (At one time church members were urged to disdain politics as worldly, and my parents never paid their poll taxes—a requisite for voting in Texas then—until they left the Church of Christ.) For several years the Abilene *Reporter-News*, under editorship of a member, went so far as to make it a style rule that the formal name always be made lower case, to wit: church of Christ, in deference to feeling that theirs was not a denomination but THE church of Christ.

The Church of Christ is not to be confused with another group (the original one, in fact) which evolved from the leadership of Alexander Campbell, the Disciples of Christ. This is a much more liberal body, also quite numerous in West Texas, although usually called "Christian" rather than "Disciples." A rare present-day Church of Christ building (one at Weatherford comes to mind) will still have "Christian Chapel" or some such designation on the cornerstone from the days around the turn of the century before the two completely parted worshipping company, a schism which began primarily over the use of a pump organ in the church house.

Those unaware of this deep split, which has widened with the years until there is scarcely any relationship between the two bodies, can become badly confused if they ask a member of the Church of Christ, "Are you a Christian?" and are assured by that member that he or she is not.

The Church of Christ has gained the reputation of being the most strait-laced church in West Texas. Any deviation from its image shocks you. Once when I was a college student, I was visiting a Church of Christ in a small West Texas town on Sunday morning and, in the middle of the sermon, was startled to smell tobacco smoke in an immediate and pungent way. Looking around I discovered an old man seated in a rocking chair, to one side of the pulpit, puffing away on a cigar. In disbelief I nudged the boy with whom I had come. He smiled and whispered calmly, "That's Grandpa Box. He owns the church house." Which was true. The Churches of Christ, having no recognized central administration, are separately owned and at one time the titles to a few buildings were still in the names of the original elder or deacon who had led his sheep out of the Disciples of Christ fold.

THE THING that broke my mother from the Church of Christ was prayer. She longed for an electric refrigerator and one day, at a women's prayer meeting, she voiced this desire in her petition to God. After the meeting one of the leaders chided my mother for asking such a selfish thing —the Church of Christ not holding too firmly to the view that a passionate personal identification can be made with Divinity. If my mother had earned an electric refrigerator by the way she lived, this woman pointed out, then God would already have anticipated her need and would have seen to it that virtue earned an icebox. It seems hardly necessary to note that the other woman, a good deal wealthier than the Greenes, had long owned an electric refrigerator as well as other material blessings denied my mother. So, facing a bleak future if it had no miraculous God in it to answer personal prayers (for by then she could see that my earthly father would always be a well-liked rather than a well-paid man), my mother began attending what she considered a more understanding church. Some time in that latter period the family came into possession of a Frigidaire with the motor on top, and although my grandmother, my great-grandmother, and my Aunt Gerty remained faithful to the Church of Christ, my mother and father, pulling away when I was entering my teens, never returned.

ONE PUBLIC ASPECT of the power of fundamentalism in West Texas irks the traveler and newcomer more than everything else put together. West Texas is generally bone dry, liquorishly speaking. Only a few oases can be found. One precinct in Palo Pinto County is wet because of the high percentage of foreign-born brought in by mining decades ago. Breckenridge, which gathered a deserved reputation for roughness during its 1920's oil boom, is a liquor town. A municipality-within-a-municipality named Impact, at Abilene, furnished millions of dollars of whiskey, wine, and beer to that city and surrounding territory. Another wet "reservation" is a five-acre tract at Buffalo Gap, in south Taylor County, and in Concho County a German community named Lowake (Lo-*wakey*) used to draw thirsty visitors from Abilene by the hundreds each week (sixty-five miles each way) before Impact and Buffalo Gap turned wet in Abilene's front and back yards. The cities of San Angelo, Big Spring, Midland, and Odessa, along with two or three smaller places on the western side of the region, have been wet for years. Wet-dry local option elections have taken place throughout West Texas since the 18th Amendment was repealed in 1933, changing the beer or whiskey status of Baird, Sweetwater, Albany, and a dozen other places. The preachers of the cities almost always spearhead the dry vote campaigns in the face of a wet threat. Lubbock, with nearly 175,000 population, and Abilene, with more than 100,000 residents, were once the largest "dry" cities in North America. (Both, since 1962, however, have had satellite precincts which are wet, and Abilene legalized the sale of liquor in 1978.)

Some liquor dealers, with stores in or near West Texas, have had the reputation of supplying generous sums of money to help the cause of prohibition. And the Texas Liquor Control Board, which polices the sale of alcoholic beverages in Texas, is continually reputed to work hand in glove with the counteracting forces of wet and dry in West Texas, receiving "support" from the dealers who don't want to see their monopoly cut into by new wet territories or new dealerships either.

Cocktails were not allowed to be sold in public anywhere in Texas before 1971, which resulted in numerous private drinking clubs which still exist in dry areas where, for a nominal membership fee, or only for being a guest at some motel or hotel, one may get bar service. This hurts a lot of sincere West Texans whose religion really does depend on the prohibition of alcohol. It makes some of their friends and neighbors look so hypocritical, going to church on Sunday and selling, or consuming, the stuff the rest of the week.

BEFORE LEAVING the subject of God, I would like to recall two events which symbolize the general attitude of some religious groups in West Texas toward racial equality.

When I was a boy there was a famous Negro preacher called Brother Keeble who used to hold summer revivals in a big cotton warehouse. His audience would include as many blacks as whites, but the two races sat apart. And when it came time, at the close of the sermon, for Brother Keeble to exhort the sinful to come forward, a separate call was given to the whites, then the blacks. I used to wonder (motivated more by semantics than sociology) if the white people considered themselves black with sin, did the black sinners take themselves to be white with it?

And out near Loraine, in Mitchell County, lived a Negro rancher named 80 John Wallace, who got his name from herding Clay Mann's cattle with a big "80" branded all over the side of them. 80 John had come to West Texas in the frontier days, and by being shrewder and tougher than others of his race had avoided losing whatever he had to some banker or covetous white neighbor. (He was also advised by Mann, one of the old Gods of Texas cattle ranching.) By the time he was an old man, 80 John was quite wealthy and had earned the respect (as the white people put it) of everyone around him. One day a delegation of white men who were of the same religious persuasion as 80 John (most persuasions in Texas have black and white branches), came to him and asked if he would contribute to the erection of a badly needed new church building for the whites. 80 John not only contributed but almost singlehandedly paid for it. In gratitude the white congregation voted to let him attend services there and built a special place for him and his wife to sit.

Years later, long after his death, the Mitchell County Historical Society raised a granite monument to 80 John at his ranch, but to me this church was monument enough—to him and to several other things.

11

Beyond the Old One-Hundredth

GOING WEST AGAIN. . . . Eight or ten miles out of Abilene you come to a famous but invisible landmark. You are most likely simply to pass over it or through it, whichever is more applicable, for it is the 100th meridian, the place where Bernard De Voto, Wallace Stegner, and a host of other writers have said the American West begins. De Voto based it on moisture, the 100th meridian marking the general line where average annual rainfall drops below twenty inches. Stegner bases his contention on history, the 100th being where the settlements stopped and waited for so long before the final civilizing push claimed it all.

Driving on the wide, modern highways across that unseen line, one may still observe some almost startling changes. In the matter of rainfall, I have been traveling west and had the rains stop at that line almost as if controlled by some giant hose. The land around it also changes. The soil, which has been adaptable to farming most of the way from the Brazos River, now turns purple and dry with alkali outcroppings evident—in fact, a few miles west of the 100th meridian lie enormous deposits of gypsum which provide a profitable industry but which contaminate the waters of both the Clear Fork and its mother river, the Brazos, as they flow through the stratum.

The horizon expands, the sky tilts away from you, the dryness of the air makes it more bracing and the sun more broiling.

Oil, while of more historical importance to the portion of West Texas lying eastward, now becomes more evident as a present economic fact. Horsehead pumpjacks as tall as three-story buildings can be seen working away on every horizon like men chained to lift up, then push down, up, down, up, down, in slow but powerful strokes. These pumps, named for their steel-shaped resemblance to a horse's head, are as good a symbol of oil as exists, their smooth, shiny sucker rods pulling away at the crude petroleum trapped in the earth sometimes miles below.

Merkel, just over the 100th meridian, used to be a cattle town. Now it is a bedroom suburb for Abilene. My father's family settled at Merkel originally and I had another great-grandmother, named Nancy Sandlin, who lived there in a big, unpainted wooden house where a huge galvanized cistern supplied the drinking water, causing

the iced tea of a summer to taste like cedar shingles because the water ran into the cistern from off the roof—the family being careful to divert the first flow of a rain so that the roof would be washed before the little crank handle was turned which sent it pouring into the cistern. Granny Sandlin came to West Texas in an emigrant car with her Confederate veteran husband, James, and they now lie together in the Merkel cemetery which, for no visible reason, is called Rose Hill.

Beyond Merkel the country was once all grassy plain, with curly mesquite and buffalo grasses native to the soil. And it was superb buffalo country indeed. By the 1870's the northern herds had been wedged down into Texas by the hunting in Kansas stimulated by the rail lines pushing west across the prairies, and West Texas beyond the 100th meridian became the great hide bonanza of the nation. It lasted less than a decade. The Sharps and Henry rifles made a ruthless, quick thing of the buffalo-hide era, and no one can competently guess how many buffalo were slain between what is now Abilene and Big Spring, from the Callahan Divide on the south to the Cap Rock to the north. This wide prairie basin saw hundreds of hunters flood out onto it, shooting the beasts for their hides alone and sending huge stacks of flint (untanned) hides back east through Fort Griffin, in Shackelford County, to Fort Worth and Dallas or north to the Kansas railheads.

It was this slaughter of the buffalo almost as much as Ranald Mackenzie's final raids by the U.S. Bluecoats that ended the Comanche domination of West Texas. At the end of the 1860's, out beyond that straggling line of forts near the Brazos River, there was no continuous survival for the Anglo-Saxon. The Comanche Barrier, as Rupert Richardson, West Texas's foremost historian, has named it, was more awesome than the Rockies or the Arizona and California deserts as an impediment to civilization. Most writers of the nineteenth century, describing the heartland of West Texas, offered little hope that it would be settled, the majority dismissing the vast country as impossibly dry, unbearably hot, and unprofitably sterile. We can realize now that what they really feared was the Comanche in that country. To dismiss it as unfit for farms or cities made the Indian problem secondary to good sense.

But the slaughter of the buffalo ended this because it ended the domination of the Comanche, who depended upon the buffalo for everything from his war shield of iron-textured rawhide to the jerked meat which he carried with him on raids. Even the Comanche religion (which was about as minimal as any nomadic tribes') was centered on the buffalo because it revolved primarily around the hunt, and the buffalo was eighty-five per cent or more of what the Comanche hunted. So when the buffalo went, the Comanche went. And the buffalo went fast, and completely. Where millions of the beasts had flowed across the prairie every year, cutting deep, narrow trails into the very earth itself and gouging out wallows so deep and wide that even today, from an airliner flying over parts of West Texas, these saucer depressions stand out like pockmarks on a human face, none could be found after the seventies. As a boy my only direct contact with the buffalo was at one corner of a dusty enclosure down at Abilene's Fair Park zoo where a herd of eight or ten was kept, mainly to supply the old-timers with meat for a buffalo barbecue every Fourth of July.

The hide hunters were mechanics, not adventurers. They operated like an investment fund. Most of them, originally, were not frontiersmen. They came down from Kansas or from the East in companies or corporations, organized with wagons, special rifles, designated percentages of the profits, and all the modern concepts of money-making investment. They left few marks on the land, and those were mostly the names for creeks or canyons or other natural occurrences. Up near Rotan, in Fisher County, a sort of headquarters for the West Texas hide hunters sprang up, called Rath City. But it was never intended to be anything but a temporary locality, offering only supplies, food, and a little liquor and gambling to the teams of buffalo killers spread out for a hundred miles in all directions. Charlie Rath, for whom this spot was called, was a storekeeper and wholesaler, not one of your romantic heroes of Texan fame. Rath City matched in grimness the expert coldbloodedness of the hide hunters. Today there is no trace of it to be seen on the surface. The whole establishment was reputedly packed on forty horses and hauled back to Kansas after two years.

The hunters used powerful big-bore rifles which would hurl a bullet as big as the end of your thumb with lethal impact for the better part of a mile. In fact, at the second battle of Adobe Walls in 1874 (which involved buffalo hunters and Comanches) Billy Dixon, sighting down the heavy hexagonal barrel of his Henry, claimed to have made a celebrated shot which dropped an Indian horseman who had thought he was safe because he was 1,500 yards away from the trading post where the hunters were under siege. True or not, its acceptance into legend shows how people felt about the prowess of the hunters and their guns.

The buffalo hunter, going after the beasts, crept up on the down-wind side of a herd, set up his gun mounts, and began picking off the animals as fast as he could fire. Buffalo, while noble in certain aspects (they always face the gale), have some qualities which humans are prone to call stupid. For one thing, shooting into a herd, if done with some discrimination as to the proximity of others, would not usually disturb those around the victim. This meant that a hidden hunter might drop from five to a hundred unwary buffalo before some sense of their danger aroused the animals. And there have been cases where whole herds were killed at one stand. A hunter could kill dozens, even hundreds, of buffalo daily. Several individuals, writing of their ways and lives in later years, recalled killing six or seven thousand animals in one hunting season.

Although the sum of the number of buffalo in North America seems to rise a few million every time a new historian writes on the subject, it is still hard to really grasp the reality of slaughter implicit in the fact that ten years could write the finish for the herds.

Something not involved in the killing has bothered me for years—what happened to all the buffalo hides? Even now, shouldn't there be some sizable remnant around, thousands still being used or stored in trunks? But there aren't. I have seen just one buffalo robe or skin outside a museum in West Texas.

Although the shocking slaughter still upsets a reader when he finds the details—not just the numbers but the casual view of the consequences—it can be seen that the buffalo had to go if West Texas was to be settled. Elimination of the roaming herds was a blessing, and no support for saving the beasts was found in West Texas until many years later when they had all retreated to Canada. In fact, the last, lost herd still wild, some eight or twelve individuals discovered in a box canyon early in the eighties, was dispatched by gun immediately on being found. Charles Goodnight, for sentimental reasons, preserved a herd on his Panhandle ranch.

On a lesser scale, and for different reasons, this process of *annihilation* was practiced later on the little barking, whistling rodents called prairie dogs. Until World War II there were many square miles of what we called prairie-dog towns in West Texas—acre after acre of holes where the rodents lived. What shocks you is not their destruction (they are a pest to agriculture and livestock raising) so much as the fact that they were eradicated by the millions with poisoned bait and lethal gas and nobody cared to preserve any; and were it not for the chance that a few "towns" lay within city limits or were fenced and exhibited in parks (like Lubbock's Mackenzie Park), the prairie dog would be extinct. Now, as with the buffalo a couple of generations back, zoologists are having to bring back specimens for exhibits in areas where, thirty years ago, the prairie dog was numbered in his millions, too.

Wolves and coyotes, the former scarce, the latter easily come across in West Texas, are still pursued by bounty hunters, the counties offering a stated amount for a pair of ears and some even hiring an official county hunter. This job, like that of public weigher in certain counties, is a political plum. The public weigher in Haskell and Knox counties, where high-grade, long-staple dry-land cotton is raised, used to become wealthy due to a clause in the description of his duties. He was empowered to dig and keep a sample out of each bale of cotton brought to be weighed (cotton weighing a slightly different weight from bale to bale) to see if the quality of the outside carried through the bale. The weigher became expert at slashing deep, and at the end of a season possessed as his own a great many bales of ginned cotton which he sold for thousands of dollars. The public weigher in such counties was apt to be someone's son-in-law or ne'er-do-well son, preferably (and usually) that of a big cotton grower.

Only after the middle 1950's did this position become a salaried office in the High Plains and dry-land cotton counties.

Just north of Rotan are twin landmarks which guided Indians, troopers, Spanish traders, California emigrants, and settlers from the discovery of Texas until the days of highway signs. Called the Double Mountains, the peaks are not so high as they are eruptive, jutting up 2,500 feet solitarily from the surrounding plains which lie at 1,500 feet, so that they look like they should be snow-capped in their height. Robert E. Lee, in an unsuccessful chase out of Camp Cooper after some Comanches in 1858, camped at the Double Mountains and was impressed by their noticeability. Today they are part of the Double Mountain Ranch, owned by Sammy Baugh, the legendary professional football player who, like a good many other professional sportsmen, comes from West Texas. The Double Mountains are so well known that a branch of the Brazos River is named for them, and the buffalo hunters referred to them for locations fifty miles away. They are a beautiful sight, coming at you of a sudden when the highway makes a bend in their direction as you drive north from Rotan. They take on a blue tint, from a distance, even in the summer-time, and from their tops you may see twenty or thirty miles in all directions because their only visual obstruction is each other. Treasure hunters, reading of them so often in memoirs, diaries, recollections, and official histories, are sure that somewhere on the slopes or buried at the feet of the Double Mountains is a treasure of immenseness waiting to be found electronically or by virtue of thorough digging, and the owner has to battle these modern gold seekers with the same persistency as the old-timers fought the rustlers and brand changers.

In the reaches beyond the 100th meridian the loss of

vegetation from the landscape is remarkable, and if Saint Anthony had wanted a place in the New World to go alone to meditate on his sins, some spot in this broken country would have suited his purposes well. None of the Cross Timbers foliage, which is thick even to Cisco, goes west of Sweetwater, except along watercourses that hold a fair supply of moisture. The cottonwoods hold along the rivers but begin to disappear by the time you have reached Big Spring. Willows and elm trees grow along the creeks and draws but seldom reach a decent height, remaining for the most part bushes. Salt cedar, a tough, dusty-looking evergreen, is a pest on the far Pecos edge of West Texas, and eradication programs are undertaken against it to match those against mesquite and prickly pear.

For the most part, out in the western half of West Texas, trees are found only where men have planted them, especially when you come up on the level prairies just west of Big Spring where the Callahan Divide begins falling off into a series of bluffs, breaks, and red-dirt washes. Just west of Odessa, after the prairie has given way to sand flats, is a tiny community named Notrees, and the few which grow there were planted by nostalgic settlers, for the name fits perfectly the inclination of the countryside.

While the rainfall totals drop sharply, down to twelve inches per year at the Pecos River edge, the wind increases in steadiness—or does the unbroken landscape only make it seem that way?

The wind. It is the greatest natural resource in West Texas, yet it becomes the cause, or the excuse, for most of what is called uncomfortable, abominable, and harsh about the country. In the winter the wind penetrates with the cold so that even freezing seems like an Arctic day. It penetrates with gritty dust in the spring and there are more sand-storm and dust stories in West Texas than there are drought tales. (Canned spinach is grittier after going through a West Texas dust storm.) But this land—particularly this farthest part—would lose a great deal of its charm and its possibilities without the wind.

It clears the sky and by changing direction prepares the whole atmosphere for abrupt shifts in weather so that, like a mad drama where the scenes are shifted out of context with the play, there is no sequence of warnings or causes.

It moves things over the surface, men and animals as well as tiny pollen and large tumbleweeds. It changes the seasons with the speed of its wings, tumbling an autumn day from Indian summer to dangerous winter at forty miles an hour, or blowing out the snow and cold of a freezing morning into a semitropical afternoon as it wheels and blows from another quarter.

If you cannot live with wind you cannot live in West Texas, yet it might be hard to arouse in most West Texans any particular consciousness of its presence, once they have lived with it for a while. Then they come to depend on it to perform beneficial services and disregard the inconvenience and hazards of it. Windmills still whirl up water out on the cattle ranges where the wind is dependable and strong, and just before the Rural Electrification Administration program appeared, the wind-charger electrical dynamos had become extremely popular on West Texas farms and ranches without access to power lines. The wind moves the wildflowers around, blowing a hillside of Indian blanket or paintbrush up and over an adjoining slope so that after four or five years the colorful panorama has moved on, being wind-replaced by another flower. The bluebonnet, which grows mainly on the south and east sides of West Texas, is particularly vulnerable to wind-shifting and one can almost see the sweep of blue, in the spring blossoming time, moving away with the wind.

The wind supports the vultures (or buzzards, as they are generally called in West Texas), allowing them to tilt and sail all day without seeming to flap a wing once. It sends the hawks sweeping back and forth over the long, brown grasses of the pastures, holding them aloft in their precise use of its currents and seeming to throw them down with a deft hand when they fold their wings and drop on prey. It adds to the deadly, silent glide of the owls that pass low over the pastures, from mesquite to mesquite, pursuing the field mice, rodents, and snakes that hide in the clumps and bushes, and in the spring the sky boils with the high convocations of crows (my great-grandmother said they were going to church) by the hundreds, flying in a milling, turning ball for what appears to be the pure windy sport of it.

And yet the wind is not an obtrusive force, except in early spring. The stranger steps out of his automobile after a long drive or gets off an airplane and thinks, momentarily, that some extraordinary kind of pressure has smitten him full force (I have even had this tendency to panic overcome me when I had been absent from the steady wind for a year or so), but within a few days, once the high gusts of March and April are done with, the presence of the wind is relegated to certain automatic gestures—the women pushing back their hair or holding down a skirt without considering that they are combating an unnatural force, the men pausing to run a comb through their hair each time they enter a building, because the wind has always lifted a few strands out of place. Cooperation with the spring wind is more sensible than resistance, except in Midland or Abilene where there are enough tall buildings to form canyons down whose concrete and asphalt gullies the racing currents can throw a staggering blow at you and sometimes seem too rough for playfulness, actually holding you helpless as you attempt to turn a corner or open an outside door against them. Then the girls clutch their skirts, not just for modesty but for survival, feeling the wind to be altogether capable of lifting them bodily and dumping them, at best, in an undignified sprawl.

But to speak to a West Texan of the wind as though it had no right being there is like speaking to an islander of the ocean as though it would be highly desirable to dry it up and remove it from surrounding the land. The wind is essential in its own way to the creation of West Texas. One might even speculate that it is just as essential that it be unpleasant at times as that it be the salvation of a summer day or the natural air conditioning of most summer nights.

Back in the 1920's a talented novelist, named Dorothy Scarborough (she had lived in Sweetwater as a girl), wrote *The Wind,* a story of West Texas in which her heroine eventually lost her mind from having to live with that constant blowing—that was the symbolic theme; there were other negative factors involved. West Texans reacted with rancor and much spite, and even forty years after publication the generation that felt itself caricatured by *The Wind* would not give the book any of the literary credit it deserved.

THE BACKBONE of settlement, the spine of habitation through West Texas, is the T&P Railway, U.S. Highway 80, and Interstate 20 going from east to west (I speak of them as a single unit, as they generally lie within a few hundred yards of one another). A map shows that all the cities of size in West Texas, with the exception of San Angelo, lie along this route. From Abilene westward, we encounter Sweetwater, Colorado City, Big Spring, Midland, Odessa, Monahans, and, on the bank of the river, the city of Pecos. The only other such highway lifeline is U.S. 180 which parallels it to the north by a distance of twenty to forty miles. On it are Mineral Wells, Breckenridge, Anson, Snyder, and, sitting on the edge of the Cap Rock, Lamesa.

San Angelo sits alone and lives the alonest. It is unlike most West Texas cities in that it is a sheep and goat town.

In the annals of the West much has been made of the enmity between cattle raisers and sheep raisers. "Sheep herder" is still a term of some contempt in the cattle-ranching parts of West Texas. The word "shepherd" is almost never used, even in the sheep district; in fact, I am not sure but what most West Texans would think you were discussing a passage from the New Testament if you mentioned shepherds tending their flocks or made some such usage.

But in reality, as compared with tradition, West Texas, at its south edges, is the nation's greatest wool and mohair producer, furnishing ninety-five per cent of the nation's and half the world's supply of these clippings from the sheep and the goat, respectively.

San Angelo has been, for years, the nation's leading market for wool and mohair, but nowhere in the world where sheep and goats are raised, I venture to guess, is there so much resistance to eating mutton, lamb, or goat meat. Despite intensive campaigns from time to time on the part of the Sheep and Goat Raisers Association to get Texans—any Texans—to eat this meat, the per capita consumption in West Texas is virtually zero pounds. Only now and then will a party be given cabrito, a form of barbecued kid prepared, in Mexican fashion, over mesquite coals. Cabrito is made from the flesh of Spanish goats, not angoras, but even so the host is wise simply to serve it and not comment on its origin. No restaurant in West Texas would think of trying to keep roast lamb, leg of mutton, lamb chops, or goat on its menu and only in a few larger eating places in the larger cities will lamb chops be offered the public. The same thing is true of meat markets.

Some people who raise sheep and goats say the reason they can't enjoy the meat is because neither animal is a particular joy to be around. Not for nothing do we call stupid humans "muttonhead." (I would defend the Spanish goats, however, as being beautiful, agile creatures whose only vice in the wild is a rank smell.)

West Texans are not adventuresome food eaters. Until enough servicemen from other parts had been stationed there in World War II, steaks were customarily cooked until dark gray throughout, and roast beef with a tinge of pink was regarded as raw. My grandmother Cole sent back more than one hamburger for recooking because the meat "wasn't done"—a term that implied a uniform brown quality. Even now, most cattle ranchers will have their steaks no way but well done.

As for such dainties as rattlesnake steak, armadillo, jackrabbit, or venison, few such fancies are tolerated. Hunters, often as not, give away the spoils of the chase rather than bringing it back to West Texas.

San Angelo is a pretty town with two branches of the Concho River coming together at its heart—the Concho, unlike other West Texas rivers, having clear water that almost never runs dry. Two large, man-made lakes sit near the town and its has wide streets and a quiet air of dignity, money and pleasure in itself. However, in San Angelo one tends to feel the way one does in certain cities which sit on the edge of a desert or some other form of Great Beyond. San Angelo is cut off from heavy highway traffic because few people go through except toward the remoter Edwards Plateau sheep-and-goat country, the Big Bend, the Davis Mountains, or northern Mexico. I think the pleasantest little story about San Angelo involves its name. In 1867, when the U.S. Army established Fort Concho (part of the post is preserved on its downtown location), an enterprising merchant named Bart DeWitt built a trading post opposite the fort and it was called, with frontier directness, "Over-the-River." When it gathered a town around it, DeWitt named the settlement Santa Angela, in honor of his wife's sister, who was a Mexican nun. But West Texans couldn't live with the stop-and-go tongue motions of "Santa Angela," so they anglicized it to Saint Angela, then San Angela. When the government was setting up a post office, some purist in Washington objected to combining the masculine "San" with the feminine "Angela," so he changed it to San Angelo to conform to Spanish grammar.

West beyond San Angelo is a strange country, so completely open and dry, so sandy, gravelly, and scrubby as to qualify in most people's minds as a true desert. But it is not an unappealing land, it is, in fact, quite inspiring to travel, with rolling, bare hills, long, wide vistas, and the eternal promise of a blue uplift at the horizon. Its high, lonesome charm is enhanced by its claims for healing such diseases as tuberculosis (a large state sanitarium for lung diseases was in western Tom Green County). Back in the early part of this century, hundreds of weak-lunged, weak-eyed sons of wealthy families were sent out to this region to regain their health—and a good many said they did.

The scattered vegetation is mostly cacti, greasewood, and scrub mesquite. Out near Monahans, in Ward County, there is a singular series of miniature forests consisting of oak and mesquite trees no higher than three feet. But these dwarf woodlands bear heavy crops of acorns and mesquite beans. Most people, finding such woods, do not realize the true nature of them because from a distance the trees look like nothing but thick bunches of bushes.

The late Roy Bedichek, in *Adventures with a Texas Naturalist*, wrote: "I venture . . . that in no other forested section, the Amazon Valley not excepted, is there to be found a higher proportion of fruit to wood than in this Lilliputian jungle in the northern portion of Ward County. Vegetatively considered, it is as much a natural curiosity as the Painted Desert or the wonder-areas of Yellowstone." (Part of this forest is now in the boundaries of the Monahans Sandhills State Park.)

On the eastern edge of this wide, westering sub-

region, however, the watercourses support some magnificent live oak trees, one in Irion County having proportions of one hundred feet across the crown with a trunk circumference of twenty-four feet.

But the country's charm and appeal unfortunately bear little relation to the difficulties of making a living there. So no matter how accustomed or attracted to rolling hills, high, dry air, and glittery sunlight one might be, Irion, Reagan, Upton, and Crane counties (in contiguous western procession from San Angelo to the Pecos River) all show a drop in their already scanty population figures with each year's passing. Irion County, for example, saw its greatest number of inhabitants at the time of World War I. Except for a little irrigated land, farming is a hopeless undertaking in general. Cattle and sheep ranching, both of which demand vast reaches of acreage, are the only natural pursuits, so a few relatively wealthy ranchers stay, and the little towns dry up.

There was a period, in the twenties and thirties,

when oil brought a sudden burst of humanity and wealth to this portion of West Texas. Crane County, still a big producer (although the manpower required for production now is a fraction of what it was), has pumped over 7.25 million barrels of oil since 1923. Upton County had a record of 350 million barrels, and Reagan recorded 226 million by the mid-sixties. Three of these big counties have only a single town within their borders. Crockett, with 2,800 square miles, has only Ozona, "the Richest Little City in America" according to the chamber of commerce, which claims there are more millionaires living in Ozona, per capita, than anywhere else. Crane County, of 800 square miles, has only its county seat, Crane, and Schleicher (pronounced *sly*-kur), which lies directly south of Tom Green County, affords only Eldorado. None of these counties has more than 4,000 inhabitants, most of whom live in the town. So the land may not be lonely but it is empty.

IN OTHER REGIONS, where forests and grasses clothe the terrain, the sense of antiquity comes most often from seeing man's works, from tracing his old achievements that have left marks on the earth or monuments from his hand. It is seldom given to anyone except the professional geologist to wonder what lies on the subsurface page.

But the gaunt, eroded landscape of this western end of West Texas is measured in aeons. This seascaped country looks as if the waters had only been dried up in our decade, as if those little conical hills standing in the pastures like the islands they were, had felt the waters lapping their crowns in our lifetime. Driving through the nude hills, smoothed and shaped as if some huge child had been constructing mud castles, topping them with a carefully chosen flat rock, one clearly sees where the ancient waves deposited loess gravels, sees how the sedimentary layers were put down, compressed, overburdened, fused into solid sandstone and limestone. In this driest of lands the marks of water and its handiwork are everywhere. The shorelines of those oceans, taking millennia to recede, created little beaches in unmistakable series on the land, and where the highways cut through a hillside gap one may find marine fossil evidence of that watery time.

Thus, West Texans are earthy in a direct way. The very clay itself exerts a tremendous pull on them. Naturalist Bedichek quotes Alexis Carrel in this context: "Man is literally from the dust of the earth. For this reason his physiological and mental activities are profoundly influenced by the geological constitution of the country where he lives, by the nature of the animals and plants on which he generally feeds."

In West Texas man feeds mainly on the animals he brought with him, and plant life, like his food animals, must be grown by him and not left to nature to supply. So there is only the land with which to feel this corporeal identity.

Colorado City (which has swung to and fro between using the "City" part) was one of the few places in deep West Texas that was there before the T&P Railway came. Cattlemen, always seeking more free range, because overstocking was killing off grazing lands faster than the frontier could open up new country, began trying to run cattle ever farther west. By 1880 operations were being tried along the Colorado River and Colorado, the town, became a supply point for the ranchers. By the time the railroad got there, in 1881, it had grown to be a sizable civilized spot. Several Fort Griffin merchants, seeing the handwriting on the wall for their town when the fort was abandoned in 1881, put their frame store buildings on skids and pulled them across country over the rough one hundred miles to Colorado. By 1883 Colorado claimed 5,000 inhabitants, making it by far the largest city between Fort Worth and El Paso if these figures are true, as probably they are not. Regardless, Colorado was populous for that day and amazingly advanced. By 1883 it had a telephone system and, according to the *Texas Gazetteer* for that year, a long-distance line. History is vague as to how long the distance was, but as Colorado sat nearly three hundred miles from Dallas and Fort Worth, it was not to those metropoli. Be that as it may, Colorado was by far the most remote farthest west city in Texas to have telephones so early.

Colorado also had a streetcar line about this same time. The cars were pulled by mules, and the line ran from the T&P depot a mile or so east to a spot recorded only as a beer garden. (A cemetery is there now.) To get there the car line had to make a steep up-and-down piece of trackage traversing Lone Wolf Creek, and it is said that the mule was allowed to ride down on the return trip from the beer garden, while on the trip out, mule and passengers alike pushed and pulled to make it up the steep creek bank.

When my uncle Grady Cole went to Colorado in 1930 to open the city's first airport he found the ensuing years had taken away that keen spirit of experiment which brought a "long-distance" line to the place in 1883. His airport attracted few students and transient flyers, so he closed his big sheet-iron hangar, on the east side of town, and came in to run a battery shop which featured nothing more awesome than an orange and black Baby Austin delivery car.

My father and mother moved to Colorado for a short

period, most of which time was spent, as I remember, in running back to Abilene on emergencies. All I clearly recall is one third-grade teacher warning me that Colorado wouldn't put up with my smart-alecking just because I came from the big city. I was so flattered at the notion of being "big city" that I behaved myself from then on.

MIDLAND AND ODESSA have one excuse for being there, with their rather impressive skylines and long avenues of fine homes. The excuse is oil. Oil has made Midland quite a cosmopolitan place, and a high percentage of its population is not only non-native but non-Texan. Odessa, only twenty miles west, is the bedroom city for the oil industry, being larger than Midland but lacking that city's polish—and pretense. The country surrounding Midland and Odessa is almost completely flat and, until you leave the urban squalor that passes for progress, has no charm at all. So one must look up and breathe deeply to take in as much of the sky and the bracing atmosphere as possi-

ble. (A Midland bank once commissioned a regional history which was titled *Land of the High Sky.*)

Midland was originally named Midway because of where it was located by the T&P between Fort Worth and El Paso. Both Midland and Odessa were for decades cattle towns, peopled by immigrants of a slightly different stripe from most of West Texas—the Pacific Northwest furnished one large early group for Midland, and Odessa was envisioned as a religious colony. Both faced modest futures until the 1920's when oil was hit, and eventually the area around the two cities became the economic capital of the unbelievably rich Permian Basin oil field—the richest in North America. Only in the 1960's did the oil play taper off and the marvelous growth rate (from 9,000 in 1940 to 63,000 in 1960 for Midland; 9,600 in 1940 to 81,000 in 1960 for Odessa) slow down.

But of all places in West Texas where "outsiders" have been sent by armed forces, oil companies, corporations, and chain stores, Midland probably has seemed more like home. Its ideas and, in most cases, its execution of ideas, are metropolitan. Its civic ties are with Dallas, not Fort Worth—symphony and theater, not rodeo and cowboy boots. Today, with the two cities being essentially one municipality, they share each others' future, if not their past.

IN THE 1920's oil production became more important than cattle raising over most of West Texas, and a new pioneer hero was developed—the independent oilman.

Doing business with a handshake, tough but fair, tossing the dice with fate and, win or lose, laughing about it, the happy-go-lucky adventurer threatened to take his place in legend with the West Texas cowboy.

But the cowboy never got rich, and the oilman did.

The cowboy remained indigenous to his geography, while the oilman became a world figure with no easily defined home country.

The oilman became entangled in politics, sacrificing, in the public eye, his humanism and sense of humor for a thing called the depletion allowance—a legal device that enabled him to take from the top the first twenty-seven and a half per cent of his income and shelter it from taxation. From being a folk hero the oilman became a villain, seen as the creature of lawyers and bankers.

The cowboy remains the true American primitive. He has strength, innocence, earthy wisdom, honor, and color. In the American mind he is always direct, fair, modest—and poor. American folklore, rightly or wrongly, can only identify with being poor. Get rich (in pocket or in pride) and you lose.

12

What Time Owns

In the middle of the nineteenth century the Texas legislature, playing with the unmapped and empty lands of its frontier, created a strip of counties in West Texas which were all approximately thirty miles by thirty miles in size. The legislature stipulated the county seat of each was to be located dead in the center and that it was to carry the same name as the county.

These latter guidelines were often disregarded when the counties began to be settled. Only five of the twenty or so still have similarly named county seats, although on some old maps there can be found towns which never existed, like Taylor City, which the mapmakers gambled would be built in accordance with the legislature's wishes, or some like Runnels City, which were built but failed to survive.

Shackelford was one of those thirty-square counties but while properly locating its seat in the center, it forgot about the legislature's instructions and named the town Albany—for Albany, Georgia.

Shackelford County is a historical laboratory. From the turn of the twentieth century its population (with the exception of the few years of an oil boom around 1930) has been four or five thousand—half of the people concentrated in Albany. The land of Shackelford County is still owned, in a high percentage of cases, by the descendants of the families that came out to the frontier to settle a century ago.

The area around Shackelford County—with the southern half of Throckmorton and the eastern edge of Jones—was the cradle of West Texas. This was the brink beyond which no one but soldiers went unless something more urgent than travel compelled them, and it was the last place on the long and bloody Comanche frontier line that anyone tried to settle before the Civil War. Today you may see the ruins of a rock house and a large, stone-fenced corral far out in the middle of Lambshead Ranch at the southern edge of Throckmorton County. It is a wide and lovely view, looking west across a tremendous flat valley, and except for the road you arrived on, the valley is untouched by anything of modern man. No fences, no utility poles, no plowed fields or pipeline right-of-way can be seen. Walk northwest over a line of slight rises and you may avail yourself of the rare chance to turn 360 degrees, looking out, and see nothing of man until you glance down at your own shoes—or a jet plane pluming a contrail over your head.

This rock ruin was the main house of the Stone Ranch, built in 1856. For more than a decade following its construction, the Stone Ranch was the most exposed, farthest from civilization, and most dangerous home in Texas.

Shackelford County is a different kind of place. It is one of the few counties in central West Texas that was not the product of a railroad. It was not wrenched from one history and set bodily in another by an oil boom (its boom was mild and easily absorbed), and it has not reached out for industry or wholesale distributors or foreign investments to bolster its economy. It has remained what it was settled to be a century ago, cattle country. It has also remained its own world, holding its own moral standards, making its own social demands. But it is not an antique culture, worshipping only the past. It is not so much ingrown as enclosed. In another sense, it is a kingdom, a feudal system where county records, as late as 1960, showed that seventy-six per cent of the land was owned by twenty-seven individuals.

Albany, the county seat, is the center of life in and for the whole county.

YOU CAN COME into Albany from six directions but the first thing you will see, by any route, is the spire of the courthouse. I like to come up from Abilene, which is thirty-five miles southwest, early in the morning. Then, as you pass over the high ridge that surrounds the town and loop and twist your way down, Albany lies below you etched from the east with the first low sunlight which picks up the edges and outlines of the buildings, houses, and trees like a suddenly uncovered jewel. Albany's profile hasn't changed much since her picture-book courthouse was built in 1883. I have seen an old panoramic photograph taken that year from the front porch of a house that is still standing. All these years later you can find most of the roof lines; the same chimneys and housetops, and the same courthouse dominating it all as you stand in the spot where the photographer stood.

Albany sits in a bowl—a saucer, if you must reduce it to more precise comparisons. This saucer is depression enough to create difficulties for radio and television reception. (Highway patrol units working Albany used to have to drive out west of town a few miles to the top of the last ridge in order to raise district headquarters in Abilene.)

This being situated in a bowl also means that from

the top of the courthouse clock tower you can see all around but not out. And the view has an exciting quality about it, for the viewer is denied the necessity of there being any other world except the world of his bowl—which is exactly the way Albany sees a number of things. Not many people have the luxury of that visual circuit of Albany because to get to the pinnacle of the tower you have to clamber out onto a rococo summerhouse of an affair, then take your mortal chances over a slick strip of sharply tilted copper roof, and, finally, share your summerhouse with the big bell that makes a clangorous outcry every half hour, scaring you out of your wits, because no matter how conscious you are that the bell is beside you and the clock face just below, you can never quite associate the two contrivances with time. Then, what has been melodious and almost remote, when heard on the ground some hundred feet below, becomes a wild, discordant alarm when set going at your elbow.

While not many people need this warning because not many will ever make the climb, the clock and the bell themselves are another matter. They are the heart and the pulse of life in Albany and have been since the courthouse was completed. I have a feeling that the clock and bell are what Albany treasures even more than the building. The face of the clock, restored by the late Robert Nail, who was the guardian of history in Albany, is the original. Only in the 1950's was an electric motor installed to wind the clock. Prior to that it was kept wound by the action of a big chunk of roughly squared limestone which, suspended by a rope, slid down a long, grooved chute, pulling the clock spring taut as it did, and taking several days to make the descent to the floor of the clock tower. Then some special guardian of the town's time had to go and ratchet the stone back to the top of its slide and let gravity start its job over again.

The courthouse, which is the jewel of Shackelford County's heart, is frontier-elaborate in design, just missing the awful Gothic clutter of the Victorian Age but carrying enough decorative scrollwork to show the architect knew finery when he saw it. The building rises rather stiffly but substantially, built of carefully dressed limestone with carved stone sills and lintels on its tall, narrow windows. There is not a crack in its walls or its fourteen-foot-high ceilings, and I was astounded, when shown the architect's plans, to discover its foundations were only eighteen to thirty inches into the ground.

Today the building stands with its exterior not only architecturally intact but surrounded by a public square almost as little changed. Most West Texas courthouse squares were plowed up and asphalted for parking space long ago. Only a tall antenna for the sheriff's short-wave radio and his television set sticks up above the Shackelford tower, annoying at first glance but, on sufficient reflection, having an assuring quality, telling us that Albany will not destroy one world so long as it can be accommodated in another. A lot of cities reverse the philosophy and tear down the old courthouse in order to have a tower in keeping with the television aerial.

A FEW MILES NORTH of Albany, atop a wide plateau which was called Government Hill, lie the ruins of Fort Griffin. Just at the eastern foot of this mesa, which breaks off steeply and drops a couple of hundred feet, is a long, plowed field with fence rows grown up in mesquite bushes and a few big trees down at its north end. This was the Flat, and under the thin covering of chocolate loam of the field lie most of the reminders of the civilian town of Fort Griffin—broken, sun-purpled glass, smashed bullets of heavy caliber, square nails, and odd pieces of metallic hardware which turn up now and then from the plow. Come here at dusk (or camp at night in the state park just across the highway) and you will occasionally hear the coyote talking from the little hills around or, early in the morning, you might even see one heading back to its den—although you are more likely to find a wretched, bloody carcass of this beautiful dog slashed across the highway where it met the fate so many West Texas animals are consigned to, than you are to see it alive and free.

A lot has been written about Fort Griffin, more about the town than the military post. The fort was built in 1867 at the urgent behest of a frontier society which was reluctant to beg Yankee soldiers to protect their late Confederate hides but which otherwise faced extermination (it feared) from the Comanches. The federal government, as if to rub salt into the late enemy's wounds, garrisoned the post throughout its history with Negro soldiers. This must have worked out better than might have been predicted because after the fort was abandoned in 1881 a colony of descendants of these "buffalo soldiers," as the Indians called them (because their hair was tightly curled like a buffalo's), remained in Albany and lives there today.

When Fort Griffin was closed the town lingered on in a bored existence as a farm village after its decade and a half of hell-roaring outlawry when trail drivers, buffalo hunters (it was the hide center of the nation), professional gamblers, gunmen, prostitutes, and U. S. cavalrymen walked its streets looking for amusement—which was seldom anything decent, innocent, or safe.

I won't try to write of all the names that appeared in the Flat—Doc Holliday, Bat Masterson, Lottie Deno, Big Nose Kate, U. S. Army generals and colonels who color up the history books, robber barons and cattle kings before they were quite as rich or famous or fine as we have later made them. Television has taken the era up and gotten it so twisted that most readers would think I was wrong if I said much, and on the other hand I've seen and heard so much I might get fancy mixed with fact in too strong a proportion myself.

My Albany historian friend and playwright, Robert Nail, showed me what each remaining stone marked,

down on the Flat, and knew what every faintly traced old foundation once supported; where the stores, the schools, the Masonic Hall, the saloons, and whorehouses were—or do you prefer "cribs"? That was the word a contemporary newspaper editor applied to those shanties which lined Clear Fork River as he exhorted the decent people and the family men to drive out the Jezebels and the painted creatures of the night. But as was so often true on the frontier (especially in the old hide and soldier towns) the ladies of joy had more followers around town than the editor did.

There is one heap of earth, a sizable mound which many years of plowing have failed to eradicate, that marks the spot where the Beehive Saloon stood. The building was made of adobe on bad advice, for dry as West Texas is, it is not dry enough for that mud-brick construction material to be used successfully over any long period; so now, with years, it has melted into a pile of dirt. But the Beehive had a sign hanging over its door which, though not original in its verse, does something good to my own sense of historical aliveness. It proves that once the old people got beyond the shouting voice of the circuit rider or the camp-meeting evangelist they were fairly gifted with imagination above the sticky sentimentality they left in letters and semiofficial documents. The sign, worded against a picture of the traditional beehive, read:

Within this hive we are alive
Good whiskey makes us funny.
So if you're dry come in and try
The flavor of our honey.

The town faltered when the fort left it, then a couple of years later when the Texas Central Railroad was built to Albany, most of the Flat's businessmen moved their places down to the county seat. (The railroad itself pulled up its rails late in 1967, where once it kept an overnight Pullman coach parked on an Albany siding to take care of cattlemen going to Fort Worth or fancier points like St. Louis or Chicago.) When I was a boy there were still a couple of country stores sitting down at the north end of the field under those big trees, a gasoline pump of the "armstrong" variety standing beside one—but time has eaten them, too, except for the concrete square the pump stood on. In the late thirties Fort Griffin had another brief spurt of fame of the notorious kind. It was the only place in several counties where hard liquor could be bought. At evening the contrast between the old fort ruins, twilighted up on Government Hill, and the liquor stores, limned by neon, down along the highway, was missed by most of the thirsty people heading there not for history but forgetfulness. This final moment of glory ended with World War II when Shackelford County voted itself dry.

One of the main things that keeps Fort Griffin's name alive is a stage pageant, an immense, sweeping, outdoor thing the whole county puts on and which Bob Nail wrote and directed for thirty years. It is called *The Fort Griffin Fandangle,* and you can't play in it unless you are a Shackelford County resident. The script, the music, the dances, costumes, make-up, stage gear, scenery and parade vehicles used in the production come from the same local source—which is staggering when you project Shackelford's total population of 3,600 against the two hundred or more roles to be filled. Whole herds of cattle are moved across the stage, using one of the last surviving collections of genuine longhorns. This herd is kept out at Fort Griffin State Park and is heavily tranquilized for the show, because the longhorns are wild and mean. *The Fandangle* was formerly staged in the high school stadium, right beside the Katy Railroad's tracks (successor to the Texas Central), and every night during the performance, here would come a freight train, puffing and whistling for the downtown crossing. So Nail gave it a simple solution; next year he wrote a train part into the *Fandangle* script and timed it to coincide with the 9 p.m. freight. It was so successful that when the railroad took off that evening freight run the train part stayed in and the *Fandangle* producers built their own train. Today the Katy no longer runs at all in Albany except for this once-a-year revival on the *Fandangle* stage.

Sometimes when I am seated in the outdoor amphitheater that is now used for the production, watching a performance of the show, I wonder what the ghosts are thinking, twenty miles away, out on the dark and lonely Flat, knowing these people, many of them their descendants, are trying to resurrect them and their way of life. The show is based on good history, but it furnishes good irony, too, in that neither actors nor prototypes would change places.

IF YOU TRAVEL up the curving Clear Fork River, which passes in a loop around the site of Fort Griffin, you will come to one of the forgotten places of history, Camp Cooper. The ifs are important in that statement because, except by lucky chance, you will not find your way to Camp Cooper without outside help. Getting to the general area is difficult enough and finding the actual site, even knowing where it is, becomes even more of a problem because the grounds where the post was located are a jungle of mesquite thicket through which it is almost impossible to walk and quite difficult to see.

The loneliness of the place catches you almost immediately after you leave the Flat—which at least has a busy highway running north and south beside it. But when you cross the Clear Fork on a spidery iron bridge with wooden plank flooring that booms like a drum, and your wheels touch the other shore, you are back in the nineteenth century. The road is a narrow, dirt pathway which leads through gates and across cattle guards and finally fords the river itself. En route you may pass the site of the Comanche Indian reservation which was established in 1856 and was the reason for Camp Cooper being set up, although nothing but a granite shaft marks the spot.

Camp Cooper sits on the north bank of the Clear Fork, on a wide shelf of land which runs up against low hills. It is immediately seen, by the untrained eye of today's visitors, that this is a terrible spot to put a post—in the summer the heat runs up to 120 degrees, for one thing, and Clear Fork runs gyp (for gypsum) water much of the time, for another. And although it never proved to be the case, if the Indians had wanted to lay siege to the camp, it would have been child's play, because the only escape routes are through rather narrow gaps at each end of the string of hills.

Camp Cooper was put there to guard the Indians of the reservation from the Texans as much as to guard the settlers—reversing the role of every other fort established in Texas. It had a distinguished list of personnel, beginning with Colonel William J. Hardee, who established it, and including such military names as Albert Sidney Johnston, Earl Van Dorn, George Stoneman, Theodore O'Hara, John B. Hood, George Thomas, and Ranald S. Mackenzie. Johnston was the Confederate general who was killed in command at the Battle of Shiloh; Earl Van Dorn was shot during the Civil War by a fellow Confederate to whose wife Van Dorn paid too much attention; George Thomas became known as "The Rock of Chickamauga" at the head of the Union forces there; George

Stoneman was a Union general, Theodore O'Hara wrote a rather famous Mexican War poem, now slipping into the mist, "The Bivouac of the Dead"; J. B. Hood was one of Texas's proudest sons in the Civil War, founder of Hood's Texas Brigade, and Ranald S. Mackenzie, whose stay at Camp Cooper came after the Civil War, was the man who finally and brutally drove the Comanches out of West Texas forever.

But the most important figure in Camp Cooper's history was Lieutenant Colonel Robert E. Lee, who arrived April 9, 1856, and remained commandant until July 28, 1857.

I cannot imagine Robert E. Lee in West Texas, but the country played an important role in his life. When he arrived at Camp Cooper, the Virginia aristocrat was mortified at the way he had come down in the military world. Ten years before, in the Mexican War, he had been called "America's very best soldier," by old General Winfield Scott. He had been superintendent of West Point and had handled the assignment brilliantly. Then he was sent to this, the rawest of frontier posts, with a mere four companies of cavalry under him (twelve officers and 226 enlisted men). He was deeply embittered as he forded the Clear Fork and saw the hot, dusty tents and unfinished log and stone buildings.

"My military career is at a dead end," he wrote Mary, his wife, back at Arlington.

But West Texas did something for Robert E. Lee, and no historian has given his stay there the credit it deserves, in my opinion. A man of fifty, he had been in the Army since entering West Point at age eighteen. His brilliant career during the Mexican War had amounted to nothing except a kind of underground reputation among some of his racier fellow officers for being a snob and a goody-goody.

But Lee, brave as he had been during that war (he had been brevetted three times on that account), had never had field command experience, had never had to make the dreary daily choices which cannot be passed up or down the chain of command. At Camp Cooper he learned to decide alone and act. He learned he was not really important to the military hierarchy, and that being a member of a famous First Family of Virginia and married to another (Martha Washington's great-granddaughter) counted for nothing out in West Texas. He learned another lesson in humility—to do your best in a situation even when no one demands the best of you and neither does the situation itself. (All this you can read in his letters to Mary Custis Lee.) As he learns to love the majestic loneliness of West Texas the man finds himself, discovers the depths he is capable of probing. The remnants of bitterness and the narrow aristocracy of his background drop away—you can read it in the letters—and human understanding and patience emerge. I think it can be said with certainty that General Robert E. Lee of the defeated South, the one general held in love and respect because of his supreme humanism, could never have emerged as a person had not defeated and embittered Lieutenant Colonel Robert E. Lee spent nineteen months in a separate, demanding personal world in a place called West Texas.

ONE INTERESTING development of Lee's character also occurred at Camp Cooper. He conducted the first funeral he had ever had to handle. On June 9, 1857, the child of the post surgeon died, "and for the first time in my life I read the beautiful funeral service of our church [Episcopal] over a grave," he wrote Mary. Then, less than two weeks later, he was called on to conduct another funeral, this one the son of one of the sergeants. "I was admiring the little boy's appearance only the day before he died," Lee wrote home sadly.

Today the Camp Cooper cemetery is hard to find, in an entanglement of vines and briers, full of copperhead snakes and a kind of harmless but scary chicken snake that climbs the willow trees around the plot and drapes itself for all the world like a tree limb—and when attempting to penetrate the section one is always reaching up to push aside a branch. Lee also complained, incidentally, of the snakes at Camp Cooper and the way they would steal not only the eggs his hen laid but the hen herself, Lee having originally brought a pen of chickens and a chef with him to Camp Cooper. Neither institution outlasted the fauna, or the social climate of the place.

Visiting the gloomy cemetery, once you have discovered it, is an experience in melancholy. The burial ground is located on a point where a creek enters the Clear Fork and, being subject to periodic overflow, is a dismal tangle. Under the tall pecan trees along the river, the sadness of death lingers even for those rare visitors who might not recognize where they are. The soldiers buried in the Camp Cooper cemetery were removed to San Antonio at a later date, but the other graves were not disturbed; and while the two children's plots are not inscribed, there are two stone-marked little places which I feel sure are theirs, and one can easily hear, on the wind in the branches, Lee's quiet voice reciting those ancient lines from the Book of Prayer about "ashes to ashes, and dust to dust . . ."

One wonders how many more times this man would hear these words, or say them, in the bloody years of war which lay only months ahead of him when he left Texas in 1861 to go back to Virginia and receive the elevation of history. Strange that one remote spot in West Texas should have shaped so many parts of a Virginia aristocrat —his first field command, his first funeral service, his first true vision of himself.

CAMP COOPER, after Lee departed, was far from out of history, however. In December 1860, a company of Texas Rangers under L. S. (Sul) Ross (who was later governor of Texas) picked up a company of Second Cavalry soldiers to help them chastise some Comanches.

The pursuers caught up with the Indians about fifty miles north of Camp Cooper at the Pease River and discovered it was the main band of Chief Peta Nocona (for whom Texans later named a town in North Texas). During the battle one of the soldiers was pursuing a squaw with the usual honorable intentions of shooting her in the back, when she turned, holding up a baby, and cried, "Americano! Americano!"

Closer inspection showed the squaw to have blue eyes, and although there were some red-haired Comanches, there were none with blue eyes. This saved the squaw's life and her baby's, and she was taken back to Camp Cooper and locked in the hay barn—which building was one of the few stone structures there and was called the hay barn only because at one point, not long before, a dashing commandant, named Newton C. Givens, had taken it into his head to move Camp Cooper lock, stock, and barrel out to his ranch—Stone Ranch it was—so he could live in more comfort; and the Indians from down on the reservation had come to Cooper and stored hay in the permanent buildings that were left temporarily vacant. Givens conveniently died, or else Camp Cooper might have remained at Stone Ranch, which is certainly a more salubrious place.

Her years seemed to be about right for this blue-eyed squaw to be the Parker girl who had been captured in 1836, at age nine, when the Comanches had raided Fort Parker. Sul Ross took her to Camp Cooper, unable to get anything out of her, as she clutched her baby, and he sent word back to Birdville in Tarrant County, for Isaac Parker to come see if this could be his long-lost niece. We are not told how long it took the old man to get out to Camp Cooper, but we may be certain the intervening period was full of speculation in the camp—probably divided between those who wanted to save her if she were a white woman and those who wanted to shoot her for the same reason, having cohabited with the painted savages and refused to rejoin the white race.

(I wish I had time to tell about old Isaac Parker, for he deserves more credit than just having a county named for him. Born in 1793, he married and had four children, and when his first wife died in 1867 he waited exactly three years and married again—by now he's seventy-seven, recall—and had four more children before he, too, died in 1883.)

But at any rate, Parker rode hard to Camp Cooper and was taken directly to the hay barn where the white squaw, as they called her, was sitting on her cot. In the bare room the savage woman with the blue eyes confronted the old man with the white beard and he found nothing he recognized of the little niece he had last seen nearly twenty-five years before. She refused to speak, Spanish didn't seem to interest her, English glazed her eyes, and no one knew enough Comanche to ask the right questions.

"Cynthia?" he asked, and got nothing but a glance from her.

"Cynthia? Cynthia Ann?" he asked again.

The woman turned and looked at him then, listening to something that was trying to speak to her.

"Cynthia Ann? Is it you, Cynthia Ann?"

Her lips moved as she said the words like you taste a piece of strange, delicious fruit.

"Cynthia," she said softly. "Cynthia . . . Cynthia Ann."

It was Cynthia Ann Parker, taken by the Comanches, turned into an Indian who, at age fourteen, had refused to return to Texan civilization with some traders; who had been seen, at age sixteen, as wife of Peta Nocona; who had been glimpsed later at a battle or two, and then had gained a kind of dark fame as wife of the foremost Comanche chief. Nocona was killed in that Pease River battle, so a Mexican captive whom the Rangers released had said, although no one knows for sure, even today. She was mother of two sons, raiding warriors themselves; Pecos, whom history has lost, and Quanah, who later took his mother's last name and walked the white man's road successfully, after fighting him bitterly until forced onto the Oklahoma Reservation, the last of the Comanche war chiefs.

But for Cynthia Ann the old world into which she was born was not her world in any way, and although she and Topasannah, her baby girl (Prairie Flower, romantic historicians claim it means), were hailed by the Texans and Cynthia Ann was given a pension by the legislature, she languished. She must have known that Peta was dead, her sons gone from her touch, and that she could never go back to those she loved but must stay with these white people who said she was one of them. At any rate, Topasannah died in 1862 and Cynthia Ann expired two years later at the home of her sorrowful brother, Silas, Jr., who never could make her understand they were of one blood.

AND YET another story about Camp Cooper and then

we will leave it to the quietness that has wrapped it in a century's robe.

In February 1861, Texas hot-heads had just about gained domination of the state in their frenzy to secede from the Union. There had been, only a few months before, a good percentage of Texans who were not ready to leave the United States, but in the dark hours of the fall of 1860, when the "Black Republicans" were successful in their candidate from Illinois, Abe Lincoln, the secessionists took over with fear and intimidation and only Sam Houston, the Old Lion who never feared a thing in his life but his last, young wife, could publicly declare his opposition.

But even Sam Houston couldn't stop the tide of doom that this rowdy group wished so heartily to see drown Texas. A secession convention was called and it voted to put the question to the people—and to depose Governor Sam Houston in the process. The state-wide vote was in favor of seceding and joining the Confederacy by four to one—especially after a few anti-voters had been shot or hanged, had mysteriously disappeared or otherwise eased themselves out of the country.

Immediately after this, on February 18, the general in charge of U. S. forces in Texas, a hollow warrior named David E. Twiggs, hastened to surrender every post and fort to the interim government which had little legal basis except the law of force. Several hundred hot-bloods saddled up and headed out to accept the surrender of the various military establishments. (What would we have done had we lived then, when opposition was not only futile, dangerous and unacceptable but apt to inspire only more frenzy in favor of the rasher sentiment on every question? It is not enough to say, now, that we would have stood up for what we believed—in the face of fire, the rope, guns, and almost certain ruin, if not death. How can we, when we dare not oppose popular ideas now any more than those conscience-stricken Texans did then.)

Most of the paramilitary forces encountered little or no hesitation when they came to take the sword of the various U. S. commanders. Many of the commanders were themselves Southerners and the surrender was a token thing, with the U. S. soldiery simply joining the new Rebel group.

But not so at Camp Cooper. When Colonel W. C. Dalrymple appeared there with a large group of Texans anxious to take over the fort, Captain Stephen D. Carpenter, the commander, was in no mind to surrender.

"I was not put in command here to see the Stars and Stripes pulled down while I or a single one of my men are alive," he told the Texans. And he obviously meant it. Dalrymple stood siege for a couple of days, with more Texans riding to join him every day. Eventually he had Camp Cooper completely surrounded (I mentioned the vulnerable position insofar as a siege would make it) and he called out the young Federal captain.

"Just look around you," Dalrymple told him. "Up along those hills, atop that bluff."

Captain Carpenter made a circuit with his gaze, and all along the horizon of the hills he could see armed men, their guns trained on his smaller detachment below. It was hopeless. But even then he hesitated and finally explained his motives:

"In the present agitated condition of our country I feel compelled to regard . . . the perilous consequences of refusal that must result to our whole nation." And he capitulated.

Thus the Civil War was averted by some six weeks—to the firing on Fort Sumter instead of the firing on Camp Cooper. As it was, Cooper merely served as an outpost for the Frontier Battalion during that war. This unit was a group of frontiersmen organized as state or Confederate militia, who patrolled West Texas, now and then breaking up a collection of draft dodgers or suspected Union sympathizers but mostly fighting Indians.

But there is one reference to Camp Cooper left unexplained. It is found in that most readable of all Texas frontier memoirs, the recollections of Buck Barry, who was with the Frontier Battalion. He says, "Although I served the Cause throughout the war, the only Yankee soldiers I ever saw were 300 Federal prisoners sent to Cooper to be fed cheaply on buffalo meat awaiting exchange." The portion of history's iceberg visible from my way tells nothing else of this episode.

IF YOU WALK south from the site of Camp Cooper you enter a mesquite thicket in which it is easy to lose your way. Once the parade grounds, later a cultivated field (the implements are still in place), so rapidly and thickly do mesquites grow that now it is a thorny jungle. When you find your way out, you have come to a shallow ford across the Clear Fork which was used by patrols and wagons heading out to the prairies. The ford is only usable now by people on foot but the banks show clearly that it once had a road.

A stone ranch house, four chimneys lined up two-by-two, sits atop the slight rise just beyond the far, high bank of the river. It is a remote house with the marks of age showing clearly on it and hinting at the sorrow and mystery it has seen.

This is the Putnam ranch house, better known as the Larn place—although it has been in the Putnam family many decades longer than Larn owned it. John Larn was a handsome, dark-eyed young man, fairly well educated, who came to Fort Griffin early in the seventies, either from Kansas or Colorado. He quickly established a reputation for making money, being a deadly shot, and leading men. He also fluttered the girls' hearts, and by the time he was twenty-one had married Mary Jane Matthews, the pretty daughter of Joe Matthews, the most respected cattleman in the territory.

The countryside was split (as were most pioneer communities) between those who wanted no law that might inhibit their ambitions, and those who needed protection against superior force or unfairness. And a vigilante group had been formed to enforce what was called "law and order," although we can't be sure now whose law it enforced or whose orders it took.

In the spring of 1876 the crisis reached a point where Shackelford County was being alternately terrorized by the rustling faction and by the vigilantes, who were hanging avowed rustlers at the rate of four to eleven at one session. When the sheriff resigned, the citizens turned to Larn as the best possible replacement. He did a remarkably fast job of straightening things up, teaming with a deputy named John Selman, a man whose gun was as respected but whose reputation, at that point, was much worse.

Within six months, Larn had stopped the random shootings and loose crime in the county and had made himself highly attractive to the Fort Griffin crowds. (Although the new town of Albany had been voted county seat the year before, Fort Griffin still functioned as the center of activity.) But Larn had always inspired an uneasy fear in some people. He was too sure of himself and too little inclined to talk.

Whatever verdict history may bring on Larn, there is no doubt he loved pretty Mary very much and she loved him. She said, for one thing, that he never spoke a cross word to her, and our fleeting evidence gives us a hint that theirs was a marriage that was always a love affair. Their first home is said to have been built on that mesquite flat at Camp Cooper, using stone and materials from the old post. The cottage is still standing and is suitably remote and romantic enough, even in its tumbled state, to have been what local legend calls it today, the Honeymoon Cottage.

The first time I saw the cottage the romantic interpretation was enhanced by a large flowerbed in the front yard, the bed carefully shaped with rocks in the form of a heart. This fit the conception of the handsome young couple spending their first married days in the place, dallying with hearts and flowers. The fact is that Bob Nail and I, digging around the yard, discovered it to be divided into four equal parts, each containing a flowerbed edged in rock. The other three beds, if you haven't already guessed, were shaped like a diamond, a spade, and a club.

At any rate, Larn prospered as a cattleman and soon moved Mary across the Clear Fork, up that overgrown road from the ford and into the ranch house—which was also constructed in great part from Camp Cooper buildings. It was not, and is not, an ordinary ranch house. Some finely etched glass is still in place around its front door, said to have come from the commandant's quarters, and fancy hardware and moldings are believed to have been brought to Cooper by some of the famous officers who served there before the Civil War. At the time Larn built it, the house had a square cupola rearing up between the double line of chimneys. That cupola had a kind of bench built along its four sides which could be used for sitting and contemplating the rolling valley around the house—or maybe as a lookout and sniper's perch. By now many of the neighbors were convinced that handsome John Larn, while an effective sheriff, was a ruthless, cold, and ambitious man who, far from trying to enforce equal justice, was trying to control the county and eliminate competitors rather than rustlers and outlaws.

One approach to the Larn place, the eastern and prettiest, to my mind, is by a road which comes over a hill and picks up a tall rock wall, following it for more than half a mile. It is a good wall, put together with that forgotten skill of the dry-wall mason, still sturdy in most of its stretches and as balanced and well designed as any I have seen.

A stone wall is a rarity in West Texas. Only the oldest settlers built them. Barb wire, after all, was one of the inventions that made settlement there possible. Rock walls are from a date when there was nothing else to fence with. Not many people today know how to build a dry wall. We pile the rocks one on the other and come out either with too many large ones or end up making course after course of small ones. In any case, the old walls had a symmetry of purpose, a solid notion of strength, standing there with almost human patience, clever in the way they were intricately devised of the sizes and shapes as they came to hand. To me they are the very texture of yesterday.

Larn's wall is still the subject of legend. What is known is that two dry-wall masons, named Jones and Wilks, were offered five hundred dollars to erect a mile of rock fence along the big pasture near the Larn home. They collected one hundred dollars to start and were to be paid the remainder on completion of the fence. But when they finished the job they disappeared. Larn's enemies immediately speculated that Larn had dispensed with his debt by killing the two masons and disposing of their bodies and, in fact, two badly decomposed corpses were found in the Clear Fork but no identification was made. On Larn's behalf let it be noted that one of the men was reportedly seen alive and unharmed a few years later in Arkansas.

Larn resigned his public office a year after assuming it and got a government contract to furnish beef for the soldiers at Government Hill. His partner in the deal was Selman. Neighbors claimed that while Larn was supposedly slaughtering several animals every day to fill his contract, his herds seemed to increase rather than shrink. A group of farmers and small landholders in the vicinity, contemptuously called "the Grangers," suffered such depredations—loss of cattle, wanton slaying of horses in their pastures, physical abuse, and threats—that the men stayed in the house all day, sending their wives out to transact what little business they were allowed to pursue. Few of the men undressed at night and none would answer a "Hello the house" after dark for fear of bushwhackers. They blamed "the Larn gang."

Larn seems to have done little to dispel this air of mystery around him. He declared he was not a rustler, and pointed to his family life as exemplary, proving, he seemed to feel, that this was evidence enough of his virtue. His attitude was interpreted by many as scorn.

What we know of his private life leaves shadows. At night, around the Larn ranch house, there would be unannounced hoofbeats, coming and leaving. He would go off for days to trade for cattle, he said, and the stories would filter back of acts both outrageous and benevolent he was supposed to have performed. Some people remembered a former partner named Bryant who had been shot to death and his cattle kept by Larn "without administration," a newspaper later reported. Also, a confrontation is supposed to have taken place shortly after he quit his sheriff's job, bringing Larn and the big cattlemen together—and only his father-in-law's intervention saved

Larn, rumor said. But records are scarce, and recollections, when it was safe to make them, were vague. And practically everything said against Larn could be turned around and seen as ugly gossip. Rustling, bold and flagrant, continued.

Finally the new sheriff, Bill Cruger, took a search warrant and a detachment of Texas Rangers to the Larn place and dragged the river—on a tip. One account says they found two hundred hides sunk in a deep hole, the brands blotted out—or at least not Larn's. However, a Ranger reported only six were found. Larn and Selman claimed it was a frame-up and, for whatever reason, charges against them were not prosecuted. If Larn was bluffing even the Rangers were afraid to call it.

Two children had been born to John and Mary; one son died very young, the other, Will, made a sturdy little boy who followed his father around when he was at the ranch. Larn at home was brooding and portentous. He would order, on certain nights, that no lights were to be lit. He himself would go up to his cupola, rifle in hand, to watch or sleep. Mary would waken to hear soft conversations and movements around the house which she must have learned to accept without coming to doubt her husband. Larn depended more and more on Selman, and Selman, who had lived with the settlers of the area since the middle of the Civil War, had long had the reputation of being what we might now call a punk. But he was tough and dangerous, as was shown when he later killed John Wesley Hardin.

At any rate, the situation grew tenser. The Rangers wrote that even their mail was being opened. There is an undertone of "more than meets the eye" to their reports. One Ranger lieutenant wrote his superior officer, "I could give you some names . . . that would make you shudder at the thought of such in the standing that they are of being in such business . . . the majority of the officers of the county who is and has been into a secret organization . . . sworn to stand up to whatever was done by any of his party." Eventually something had to be done about Larn. And eventually something was.

Larn always carried a gun and was known to be an impossibly deadly shot—one of those rare frontier kind who really *was* a marksman and a quick-draw artist, and who really *did* carry a gun. (It is amazing to us when we find out how many frontiersmen, even in times of Indian warfare, didn't carry arms unless hunting or out on a particularly dangerous errand.)

But Sheriff Cruger got eight other men to go out with him and try to arrest Larn. (One of the men was Mary Larn's brother-in-law.) They went in the night, fearful of that watchtower cupola of his, and in the morning when he went out to milk (he was a family man, remember) he left his guns in the house. Three of the posse rose from hiding and Sheriff Cruger said to Larn that he had a warrant for his arrest. One version says Larn was armed and surrendered his pistol without a fight, then realized he had made a mistake when he saw the warrant was from Albany and not Fort Griffin, where Larn's gang centered. Another story says Larn offered Cruger five hundred dollars if the sheriff would let him go get a gun and fight it out. The posse wasn't that romantic, if the story was true, for they handcuffed him and set him in a wagon, taking the trail to Albany instead of the more public road by way of Fort Griffin.

Mary, discovering he was a prisoner, sensed what was to happen. She got little Will and hitched up a buggy and she, too, drove south. Some say Larn, fearing a mob, talked the posse into letting her and Will accompany him for safety's sake.

Larn must have known his time was short. He had,

after all, been a vigilante leader himself and whether he was a rustler or not, he had helped dispatch several unwanted persons in the past. The party got to Albany amid hot waves of rumor. Mary got a room in a house just off the present courthouse square (the house is still there) and John was taken to a log cabin down on Hubbard Creek, two blocks away, which was being used as a jail. The prisoners were fastened by chains to big staples driven into the wall.

Mary got a lawyer and tried, but failed, to get her husband out on bail. Later the justice of the peace wrote that a hidden vigilante was listening to the proceedings and if he, the JP, had accepted bond for Larn, the vigilante was under orders to shoot the JP.

Mary, awake at midnight, heard a burst of rifle fire from along the creek, and she screamed. Down in the jail two other prisoners, chained to the wall in the single-room cell, rolled over and hid their faces. A band of eleven men, masked and wearing the long, yellow slickers of the range that dropped to their ankles, had appeared at the jail, bound the jailer, and marched in where Larn was. Giving him just time to call them murderous cowards, each lifted a rifle and fired into him.

Mary was given the body and she took it back to the ranch and buried her husband beside the child who had died. There are just the two graves there now, out on a windy point that overlooks the Clear Fork valley to the west. It is set about three hundred yards from the Larn house, with a handsome, tall stone over Larn's grave and a waist-high stone wall squaring off the plot. Nearby, at the edge of the river bluff, from the evidence of hundreds of flint chips, we know the spot was well used by Indian craftsmen long before Larn.

We will never know what Mary felt in her heart. As did everyone else, she heard that one of her brothers was in that midnight group. We know she went back to her family and nothing survives for us as to what went on between them or whether she rejected some members and accepted others. She lived a good many years, and she kept close counsel.

But we have a clue. When she did marry again it was to a vigorous frontier preacher, a man named Brown. He was fervent but well educated, a student of religion. And it is interesting that he forthwith set out to spend many years proving that Larn, his wife's former husband, was not guilty of the crimes told against him. Brown even wrote a book to that end, a rare volume which had to be kept secretly in those few Shackelford County homes of that day which had a copy.

The Larn tragedy is still a mystery, although we can be more realistic about him. It seems probable that Larn had some understanding with a group which wanted to get rid of the Grangers and, as the Ranger stated, he was also connected with the secret vigilante organization that involved just about every official and powerful landowner in the area. But he must have gone too far, presuming on his knowledge to keep him safe from both sides, knowing that, if he wanted to, he could destroy almost any reputation in the country. When it finally became necessary to arrest him, his fate was certain, for he could not be allowed to have a trial. If Larn himself wouldn't testify, some of his intimates might. Certainly a connection was there, and with Larn's death everyone pulled a quick cover over the affair. Even Selman, arrested and brought back, was unofficially but firmly allowed to "escape" and sent fleeing.

The Larn story lives vibrantly in the Albany country. Until the postwar generation of our day it was not often mentioned at all because there were those living who knew the realities and not the myths. Only after the old ones were gone did stories with authentic substance begin appearing.

Larn's son Will roamed the West, then came back to live with his mother's family, and he turned out to be a person as strange as his father. A handsome man, he lived a restless, uncontrolled life as soon as he reached manhood, going from job to job, spending large sums of money freely, never able to cease from movement, disquiet, and despair. His final years were troubled by disease and the inheritance of history.

Today it is safe to tell the story of the Larn affair, to speculate, even to take sides—although the families involved are still notable in Shackelford and Throckmorton counties. The generation alive now has finally lost the haunting presence of the affair. It was an unhappy history but one duplicated, in form, if not content, at many other places in that frontier era we can never really understand.

13

The Butterfield & I

West of Fort Griffin lies a huge spread called the Lambshead Ranch. It is owned by the Matthews-Reynolds family, a group which has been in West Texas for well over a century and has so intermarried and combined as to be, in effect, one family, although there are separate Reynolds and Matthews both living in the area.

One of the most accurate and certainly the most charming books concerning early-day history of that area is Sallie Reynolds Matthews's *Interwoven*. It bears that title because the early history of Shackelford and Throckmorton counties is pretty much the story of these two interwoven families.

Lambshead Ranch was the headquarters for the Matthews ranching activities and was Sallie Reynolds Matthews's home. Today it is considered probably the most efficient cattle ranch in Texas, and a good many national magazines have done stories and pictures based on its operation under Watt Matthews, Sallie's youngest son. (The Lambshead Ranch was also used extensively in television ads which told of a fabulous Western country connected in some mysterious way with a popular brand of cigarettes; therefore, millions of Americans have visited the Lambshead without knowing it.)

But for all the historical association of the Matthews

and the Reynolds families with West Texas, and despite their having come out to the Clear Fork and Albany country before almost anyone else, the name Lambshead comes from even earlier in history. The ranch name comes from its being situated in Lambshead Valley, which in turn got its name from Lambshead Creek that flows into the Clear Fork at that point. And Lambshead Creek got its name from two English brothers, one of whom, Thomas Lambshead, was in the country at the time and became manager of the Butterfield stage station in the vicinity in 1858.

The Butterfield stage line marked the first real look at West Texas given the rest of the world. There had been earlier explorations—notably Captain Randolph Marcy's expedition of 1849 which found a route for the California-

bound Gold Rushers—but none had provided a constant contact. This the Butterfield stage line, with its biweekly schedule, did, bringing out news of West Texas to the outside world and bringing in news of the outside world, so that what few persons were there could feel a contact with civilization. So one may say that the social history of West Texas began with the Butterfield stage line.

WHEN JOHN BUTTERFIELD got a contract in 1857 to carry the U. S. Mail from Saint Louis to San Francisco, he sent out a line of advance men who went about their pioneering in scientific fashion, chopping down trees in the path to a uniform height, cutting down river and creek banks, and finding river fords which were rock-bottomed and reliable enough to accommodate the stage schedules and not eternally be washing out, leaving one party stranded on the east bank looking at another on the west bank every time it rained.

John Butterfield, it must be remembered, was not a frontiersman, not a Texan, and not even a Westerner. He was a Utica, N. Y., businessman who had made a career of hauling people, freight, and other valuables in a businesslike manner. So when he got the Southern Overland Mail contract at an income of $600,000 per annum he knew nothing much of what it entailed except that he must deliver so many times per week on a guaranteed basis.

It is a shame, maybe, that more pioneers weren't like Butterfield. He took a lot of the romance out of it (I suppose there are more myths connected with the Butterfield stage than almost any single Western episode except Custer's last battle), but he made it work—and unfortunately, this was seldom true of the raw-gut, rawboned pioneers who set out with ax and rifle to conquer the frontier. I saw some of those relics from that other age, all of them elderly and most of them quite lost in the modern world. But the thing that stays hardest in my memory is the idea that dominates all others: they were failures. Most of them were driven back from the frontier a time or two before they finally found a sticking place; driven back by drought, the Indians, grasshoppers, or plain bad practices of farming, ranching, or trade. The frontier drew the misfits and in a way it helped them survive, but it never prepared them for the new age that burst on them with a successful suddenness that left them isolated and bewildered, the first of the lonely crowd we think we presently have a monopoly on.

Only gradually did the white men, poking their way inward on the continent, learn how to live and compromise. And countless of their number went under, their lives forming a foundation for the names history recognizes. These men, like the animals they brought with them, came to be valued most for what they did not demand to have done for them. West Texas owes more, or at least as much, to the mule as to the fiery stallion. In men I suspect the same thing is true, although we seldom read the names of these mules and other workaday beasts of society who peopled the place.

Instead, we read of the colonels, majors, and cattle barons who held the swords and wrote the checks, naming the cities for themselves and blowing clouds of powder smoke over their history. John Butterfield's stages carried his name, and history gives him an association with the West that reality flatly denies—but what was actually "the Butterfield stage" was men at lonely passes, stations set on the prairie in a treeless midst, brackish or gyp water, drivers at midnight, conductors who pledged their lives to a schedule.

Thus, the Lambshead brothers (who, most appropriately, kept a few head of sheep) were making history for John Butterfield but being denied their own place in it. History seldom lets the chips fall where they may or designates which chip shall become embedded in the amber of its record.

THE FIRST RUN of the Butterfield stage (or, officially, the Southern Overland Mail) started in St. Louis on the morning of September 16, 1858. It was a historic moment and, unlike so many historic moments, it was well documented. Waterman Ormsby, a reporter for the New York *Herald*, had been sent to make the entire passage to San Francisco and he seemed to sense the historical significance of his mission.

"I looked forward in my imagination," he wrote, "to the time when . . . instead of having to wait over forty days for an answer from San Francisco, a delay of as many minutes will be looked upon as a gross imposition, and of as many seconds as 'doing from fair to middling.'"

The route to Texas lay through Arkansas and the Indian Nation, which was not particularly dangerous at that time except for renegade white men, the Indians being Choctaws, Chickasaws, Cherokees, Creeks, and Seminoles—all civilized tribes with their own governments and their own police. So the frontier, and adventure, didn't really begin for the Butterfield passenger until he reached Texas, which he did by crossing the Red River at a point called Colbert's Ferry, very near the present North Texas town of Denison (the birthplace of President Dwight D. Eisenhower some thirty-two years later). Even this passage was no great adventure, Mr. Colbert being a businessman, part of whose business it was to see that the stage and its passengers made the voyage as eventlessly as possible, since any events that took place were likely to be unplanned for, and therefore, in most cases, disastrous.

The first real landfall below Colbert's in Texas was the town of Sherman, about ten miles south. The first trip reached there September 21, and the stage was thirty-one hours and fifty minutes ahead of schedule.

From Sherman the stage line went westward on a new road specially built by the Butterfield engineers. At Gainesville, which was getting rather far out of civilization, Ormsby noted, "We travel night and day and only stop long enough to change teams and eat. Though the country through which we passed [the Indian Nation] was but sparsely peopled, it seemed like leaving home to bid farewell even to these settlements and proceed through the wilds of Texas, along its lonely plains and barren hills and dangerous frontier."

Right about this point in the Butterfield stage saga is where so many latter-day historians and painters have gone astray concerning the vehicles and animals. By the time the schedule hit Texas the beautiful, heavy (3,000-pound) Abbott coaches, with their red or bottle-green bodies and yellow-striped running gear, their russet leather interiors and wide leather straps, which underslung the bodies for spring action, were usually left behind. Instead, the passengers had moved into much lighter nine-passenger vehicles with frame tops covered with ducking, called "celerity wagons." The Concord-type coaches were too heavy, too slow, and too liable to upset in frontier travel, so they were mainly used on the Missouri-Arkansas and the California ends of the run. Not only that, but by the time the Butterfield stage had reached Diamond's station, some twenty miles out of Sherman going west, the fast, sleek horses had been replaced by mules. Entering the wild Indian country, as the line did a few miles later, horses were considered too great a temptation. Indians would brave almost any danger, even death, to get a good horse but looked down on mules, because they were too slow to ride. (Some would eat them, however.)

The initial trip reached Fort Belknap, in Young County, on September 22 at five twenty-five in the morning. Ormsby wasn't inspired by what he saw. "The fort is not very formidable," he reported for his New York readers. And when the stage forded the Brazos River, just west of the post, he noted "the dirty red water was not any deeper than an ordinary New York gutter." The stage came out of the Brazos valley and up on a long plain which the reporter characterized as "the dreary spectacle." Dreary or not, Ormsby had arrived in West Texas.

There is one notable coincidence about the route of the Butterfield stage through West Texas. It is as lonely today as it was in 1858. In fact, once you cross the Brazos you were certain to have met more people then, following the route of the stage line, than you might by following the same route today—understanding, of course, that today there is no road and few traces of the road that was.

Coming on west with the stage across the open spaces and the thinly timbered flatness of Young County, the Clear Fork station, in Throckmorton County, is now the site of a ranch house, but an old well curbing remains from the Butterfield days. Just below the brow of the slight hill on which the station sat runs the Clear Fork River. Ormsby was not the first, and certainly not the last, to note the paradox of the name, recording his mild objection that "the Clear Fork of the Brazos was not very clear." But he allowed that even its muddy waters were "a grateful boon for a bath," presumably the first such chance in the eight days since the coach had left the Indian Nation. Ormsby took a bath in the Clear Fork here, nearly getting left behind because the station manager had things in such a fine order of preparedness that the stop was shorter than predicted. Ormsby doesn't write it so, but we may safely presume that the stage, with no women aboard, stopped in the middle of the broad, shallow ford and let him come aboard *au naturel*.

Led by the spirit of historical inquiry, I bathed where Ormsby bathed, this particular ford being easily found today. I suppose the passage of a century or more altered our notions of what constituted a suitable "boon for a bath," but I found the spot most unsatisfactory. Not only was the water red gyp and too hard to lather, but certain manifestations of bovine occupancy kept intruding on my efforts.

In crossing the Clear Fork the Butterfield line ventured into country which had seen few white men of any sort other than heavily armed troopers. The trail, immediately beyond, ran through lovely, rolling grassland country with its western edge framed in low mounds called the Antelope Hills. But Ormsby thought little of it, saying it was "a sorry landscape, I assure you." The New Yorker notwithstanding (his attitude toward West Texas is reflected faithfully by most of his descendants, I might observe), the twenty miles or so from the Clear Fork station to a place somewhat southwest called Smith's station, is delightful and even if you can't abide the thought of so much open space and timelessness surrounding you, it is a remarkably fine country for observing the thin, white fingerprints of the jet airplanes as they speed through the West Texas atmosphere, pulling contrails from their wing tips. The twentieth century finds ways, even in wilder West Texas, to remind us that the river Time is endlessly flowing and mixing its waters pretty thoroughly at one spot or another. Picking up a flint point, made by some prehistoric hand, while watching a jet bomber perform at 60,000 feet above you, is so ordinary as not to make much of a coincidental connection in your mind while you are doing it.

THE SITE of Smith's station is on a little watercourse called Chimney Creek. I have always been puzzled as to how the name was derived, because this was the name given it from the first of Butterfield's operations. History doesn't give us much encouragement to suppose that anything so substantial as a chimney had been erected then at a point so exposed to Comancheria. The creek itself passes through almost featureless country—that is, nothing in the way of a natural rock formation might qualify as looking like a chimney. So whence the name? Another of the mysterious coincidences of history in West Texas. I call them coincidences as though human understanding were the only standard of history. It could be that legend, or folklore, or myth is more accurate, or more persistent, than historical records. Possibly there was someone who had come to this unbelievably remote spot earlier and built a cabin, erecting a rock chimney (flat, easily handled limestone is abundant along the very banks of Chimney Creek, already cubed "as if prepared by some great Natural Mason," as Captain Randolph Marcy noted in passing through the area in 1849). History has dropped that pioneer's identity, but presuming his chimney was still standing in 1857, the name sticks.

Or it could be another mysterious West Texan, one Jesse Stem, an Indian agent from Ohio who farmed, in 1852, rather near Chimney Creek. Stem was one of those rare white men who seemed able to live in peace with the most notorious Indians, and his farm was set up for experimental purposes. He was determined that West Texas could grow crops; vegetables, melons, corn, and the like, and that its Comanches and other tribes could thus make their own living on adequate reservation lands. And he spent over two years with his wife and four daughters out there, isolated and remote to all white traffic in proving his contention. (One account says he had eight men putting in crops for him and one year made $4,300 "on the ground," which implies someone came and hauled his produce away.) The location of Stem's farm and store are hazy. A writer who is quoted most often says his location was six miles "below" present-day Lueders (a little Jones County town) "on the right bank of the Clear Fork." Most of the few historians who have paid much attention to Jesse Stem have interpreted "below" as being south. However, I feel the description was via the river itself, and since the Clear Fork runs south to north, "below" Lueders would be over in Shackelford County. I am supported indirectly in this conclusion by Sallie Matthews who tells about her husband buying land from Stem's widow and how fertile the fields were, without even so much as a stump to hinder the plow.

But wherever he was located, Stem made a simple discovery which thousands of other West Texans to follow made for themselves, and often to their sorrow. If it rains in West Texas, almost any kind of produce thrives; if it doesn't rain, it dies. Even hauling water from the river, as he is said to have done, won't keep things alive. Unfortunately, Stem turned out to be the victim of the Indians he understood so well. But not necessarily from a malicious act so much as a casual one, a characteristic of both fate and the American Indians. Two young Kickapoo bucks—and the tribe was never so inimical to Texans and other white men as most plains Indians—disgruntled or perhaps intoxicated, or maybe, as West Texans still describe certain undefined but mean attitudes, just "ornery," chanced across him and a companion and killed them. His wife, who could never quite understand what motivated her husband, took his death philosophically, for she had foreseen it for years, and on their last trip back to Ohio she had extracted a promise from him of a change of occupation.

The Indians took his death strongly. The tribal chief pronounced a death sentence on Stem's slayers and a contemporary account by a white man says one of the bucks was killed on sight by some of his tribesmen and the other was taken out and tomahawked to death by his own brother—on a sort of voluntary basis. But Jesse Stem was dead too soon, and not many of the white men who followed him to the West Texas frontier held his views or sympathies, as the Indians learned.

However (returning to Chimney Creek), if it was named for something Jesse Stem left in the wilderness, then it is possibly misnamed, for Stem's dwelling was a good many miles farther north, and Chimney Creek dumps its pitiful stream into the Clear Fork after running not nearly so far. I prefer to keep the vision of an even earlier, even more mysterious inhabitant as source for the name.

At Chimney Creek is one of the rare places where you may actually ride in the ruts of the old Butterfield stages. One summer day, a few years ago, I managed to do so in an old Chevrolet, accompanied by Robert Nail and Shackelford County rancher, Robert Green. We were driving through rather high pasture grass, trying unsuccessfully to discover some trace of Smith's station. We had already dismissed a nearby ranch house which was held to be "the old stage station" by some of the half dozen or so people living in a five-mile radius. The house, picturesque and old by frontier standards, looked like a perfect Butterfield station but the owner, showing the three of us around, smiled and said he didn't exactly discourage the Butterfield station legend for it seemed to please not only the neighbors but the ranch hands—but his house had been constructed in the 1870's and there wasn't much question about the date. The fact that this particular house had been built into the side of the hill that afforded a deep cellar, supposedly used for penning horses under the house, is probably the basis for the Butterfield affiliation. On the other hand there were other, later, stage lines through the country and the ranch house lies right on the direct route from Albany to Abilene, so it could have been a way-stop.

But all this aside, my two Robert friends and I were

nervously nosing the old Chevrolet through the high grass, which completely hid anything and everything before us, when I felt the steering wheel give a jerk and the front wheels lock in on something. (Can you remember letting your car be guided on certain avenues by the old streetcar rails in the pavement? It was that sensation.) The next thing we knew we were being controlled by the ruts of the Butterfield trail. Not only that, but before many yards we had hit something too substantial to drive over, and when we got out to inspect the barrier we discovered a pile of dressed stone, a wide hearth still in place, and the discernible outlines of a building that had been Smith's station. And we had run into it to find it.

We recalled from reading that monumental work on the Butterfield trail written by Roscoe Conkling and his wife, that at the same time they visited (in the 1930's) they had found an old rock corral nearby. There was no evidence of it and by rights it should at least have left a great many piles of rock, even if thrown down from their former positions as walls. The mystery was cleared up a few weeks later quite by chance when I was buying gasoline twenty miles or more down the highway at a filling station on Deadman Creek near Hamby. The proprietor and I got to talking about how the creek got its unusual name (there's no mystery about it; a dead man was found floating in a pool along its length). One creek carried into another and I mentioned Chimney Creek and was surprised to hear the old man say he had been foreman of the ranch on whose acres the Smith's station ruins were found. I asked him if he recalled the rock pen and he said he certainly did, it had been there from the first day he ever rode the ranch. My heart sank a little because, as I told him, we hadn't been able to find the corral, therefore must not have found Smith's station.

"Oh, that?" he said, shooting a wad of tobacco spit

out toward the highway. "Well, just before I quit there the Highway Department come by wantin' to know where they could dig out some rock to crush for new roadbed. I told 'em, 'Hell, don't need to dig. There's a long line of rocks down there in that Chimney Creek flat that you're welcome to.' "

So the Butterfield corral at Smith's station was scooped up, crushed, and put down as part of the roadbed for State Highway 351. Maybe it was appropriate, despite the injury to history. Using a Butterfield ruin to create a new road is gloriously just, as symbolism goes.

BEYOND CHIMNEY CREEK the countryside is remarkably unchallenging, although a few miles to the south or east lie some magnificent West Texas ranch vistas—and I shall presume a ranch imparts a different look to the landscape, if I may. However, another mysterious, or at least curiously unrecorded, site lies between Smith's station and the next Butterfield stop, which was at Fort Phantom Hill, about twelve miles southwest. This mysterious location was the site of the former town of Rising Sun. I lived within twenty miles of that site for many years (and in West Texas, twenty miles is almost next door) and I have never been able to find any but the scantiest information on the forgotten city of Rising Sun. Even though it was still shown on U. S. topographical maps of 1893, I have never met anyone who had lived there or was born there. Today where Rising Sun stood is a plowed field, not even reached by a highway or public road of any sort. I would suspect that in its heyday Rising Sun had the ubiquitous fortune of Jones County towns to have a cotton gin, a post office, some stores, maybe a bank, and certainly a Baptist and Methodist church. The

Jones, Taylor, and Fisher County area is rich with names of cities that have disappeared as completely as Rising Sun, insofar as physical evidence is concerned, but not so wholly unremembered by history or man. A lost city has always seemed to me to be the most tragic of all social disasters, unless, as has happened, the lost unit is an entire nation. A city represents so much decision, so much change, and so much destination—even a small city. It is also possibility, not only collectively but for any single one of its inhabitants.

We speed through little towns on the wide, unceasing superhighways, and if we think of them at all, our reaction is to ask ourselves how anyone could tolerate living in that elbow. But how many lives have been lived out in any single village; how many generations have never left for more than a day or two at a time, except to hurry back. So when a city dies, so much dies with it that was formed in a pattern, that had assumed a tone and weave which cannot be repeated, even by using the same strands in another setting.

FORT PHANTOM HILL was already legendary by the time the Butterfield people located a station there in 1858. General Persifor Smith had designated the site after Marcy had explored the area when he traced a route west from Fort Smith to Doña Ana, New Mexico, in 1849. Marcy's trail was to help the California-bound gold seekers, and there are numerous "California" landmarks which pop up across Texas. Just a dozen miles north of Fort Phantom Hill in Jones County is California Creek. California Crossing of the Trinity River is still used daily by Dallas drivers who are so used to the name that few wonder why it is 1,800 miles short of its goal. There is a California Mountain farther out across the Pecos, and an-

other California Creek—all on one of the trails to the gold fields, and all witness to the surging excitement the Forty-niners took west with them.

When the fort was established in November 1851, it was officially titled "Post on the Clear Fork of the Brazos." How the place got the name Phantom Hill has been the subject of about as many stories as one might guess such a name would inspire. The most popular has to do with four phantoms who (which?) appeared to the soldiers the first night they camped on the site. One version has it the phantoms were Indians in robes which looked white in the moonlight. Another story says military phantoms march about the ruins of the post in retribution for having burned it. These tales don't take into account the fact that the site was known as "Phantom Hill" before the soldiers got there. In a letter written the very night they arrived to build the post, a lieutenant wrote his wife that this was what it was called "locally." (By whom, I have often wondered.) As for the burning, most people, including historians, think it was deliberately destroyed the day it was abandoned in 1854—reputedly by some soldiers sent back by our old friend Lieutenant Givens, the last commandant. He is said to have given a secret order to burn the place so no more troops would have to worry about being stationed at the arid spot. However, logic turns me another route, and I can easier accept a report that the Indians burned the abandoned post to discourage anyone from returning to a place so intrusive on their hunting grounds.

As for the name, its derivation is simpler, I propose. I made my discovery in the same way I am sure whoever originally named the hill made it. I came at the old fort's ruins by way of the former Butterfield trail, a road it has been impossible to drive for several decades; it must be walked. From afar the mound on which the fort sits appears to be quite an elevation, but once you arrive on it the hill has disappeared. In other words, a phantom hill. Or is that too simple for history? There are other legends that the spot was holy to the Indians, a hill of healing magic, of religious importance. Even the Aztecs were supposed to have made visits to test the hill's powers. Mrs. Emma Elkins, who was born there, wrote a little paperback book back around the turn of the century about West Texas Indian fights and she said the soldiers considered the location haunted throughout their stay.

I would like to accept the ghost legend, especially if it were based on Indian belief and involved the Aztecs. I would also like to think there was something more eldritch about Chimney Creek's chimney, and that there, on the lower reaches of Deadman's Creek, a new Rising Sun is repeopled from time to time without our knowing it.

But somewhere the facts exist to kill off us romantics. Phantom Hill is a phantom hill, and one James Moorehead froze to death along that little watercourse to which he bequeathed the name Deadman.

The Butterfield trail (to get back to reality) becomes a very plain road, a wide depression clearly defined by the eye, as it nears the Phantom Hill building that was used as the station. It makes an easy bend which no automobile road would tolerate, not needing the space to turn two or three teams. Ormsby, on that first trip, came to Phantom Hill by gaudy circumstances. The ghostly chimneys of the burned fort were bathed in the light of a full moon, well becoming the "phantom" title.

Those tall stone chimneys are still standing, much as they were when Ormsby saw them. In fact, once you replace the log structures and the jacal huts (made by driving thin stakes in the ground and plastering between them with mud) which were burned, Fort Phantom Hill is marvelously preserved. Ormsby notes that the magazine is "so little injured that the district manager took it for a company storehouse," and this could be true today. It is a tough, thick, squatty little building whch was supposed to have been lined with copper originally. It has a vaulted stone roof with a cactus growing from one corner of the roof and small firing-slots in the walls. When I was a youngster no more than four or five years old, I can recall seeing the magazine for the first time. My father told me it was the jail. I later considered this to be another of his jokes, but now I am inclined to believe he was sincere. It looks more like a jail than a magazine. Only one building does Ormsby mention which I have not been able to find or trace. He says there was an observatory among the buildings standing in 1858. One must marvel slightly that something so scientific as an astronomical installation would have been erected out on the sword-edge of civilization like that, but it must have been a wonderful place from which to study the stars.

THAT FIRST SIGHT of Fort Phantom Hill took place as my family was making a Fourth of July fishing week-end to a stretch of the Clear Fork that was near Delk. (Another forgotten city for you.) Yes, the Clear Fork, which sees both Camp Cooper and Fort Griffin in its wanderings through Shackelford and Throckmorton counties, also curves alongside Fort Phantom Hill to form the aortal vessel of West Texas history. The reason so many early-day installations were located along its banks is no mystery. It is the only watercourse in that part of the country that has a constant flow.

In the years when we made our July Fourth fishing expeditions practically the whole family would go—uncles and aunts from both my mother's and my father's side—and the caravan made a fairly impressive length. We would leave Abilene well before dawn when only the streetcar men would be up, marshaling their little fleet of four-wheel trolleys to get ready for the motor races out at Fair Park. My immediate family was packed into an old wooden-spoked Dodge which my father owned for a while, or maybe it was one of those solid-wheel Chevrolets; at any rate, it was not our ordinary vehicle, a high, thin-tired Model T.

The road from Abilene north to Fort Phantom Hill was through a very sandy band of land whose vegetation was scrub oak, mesquite bushes, and prickly vines that grew in clumps. This was called (the voice registering in tone a proper name) "the Shin'ry." This was another of those times when I took a word to be a personal, regional possession and discovered, embarrassingly late in my life, that there are thousands more shinneries scattered over the United States. I was well into high school before I accepted the shock that the Shin'ry up around Fort Phantom Hill was not unique in the western hemisphere.

If you got out of the ruts, driving through the Shinnery, you were in for some shoveling and other back-labor before you extracted your car. One of my father's brothers, Roy (a great hero in my eyes because he had won the French "craw-de-gear" in World War I), was a shinnery expert; that is, a sort of extraction engineer who was always called in to supervise the job when someone let the car get loose and drift into the deep sand. Another uncle, Aubrey, had what the rest of the family thought of as an affliction in that he was so much in love with his young wife—having married a few years later than his brothers—he used to let her do things the family felt should be reserved for the male. One of these things he let her do was to drive their car in the Shinnery, and oh, how it irritated the rest of them. For she would nearly always manage to hold up the caravan by failing to fight the big wooden wheel of their heavy touring machine—I am inclined to remember it as an Oakland, although the Oakland was of a relatively modest size and I know this uncle's vehicle was a hairy sort of motor beast.

Sooner or later, as everyone was happily chattering along in his individual prairie schooner, some seeing each other for the first time that year, and the sun was coming up good, and we were about out to the fort, which was two thirds of the way to the fishing hole, someone would happen to glance back and then would call, "Wait, Carl . . . wait. Aubrey's motioning for us to come back. . . ." And my father would grumble something under his breath, one of the unprofane cusswords he resorted to in lieu of the real, but sinful, articles. "He's lettin' Christine drive . . . looks like he'd know better by now. . . ."

And the long line of autos would hump to a halt,

someone in the rear backing the distance to the stranded vessel (there usually was no way to turn around on the single set of sandy ruts). The rest of the men would be hiking their way back to where Christine sat smiling, not showing a trace of embarrassment, and her adoring husband already out at a rear wheel, his shovel ineffectually tossing the greedy, dry sand which rushed back with the fluidity of water each time he tried to remove any considerable portion of it from around the wheel.

"You might as well wait for Roy," someone would say, Roy taking the Shinnery Expert position quite seriously (and to this day I would be willing to bet that were you to say something about it to him, he would make grave acknowledgment as to his expertness).

But waiting for Roy (who always drove the point—out ahead) was something that sat poorly with the other men, especially if one of the women suggested it. They would invariably roll up shirt sleeves and send someone to fetch whatever kind of pry-board could be found, or to break green boughs with which to form a mat under the stuck wheels. In a great many spots there were no green boughs (or pry-boards), so some farmer would be deprived of one of his fence posts for the deep jobs when the wheels were really dug in. The fence pole would be used as a lever, worked up under the solid back axle, and a couple of the husky brothers would grunt and heft in hopes of beating Roy to a successful extraction. But Roy's magic seemed to be needed most times, and he would stand out to one side when he came on the scene (not for Roy the down-on-your-knees business), instructing first the driver ("Ease up . . . ease up . . . you got 'er in low? Take 'er out of low . . . drop 'er in reverse . . . easy now . . . easy. . . .") and then the team on the pole ("All right . . . let's GO . . . let's GO . . . let's GO . . . all right now, come UP . . . come on UP with it").

Secretly, of course (children being as merciless in their hearts as Spanish Inquisitors), I was praying all the time for someone to get stuck. It was better than fishing, at that age.

Delk, once arrived at, was (or is remembered as) an idyllic spot, consisting mainly of a huge, unpainted wooden building which contained a grocery and general merchandise store and had a gasoline pump of the armstrong type out front (one pump served all in West Texas, where "ethyl" gas was considered entirely too highfalutin until the high-compression motors of a later decade demanded it). For some reason, probably economic, the family used to wait to get to Delk to fill the gas tank. My mother in particular had the notion that almost anything could be purchased cheaper out in the country. This rather long string of cars pulling up on a Fourth of July morning had the proprietor of the Delk store bustling around getting certain picnic supplies for the ladies, filling tanks and checking the air in somebody's tires (some drivers let a lot of air out to travel in sand) while carrying on a broad conversation as to why he wasn't taking off for the holiday. The various uncles and other male connections would man the pump, stroking the long iron handle back and forth as the gasoline foamed down into the clear glass tank, marked inside by metal rings which showed how many gallons had been drained out. It seems to me now that one or more of the brothers knew the Delk storekeeper; anyway, he never kept a count of how many gallons were put in the cars, leaving the figures up to us. I used to have two minor boyhood ambitions, the main one being to be allowed to pump the gas up the way my father almost always did every time we drove into a filling station; the other was to be able to say, quickly and offhand-like, "Check that left rear for me," to the attendant. Left rear. It had an adult sound, an intimation of a kind of masculine knowledge that seemed to me the pinnacle of maturity. Unfortunately, by the time I was buying gasoline as a regular thing, the motor-powered pump had just about banished the hand-powered kind to those inaccessible places where I seldom traded. And to this day I cannot give a casual left-right direction. I have to stop and think, make a gesture with one hand or the other, or I will say right when I mean left, and vice versa. Thus with boyhood ambitions.

The Delk store stood a tall two stories high, its false front making it seem more like four. There may have been a lodge hall in the upper story. The store was set on an incline so that the rear of the building, as I recall, was on stilts. At one side of the building was an immense cottonwood tree, and the sounds coming from the tree—locusts chirring, birds chirping—will always be the sum total of early summer mornings in the country, fishing, and a good portion of the best memory of July Fourth.

At Delk we turned off the main road, which though unpaved was graveled and maintained with some regularity. About three lanes branched off to form an open place in front of the store and we took the one to farthest left and went down toward the river. Someone always knew a farmer who would let us use his stretch of the Clear Fork. It was a smaller society then, and a visitor from the city, even though it was less than twenty miles away, had a special identity. Besides, my father and my uncles, in our agriculturally oriented environment, kept up with the individual farmers. The women in town did, too. I have known my mother to shop three or four stores looking for butter from one of the Antilleys (farm women signed their names on the white butter wrappers) or cream peas put up by Mrs. Mancill. Certain things such as homemade sausage, chowchow, or hog's head souse were never bought except from specific farm women. The Depression changed all that, causing us to let our standards sink to the common denominator of cost. And I suppose a good many of the home-kitchen geniuses died, and their daughters failed to inherit the skill, or the desire, to emulate them. There wasn't much money in it in the first place. Egg money, West Texas farm wives called it; the little dab they were allowed to spend on themselves and the house. And pride that a certain number of city wives kept asking for your products. The impersonal glitter of the supermarket ended any of that the Depression left.

On arriving at the farmhouse the caravan would halt and after considerable honking on our part, up from the barn would come the farmer himself, wearing blue bib overalls, smiling, glad to see new faces. July Fourth didn't mean much out in the country. Visitors were as big an occasion as was the holiday itself. Most of the farmers would know my father's whole family, calling all my uncles by name and asking about the people who weren't there. Aunt Bessie, "the talky one," had married Jimmy Hickey and moved to Wichita Falls. Another sister, Hattie Lee, had married Herman Brewster, and Uncle Herman (as I always called him) was not an easy person to forget. He stood six-feet-six and weighed over three hundred pounds. He had the most enormous hands I ever saw on a human, and he was as strong as he was big. I have seen him crank two big ice cream freezers at once, after the other men had worn out. But as is often the case with huge men, everything from his voice to his smile was gentle. One meeting and you remembered Uncle Herman for keeps.

After going over the prospects for the crops there would be the annual inventory of children, the farmer always seeming to have a new name to introduce: "Yes, we got us another little girl. Named her Joyce. Lucille's in the house nursin' her, I suspect, else she'd be out here

gabbin'." And the women in the cars would make womanly noises at the news. A batch of red-haired girls in sunbonnets and little barefooted, tow-headed boys would be standing shyly over on the shady side of the farmhouse, but they never joined us.

Finally the talk would get down to fishing, although usually the farmer was too busy chopping cotton or turning under early June cornstalks to have done much. Sometimes his older boys were having good luck: "Well, Joe Fred and Billy Jack, they've been catching some good-size yellow cats on a trot line the far end of the gravel island . . . you know where that is, don't you, Robbie? River's been up a right smart . . ." And so the men would eventually get back in the cars and somebody would sing out, "All right, Carl. You lead the way," if it was my father's particular farm friend we were visiting. Our car would pull in front, taking the lead from Roy, which made me proud. And also entitled me to open and close all the gates.

The path to the river got rougher every foot of the way after it left the barnyard. The big gate that opened into the pasture was red-painted and trademarked "Can't Sag," but the rest were just barbwire. The cars plunged down a turnrow road that likely as not turned into no road at all and we were soon merely bumping from furrow to furrow through a plowed field. Few of the farmers had tractors to make any kind of path. Mules were the main source of farm power in West Texas, and they didn't make wheel ruts for you to follow. We were careful, of course, to stick as close to the fence as possible so as not to run over any of the cotton or hegira just getting to size.

Although my father and most of my uncles were city men, there was still in them an understanding, seemingly innate, of the soil and agriculture—"farming" was all it was called; nothing so fancy as agriculture. It never occurred to me then to wonder how my father, for instance, knew the names of all the crops, knew what the uses were for the farm machinery; the balers, sulkies, corn sleds, cultivators, and harrows we saw near the barn or sitting rustily at the end of a row. He knew all that, and if another uncle or a brother-in-law happened to be in the car with us they would discuss the possibilities of crops that particular season, how mean a Georgia stock plow hitched to a horse mule could be, or the relative merits of chain harness and leather as plow line. Where did they find this out? My father didn't live on a farm and wasn't reared on one. Where did they come to this knowledge? Was it in their bones or did it go back to their own childhood, sitting near but unseen around the adults? It was a reminder that our society, even then urbanized in its percentages, was only one sharp breath, one course of blood, away from the dirt, not just in our family but in the total society. And not just in West Texas, but in most of the nation.

You do not find this to be true any more, this expertness at the land and growing things among the ordinary citizens, not even in West Texas. Today, if such an expedition as ours were undertaken out to a river to fish, even if it were possible to resurrect all the uncles and aunts, the faces which have passed out of the circle, there would not be this same kind of talk, talk vitally involved in the weather, the seasons, and the fortunes of the ground. You would not ride along judging the qualities of the soils or feel the warm inner glow, without knowing why, that came to you, a city dweller, from seeing evidence that this was going to be a good year for cotton, or that the grain sorghum was heading out fuller than usual.

Today, even with the same people, the talk would be of troubles—remote wars, taxes, hateful political notions, or social ideas that would have only slight direct effect on their lives. And their happy talk would be a product of the vapid inanities of television or that kind of earnest nonsense that the advertising industry and public-relations trades have made so big and hollow a part of our daily lives. Predictability—that is a one-word condition for American conversation. High level or low class, it makes little difference except for the speaker's skill in cultivated inflection or innuendo.

Not that those conversations were of great moment or profound significance then. But at least they involved reality. It was what they thought, not something put in their mouths by an agency or influence they never knew was in operation. They could at least believe in the soil they saw, and depend on the weather being cold or hot, whether such things were convenient or not. Their discontent was with reality, not with wishfulness.

Go back, would I? Of course not. Not only the impossibility of doing it but the impossibility of capturing those wider atmospheres that surrounded us. It is just that we have lost some of the good. We have gained other goods and shed other bads, but our conversations now are selfish, pinched, haughty with personal views. We have lost the cooperative belief in life from trying (and failing) to live too many individual lives in too many collective situations; from demanding without understanding.

The farmer is not much different. He knows the soil now—although soil itself has been relegated to a somewhat lower station of importance than the fertilizers and enriching mixtures that give it productiveness—but there is something always standing between him and it. There is the crop loan which takes away a lot of the risk and its accompanying joy at winning. And there is the bank or the farm-mortgage financing firm that holds him only as a number (our New Math doesn't even deal with units as a basic premise but in "sets"). If nothing else, there is the tractor and its train of equipment which turns and touches, feels, feeds, sows, tends, reaps, and processes what he used to get down his neck, in his shoes, and on his skin. Or the men and the crews he must hire to do the work because a one-man farm is no longer profitable or possible or socially desirable. And if nothing else, there is "Washington," not a city, not a place, not even an administration, but a vast, thwarting force that is without face, arms, or fingers, but frustrates his every effort to find himself, or his soil, or his profits, or his satisfaction. In another plane he might call it history, and were he a social scientist he might call it progress. Something has removed his reality, too, just like ours, so that we have to avoid direct, positive things in order to live without them.

DOWN AT THE RIVER we found our spot, a gentle beach of sand and gravel facing a little willow island in the Clear Fork. It was a perfect place for the kind of fishing my family did, because most of their fishing was seining and trot-line fishing for catfish, sun perch, and big-mouthed bass. A few cane poles were set out for my great-grandmother and some of the other older women who liked to sit and talk and have some decent excuse for their idleness. A trot-line would be rigged down at one end of the island where the water was fairly deep and the long three-man seine would be unrolled and passed through the shallower waters near the beach for bait—and possibly something for the pan, because in those days fresh-water seining was not illegal or considered unethical.

I cannot recall that a great deal of fish was caught, but I do remember distinctly one occurrence involving my Uncle Stub because it happened in such perfect sequence.

Uncle Stub Inman was a small man who knew many mysterious things, or things about life which were mysterious to me. He was a trader, and a trader is, in Texas usage, someone who goes about making his living by swapping, selling, or buying (for the right price) almost anything. Uncle Stub was always coming up with items which, to a boy, were romantic beyond belief. Once, as lagniappe in a larger deal, he acquired a blackjack, and one time swapped for a whole, huge case of candy bars; or he would now and then give me unannounced something like an aviator's leather helmet with goggles attached. The world of the trader was almost gypsy; just a little dark, just beyond the curtain of the ordinary. One visit Stub would be driving a new Overland, the next week he would be nursing a Model A with a cracked block he had salvaged with liquid glass. A trader survived through his keen sense of the possibilities of any given moment. Once Stub, down on his luck, was so badly off that in order to drive an old Chevrolet he stuffed the porous tires with cotton which he picked from some farmer's field when the end came at that juncture. Limping back to town on these improvised underpinnings, Stub saw a gray wolf run across the road ahead of him. He jumped out of his car with that romantic blackjack, took off after the wolf, caught it and dispatched it with his weapon, and brought the pelt back to town where he swapped it for enough food to keep his family going for a couple of days—and a couple of days is all any decent trader requires to reconquer any given world.

But on this trip he was riding in the car with us, and as we approached the river Uncle Stub (whose name was Stubblefield and whose size was only coincidental to the diminutive) got into a learned discussion with my father about cottonmouth water moccasins—the stub-tailed, poisonous snake which inhabits most Texas waterways, even in West Texas. Stub's contention was that the moccasin could not bite while in the water. I think the discussion had begun when my grandmother, who never neglected finding the squeamish possibilities of a situation, had said she couldn't face going swimming, or even wading, in the Clear Fork because she stepped on exposed elm roots under the water where the current had washed the bank back and it always made her think it was fat, slimy cottonmouths her toes were touching. (There are grounds for comparison, as the roots get quite slimy and some of them, if they are free of the bottom, sort of float in the kind of independent motion one expects of snakes.)

Stub, who came from Beaumont over in the far-eastern corner of Texas where there are multitudes of snakes, spoke up to assure his mother-in-law, "Mrs. Cole, you don't have to worry about a moccasin as long as you're in the water. He can't bite in the water. Just don't run to shore."

Well, that discussion picked up steam and before long there was a list of reasonable facts assembled by either party to prove why the other's ideas were outlandish. Stub, it seemed to me, had the best position as we arrived at the fishing site itself. He had pointed out, logically enough, I thought, that if the moccasin were in the water and opened his mouth to bite he would choke or drown.

The excitement of arriving and setting up the camp (for these were customarily overnight affairs) took the adults' minds off snakes for a while, and an hour or so later Uncle Stub and my father took out the short seine to get bait for the trot-line. This seine was not much wider than a blanket and had a pair of sticks attached at the ends to allow the men to handle it easy. The two seiners waded upstream fairly far and started dragging against the current. I was watching from our wonderful gravel-bar beach when I heard Uncle Stub, a man of more quiet dignity than my other uncles, give a cry such as I had not heard before. And with the cry he turned loose his end of the seine and started making swiftly for the shore. He had to come downstream past me, for the banks were too steep and slippery where he was, so it was toward our beach he waded.

Directly behind him, with seemingly human concentration on its target, swam a cottonmouth water moccasin, the arrow-point of its head making a long V as it swam with just the head out of water. My father, still holding the other end of the seine, was left behind, and at first didn't realize what was happening, but I watched with fascination as man and snake made their strange race for the dry land, and when Uncle Stub finally sprinted onto the beach the snake was right at his heels and had opened its mouth so wide that, for the first time in my young life, I could see why it was called the cottonmouth.

The whole party joined in laughter, not only from the ironic implications of the event but from seeing Stub, who seldom indulged in the kind of horseplay that my father and his brothers were fond of, put on such a strenuous performance.

"Why Stub, you were walking on the water," my grandmother said. "Just the soles of your feet were getting wet."

My father, still holding the seine, waded ashore, laughing hugely and swearing the cottonmouth had been nothing but a snapping turtle.

"I was praying it *would be* a cottonmouth," my father said, trying to hold a serious face, "so you'd be safe. I kept thinking, 'I sure hope it's a moccasin and not a big old turtle. If it's a turtle, it'll get Stub sure, but if it's a moccasin he knows he's safe as long as he stays in the water.' "

I can't remember exactly what happened to the snake or, for that matter, much about the rest of that trip. There was an episode next morning at breakfast, when somebody slipped a few turtle eggs in with the hen eggs to be scrambled. And someone found a boat to use in running the trot-lines so that Stub could help. My grandmother, laugh at Stub though she might, became convinced every hook on the trot-line would have a snake on it.

One of those trips was my introduction to the awesome thing my mother and grandmother (and great-grandmother, too, for she was always along as a Queen Victoria figure) called "liquor." Troy, a man who worked in the same glass shop as my father, and his wife, Allie, had been invited to join this family affair, and Troy had brought along a big, green thermos jug. At supper we sat around eating, more or less, by family groups, and I moseyed over to where Troy and Allie were sitting, sipping tea from their jug, and another uncle, my mother's brother, winked at Troy and said (using a nickname only he ever used): "Give old Dago here some tea."

It was not tea at all, of course, but home brew. The tea business had been something to keep my grandmothers from having to acknowledge the presence of sin in the camp. For some reason I drank the whole lidful of the stuff. I thought it was the vilest liquid I had ever tasted and, for better or for worse, this experience kept me from drinking beer until I was a fully grown man in Uncle Sam's Marines. Even then, for years, when I turned a bottle or a stein up to my lips and my nose caught the bubbles, I went back immediately—for a moment, but a poignant one—to that hot, sun-dappled day on the gravel spit, fishing on the Clear Fork.

In the history of the West Texas frontier, one word explains more defeats and losses than all the Indians who ever fired a shot, hurled a lance, or strung a bow against U. S. troops: water. Water, and the lack of it, closed Fort Phantom Hill, Fort Belknap, and Fort Chadbourne, all within a hundred miles of each other. In each case the post had been located on what the surveying teams had imagined would be a good, constant supply: the Clear Fork, running less than a hundred yards from Fort Phantom Hill, the Brazos, within sight of Belknap, and

Oak Creek, which is at the foot of the hill that is crowned by Chadbourne. But the Clear Fork and the Brazos turned out to have bad water in times of drought, and Oak Creek was unreliable. It is significant that Captain Marcy, among others, passed through West Texas originally in a year when it had received bountiful rainfall, so it looked like a land flowing with milk and honey if someone would just get a few cows and bees out there. Marcy, in his *Thirty Years of Army Life on the Border,* makes a listing of all kinds of sweet-flowing springs up all sorts of little canyons in the heart of the West Texas country; yet frustration is the inevitable by-product of any attempt to locate them even in moderately dry years.

The Army explorers weren't the only ones who were badly fooled by West Texas in a wet springtime. Illusion continued and, if meteorological records had not been kept since the early eighties it might happen now. The land promoters brought the land seekers to West Texas in those lush, wet months and the hungry emigrants saw what looked like opportunity unbounded. It is a fact that West Texas soil, dead red clay though it looks, can produce a marvelous bounty with the addition of water. Water is the key to success so often in West Texas that one of her sons, the late historian Walter Prescott Webb, came to the conclusion (with a fair lifetime of memory to back his thesis) that West Texas was, in geographical and geological fact, uninhabitable. It is not too difficult to visualize the farm boy, grubbing away on a hard-scrabble farm in Callahan County (the south part—the north end is fertile and sandy loam), following a slow, discouraged mule, telling himself that this was no way to live, this was no land to live on, as month turned into month without enough rain to paste a stamp. But the older Webb—some fifty years later—made the mistake of broadcasting his childhood contentions through an article in a famous magazine, and all West Texans with enough intellectual pretense to read that sort of journal came to arms at the very idea that their land was not meant by God to be man's home for the Golden Future. But Webb's warning to the desert cities had its point. You've pushed urban civilization too far, he said, addressing not just West Texas but the entire Southwest. You will pay with burning cities that in time will drain your society of its life force. His ideas were strong and, to an outsider, might seem more valid than the arguments countering them—which boiled down to the simple rebuttal that here we are, and growing.

Webb wrote in the year that saw the end of the worst drought in modern West Texas history, 1957. This had been a period of five to seven years when rainfall in most sections was only fifty to seventy per cent of normal. And normal was always scant. The fact that this massive drought was broken by floods (Abilene received more rain in April 1957 than it received during the entire year of 1956) tended to cause readers to forget how many of them, a couple of years before, had been saying the same thing and asking the Lord if it was His intent that this land be inhabited. So this two-faced land which looks so fine in a wet year, so hopeless in a dry one, still confuses its critics and its defenders, according to when they choose to do so.

FORT PHANTOM HILL was an extreme case of a water supply defeating the U. S. Army in West Texas—a few posts were never permanently located, of course, after having been projected, because the water supply was found to be bad or nonexistent. The troops arrived on the hill in a rain and sleet storm which nearly drowned and froze them, but almost immediately they had trouble getting a decent cupful to drink. The temptation to drink of the Clear Fork, except at flood-tide, is one that is easily resisted if the drinker has been victim of the high gypsum content of that stream, for gyp water has a disastrous effect on the human interior, with diarrhea being but one bothersome result. The soldiers at Fort Phantom Hill even dug an enormous well, said by Ormsby (at the time of his visit) to be "a fine well, eighty feet deep and twenty feet in diameter with seventeen feet of water in it." But it must not have been a success, in spite of Ormsby's verdict. Was his visit in a wet year? The depression where the old well was dug is still visible, although filled in. It must have been a tremendous undertaking for the soldiers, and although we might question Ormsby's estimate of its dimensions (particularly the eighty-feet-deep part) the remaining depression shows us it was no ordinary bucket-and-pulley affair.

The scarcity and quality of the water was made more troublesome at Fort Phantom Hill by the lack of vegetables and greens. Knowing West Texas better than some of the historical figures who commanded forts out there, I find it unbelievable that certain greens couldn't have been cultivated successfully. I lay the whole thing onto Army regimentation. The commander had never approved of turnips or roasting ears or green peas or squash (or never heard of them being grown in his own part of the country) so he refused to experiment. At one time a doctor at the post undertook to feed the Fort Phantom Hill soldiers pickles to make up for the lack of greenstuff and ward off scurvy. But the pickles didn't turn out right. A post surgeon also tried serving the wild spring onions which dot the prairies on good years, but a rumor that these lilies were in fact the uncomfortable crow poison ruined that idea. And crow poison does grow in West Texas; and I, for one, can't tell the difference between crow poison and wild onions, so my vote lies with the reluctant soldiery. In casting back over the various governmental reports and inspector's recommendations, all I can say is they would have done well to have had my great-grandmother along to show them how to get a crop from the ground, come drought or high water. The only trouble with Granny and her vegetables was that she could only grow "hardship" foods—turnips, onions, cabbage. No delicacies such as tomatoes, asparagus, or plums. Granny could make turnips grow with just the morning dew to give water and she never failed, when I was a youngster, to have a little patch out beside her hen house. I couldn't stand them in those days when they formed, of economic necessity, the only vegetable on our table at a good many meals.

It is ironic that just two miles south of the ruins of Fort Phantom Hill is the water supply for the city of Abilene, above 100,000 in population. Phantom Hill Reservoir is a lake with nearly sixty miles of shore line; and it is also amusing to note that, even closer to the old fort, the city has installed a retention dam on the Clear Fork and in flood times it pumps hundreds of thousands of gallons of water up a slight rise and dumps it into the lake. The answer is that the Clear Fork gets its gyp content from a stratum of gypsum outcropping some fifty miles to the west and in times of heavy rain this water doesn't constitute a sufficient amount of the flow to ruin it. The gypsum beds themselves are quite valuable to the territory, as several of the biggest gypsum board and plaster plants in the United States are located on this stratum line from the Red River down to the Colorado, with immense production of construction materials at Sweetwater and Rotan.

But the search for water is never very far from men's thoughts in West Texas, and in the late 1950's the city of

Abilene and several smaller cities in the central West Texas area formed an authority to create a huge lake, between Breckenridge and Albany on Hubbard Creek, this being supposedly the last source of pure surface water in the whole region of the Brazos watershed. But when the big dam was finished and the lake began to fill it was discovered that too much salt was in the water. This salt came from oil wells that had been drilled and had started flowing salt water (that ancient sea on which the valuable crude oil floats) and then had not been properly capped. After several years this giant Hubbard Creek Reservoir is still a beautiful place to water-ski and boat, but it is a nonpotable waterhole and the ranchers only use it for irrigation. Sometimes you can't have your oil and drink it too.

FROM FORT PHANTOM HILL the Butterfield trail ran just north of Abilene and just west of the village of Tye, turning almost due south at that previously mentioned Callahan Divide, which saw quite a bit of latter-day stagecoaching after the Butterfield line. One line ran down through Buffalo Gap, and the Abilene–San Angelo stage ran through Coon Hollow, just south of View (which was the place thousands of Camp Barkeley trainees disembarked during World War II); and you can still see portions of the narrow stage road down in the defile below the wide, modern highway. The Butterfield trail climbed the Divide at a place called Mountain Pass, about ten miles south of present-day Merkel. It is interesting to note that the Butterfield trail, after leaving Gainesville, missed every town of today in Texas except El Paso, where it exited from the state. It missed even such small cities as Woodson (by one mile) and Albany (by ten) and the original Abilene city limits by three or four miles—

although Abilene will probably grow out to meet the old trail before many years. It even missed the site of Tye by a mile or so, and then Bronte, San Angelo, Big Lake, Rankin, McCamey, and Pecos as it traversed West Texas. It kept to loneliness.

Ormsby, in describing the ride from Fort Phantom Hill to Mountain Pass, writes of it as "a smooth plain dotted with the everlasting mesquite." The first landmark he saw, going south, was a promontory, a separate peak from the Divide that forms almost a perfect triangle, called (today) Castle Peak. Ormsby's description does something to explain why this name was almost an inevitability.

"The peak has a curious summit, or cap, of bare rocks, as if a work of solid masonry. At a distance they much resembled the turrets and abutments of a lofty fortress. They could be seen for thirty or forty miles of our road along the plain [Ormsby was exaggerating by possibly twenty miles], and they looked so near that one naturally became impatient to reach them."

Just to the east of Castle Peak is another of these detached hills which is called Steamboat Mountain. It has a mesa of a top on which I have, on occasion, played baseball it is so wide and so flat. But it also has a curious geologic dike or some other stone formation at the top which looks enough like the handiwork of man that I almost choose to think it is, and fly in the face of science to the contrary. However, there is a charming legend that goes with this bit of scenery. This mountain is supposed to be topped by the ruins of an Aztec temple, and this was supposed to be the farthest north any permanent Aztec outpost was made. At the time of Cortez, the legend continues, one troop, or whatever organizational form Montezuma's army had, fled north carrying certain precious vessels and sacred objects, finally arriving at the

Taylor County outpost and disappearing into the mists. No Spaniards are legended into this part of Texas until 1535, when Cabeza de Vaca may have come up from the south. Five or six years after Cabeza de Vaca came through (his path crossing the Butterfield trail approximately ten miles northwest of San Angelo), another Spaniard is supposed to have appeared, Francisco Vásquez de Coronado; although it is doubtful that he or any of his men got so far east and south as West Texas. Historians deny he penetrated the plains below the Cap Rock, but some interesting relics of Spanish origin have been found near Odessa, an ancient pistol being one of them. Did some Indian drop it there? Was some unrecorded expedition lost and wandering over the area early enough to have been armed with such an antique? Sword hilts and helmets have also been turned up over the western end of West Texas but they could be explained by some of the trading trains that traversed this land from San Antonio to Santa Fe two centuries later. Well, history has her secrets, smiling like La Gioconda over our attempts to lay them bare. I can buy such things in my heart but not in my mind.

Back to Castle Peak which Ormsby admired so much. It was originally named Abercrombie Peak after the first man who came along with the desire and the authority to name things for himself, Lieutenant Colonel J. J. Abercrombie, who commanded those first troops at Fort Phantom Hill. As a matter of fact, when the opportunity presented itself to him, our Colonel Abercrombie seemed to have named everything after himself. The Callahan Divide, at that point, was officially designated "the Abercrombie Range," and Mountain Pass was called "Abercrombie Pass," and later, when he was sent to North

Dakota, Colonel Abercrombie succeeded in getting a fort up there named for himself. Ormsby refers to the stage station at Mountain Pass as being Abercrombie Pass station, but the great proportion of timetables, news stories, and such items of the period called it Mountain Pass station. Ormsby notes that his breakfast, which he obtained at the station, consisted of "coffee, tough beef, and butterless shortcake," prepared by an old Negro woman who "if cleanliness is next to godliness, would stand but little chance of heaven." The keeper of this station was one of the Lambsheads, which was singularly appropriate, Ormsby felt, because "he had a drove of three hundred sheep grazing . . . while he was attending to other duties."

Today the Mountain Pass station is only a hearth and a few foundation stones on Mulberry Creek inside a ranch. A spring, used by the station, still feeds a pond on the creek. However, the tracks of the trail itself are very plain, hugging the foot of the hill (do not be deceived by the pretentious "Mountain" of the title, for the climb up the pass is a gain in elevation of only four hundred feet or so) and keeping east on the hillside away from a modern dirt road. From the air this part of the trail is especially plain because some peculiarity of the soil brings out the ruts chalky-white against the surrounding grassland. The Mountain Pass station had a rather exciting though not historically important existence. It might be well here to note that if your impression of the Butterfield mail-run is like mine, it tends to run to calendar art—a swaying, lurching Concord coach, drawn by a team of six speedy horses, the driver laying on the whip while the guard lies atop the coach, firing at a crowd of Indian horsemen who are pressing dangerously close; in fact, in some pictures I can recall they are getting one or two of the horses with their arrows, rifles, or whatever form of arms they are using. The coach itself, in the pictures, is plainly marked

BUTTERFIELD, and the passengers might or might not be joining in the fray.

As historical fact, this picture has limited possibilities at best. Throughout the entire history of the Southern Overland Mail route, from 1858 to 1861, only one Indian attack was made on the stage itself, taking place at Apache Pass, Arizona, in 1861. As for the other details, neither Concord coaches nor horses were used in the Indian country, and I am not sure that the canvas-roofed celerity wagon would have supported the weight of a big man fighting off an Indian attack. And at first, anyway, the equipment was not marked BUTTERFIELD but simply OMC or OVERLAND MAIL COMPANY. However, despite the fact that the stages themselves were relatively immune to attack, the stations were not; and numbers of them suffered from raids, thefts, and murders. Mountain Pass, for instance, was attacked in 1859, and a Negro cook was killed (but not the one whose godliness Ormsby suspected). In the same year, on one trip, the stage arrived just as the Comanches were making off with eight company mules (the same week twenty-eight head were taken from the Fort Phantom Hill station), and one stage found the grisly remains of a man hanging in a tree near Mountain Pass. A few years after the Butterfield operations through there ceased, an Indian ambush at Mountain Pass resulted in the death of two U. S. troopers. So this quiet little rural passage, which looks almost unbelievably peaceful now, with fewer than a dozen cars a day using it, has seen its share of sorrow, disaster, and history. History isn't always big men or big things. It is diurnal, it is minuscule, it is deceptive. If there is one thing we can safely say about history it is that it has the patience of time. I am continually struck by these long thoughts as I move about in this particular part of West Texas. Its history was deeper than the coming of the Texas & Pacific

Railway, as we can see; but it began before that, before the possible wandering of Cabeza de Vaca or Francisco Coronado might have touched it.

There is plenty of evidence that this setting was once peopled by a race of some antiquity which an Abilene archaeologist, the late Dr. Cyrus N. Ray, called "Clear Fork man." Not far from Mountain Pass is a softly rounded crater known as Blowout Mountain. The name comes from the assumption that it was once a small volcano that grew cold, and whose crater filled until it is now but a wide, smooth depression in the top of the mound. At the foot of Blowout Mountain, Roy, my shinnery-expert uncle, had a farm for many years. One Sunday afternoon I found a peculiar flint piece which looked something like an object archaeologists call a humpback-scraper, but with uncharacteristic aspects. I showed this piece to Dr. Ray, who was a bull of a man and an eccentric of legendary proportions in Abilene—for one thing he would spit on you if you whistled around him. His profession was osteopathy but his life was dedicated to archaeology, paleontology, and the pursuit of natural history. He was one of those old-timers who found everything with his feet, and I am prepared to believe he had walked every acre of at least the fifteen or twenty central counties in West Texas surrounding Abilene.

When I showed him this strange piece of flint craft he seized it in his immense, rough but tender fingers and turned it over lovingly.

"That's a Clear Fork gouge," he said, "and it's a good one. Big one. Don't see many that big."

He told me he was the discoverer of the Clear Fork culture, estimated to have existed in the area (up the middle part of the Clear Fork and along its main tributaries) some three thousand years ago. He had written several articles about it for learned journals but, he assured me, he kept back a lot that he knew "because the other archaeologists will steal your credit if you let them know everything you know." (His complaint was that because he was a Doctor of Osteopathy the Doctors of Philosophy resented his expertise. He spat on people who whistled around him because he said he had unearthed a plot on the part of a local hoodlum family to do him in; and the various plotters—the hundreds of them—communicated among themselves by whistling. The sound enraged him.)

Dr. Ray's ancient man contributed this gouge-form as his identification piece. It is unlike any other tool or weapon created by prehistoric man, and its long, tapered end fits comfortably into the palm and fingers of the hand so that we know precisely how it was held. But what was it used for? There must have been some specific use Clear Fork man put it to, maybe getting to some prized bit of meat or extracting marrow. Why didn't some other culture develop a similar tool, if that is the case? The mystery of use involves only this gouge. Clear Fork man made other flint pieces readily identified as knives or scrapers. My oldest son found a Clear Fork culture knife once when a tree was being planted in the front yard. It looked like most prehistoric knives. Somehow I feel this gouge we cannot figure a use for stands as a beautiful symbol for much of history.

THE ORIGINAL DRIVERS, stationkeepers, and other employees of the Butterfield line were almost all Easterners or men unacquainted with the West. Butterfield had learned the freighting business in the rough-and-tumble of western New York state where commercial hauling, in the modern sense, was born. He had succeeded well, putting together the American Express Company, with the help of Wells & Company and Livingston & Fargo—a neat package of great names in Western freighting.

Some evidence of this Eastern influence is reflected in Ormsby's account of things after he left Mountain Pass station and got to Fort Chadbourne, some thirty miles to the southwest. At the time Chadbourne was the most important military post in West Texas and a key fort in the southwestern military frontier chain. Few posts were more exposed to Indian troubles or more remote from white civilization, for Chadbourne lay not on the edge but athwart the Comanche War Trail to Mexico.

Yet at Chadbourne, Ormsby arrived to find all the Butterfield people tipsy and not taking their jobs or their position on the frontier with any seriousness. The stationkeepers had been celebrating the arrival of the first stage a few days in advance. Ormsby seems to have felt endangered and humiliated at what happened and this particular description marks the only time the twenty-three-year-old New Yorker turned sour in his writing from personal pique.

To begin with, the mules were so unfit for use and so unruly that it took an inordinate amount of time to hitch them up. Then when Ormsby got into the celerity wagon and the still-tipsy crowd began shouting godspeed, the mules were so wild—but Ormsby tells it wonderfully:

"The mules reared, pitched, twisted, whirled, wheeled, ran, stood still and cut up all sorts of capers. The stage wagon performed so many evolutions that I, in fear of my life, abandoned it and took to my heels, fully confident that I could make more progress in a straight line, with much less risk of breaking my neck."

The mules bucked and galloped their way into the scrub oak and mesquite brush, dragging the celerity wagon with them and at last ripping off the canvas top when they dragged it under a low oak limb. Ormsby was mightily put out, as his journal shows, and he says it was all too ludicrous to be real. After a pair of the mules was recaptured—the rest escaping into the prairie—Ormsby tried to talk the new driver into staying at Chadbourne until more animals could be rounded up. But the driver, a man called Nichols, was contemptuous, and cited to Ormsby the fact that the mail must go through, and told him that despite having lost several hours by the local uproar and it being now late at night and the Comanche War Trail "right out there," they were heading west. And off they went.

The conversation could scarcely have been warm, the first few miles, with Ormsby disgusted and Nichols angry at this young upstart, and possibly feeling his liquor. Ormsby writes that by then he had already made up his mind that to go "under the existing circumstances" would be as much as his life was worth, and his main regret was that he "had not made up a hasty will." But as the stage drummed out of Chadbourne in the night toward the Colorado River, he and Nichols did fall into grudging talk. Better for the reporter's peace of mind if they had not.

He asked Nichols how far it was to the next station.

"I believe it is thirty miles," Nichols said.

Ormsby, aghast that in the wildest part of the trip across Texas the driver was uncertain of the distance to his destination, asked, "Do you know the road?"

Nichols refused to lose his cool attitude and his answer was the kind of truth that hurts, "No."

"How do you expect to get there?" asked Ormsby.

"There's only one road. We can't miss it," said Nichols.

Ormsby cautiously asked, "Where are your side-arms?"

"I don't want any; there's no danger," Nichols replied.

At that point Ormsby seems to have come to a sort of acceptance of his fate, for he ceased to press driver Nichols about his failings or shortcomings. (And can't we read between the lines and see the older man baiting the young reporter?) In fact, in a few lines Ormsby is rhapsodic: "The night was clear and bright, the road pretty level . . . and I soon ceased to regret having started. I alternately drove while Nichols slept, or slept while he drove . . . and altogether passed a very pleasant night."

Despite the driver's assurance and calm, Ormsby and Nichols were passing through as dangerous and as bloody a stretch as the long, hazardous trail offered. Within weeks death had found its target among the Butterfield personnel and the loss of stock was tremendous. Indian attacks on the stations from Chadbourne west to the Pecos were constant and costly.

But Ormsby was possibly soothed by a September night in West Texas, which is understandable, for this is one form of natural history we can avail ourselves of today without having to make too many exceptions for the century or more that has passed. This stretch of road, lonely now as it was for Nichols and Ormsby, is wide and close to the sky with grape clusters of thick stars, and in a time of full moon the landscape lights up so that it is possible to read mildly large print without artificial illumination.

THIS NICHOLS seems to have left traces in West Texas. A century after his ride with Ormsby I wrote an account of it for a West Texas newspaper, reciting it much as I have above. To my surprise I received a letter from a reader who said her father had been a stage driver for

Butterfield and his name was Nichols and she wondered if this might not have been her father. I visited her at her farm, on the south slope of the Callahan Divide just beyond Cedar Gap, and looking west down a lovely long valley which backs up to the old Rumph Cemetery—a most appropriate setting for the home of the daughter of a Butterfield stage driver. She had a picture of her father, one of those ancient, chalky photographs which had been retouched and colored somewhat by some artist, and I must say the portrait was precisely as I would have driver Nichols to be, from Ormsby's record. A full beard added strength to the face, not benignity. Yet there was nothing sinister about that face, rather it showed an understanding of something foreseen, as though he could see into our own day and know that the country he drove that stage through would someday be flowering with civilization, and that he had been there when it started—if that is the way someone like Nichols viewed life. He might not have. I look at these faces, especially the ones that look old, yet are only men in their thirties, and I wonder if the pioneers didn't know exactly what they were doing, and liked it that way; that they cared not one whit what came after them, that empire building and civilizing were so far out of their minds as to be distasteful to them. I have long harbored the treasonous thought (in West Texas where the old generations are held sacred) that instead of heroic dreams they had a kind of heroic greed that stood them in stead of morals or ambition, that the times and the places themselves were what they delighted in.

I know that many an old-timer in my youth claimed disgust, not only with progress but with the gentleness of the country and the men around him. "You never fought in your life. Even the wind's died down for you and the soil's gotten mellow. The weather's changin'. You never felt no sleet in September or had a norther freeze your cows dead in April. Things got gentle after we tamed 'em, like a colt you've cut and broke."

This poetic old man sat on a sack of Idaho potatoes in front of Rogers's Red and White store at the corner of Sunset and South Seventh and told that, or parts of it, to the owner when Rogers came out to use the produce scales. Rogers was wont to complain about the hard times. The old man was the same one who told me it never rained from the west in Abilene; and I believed him and would not believe the rain itself, one summer afternoon, when it came marching down that same South Seventh Street, driving in hard from due west. So I ran home (which was only next door) and found my great-grandmother, cranky, unbelieving, but a solid relic of the frontier, and I asked her, "Granny, can it rain from the west?" She looked at me with annoyance and gave one of the sniffs that punctuated her every sentence. "It looks to me like it can rain from wherever it takes a notion to rain from." The certainty of the adult judgment began to slide to the temple floor for me.

The old man who sat on the potato sack and railed at our softness, that was the kind of face Nichols showed, regardless of whether this was the same Nichols who contemptuously carried Ormsby over the Comanche War Trail unarmed. It was the face of a pioneer who raged against his own time (otherwise why come to the frontier), and who foresaw a day coming when life would be gentler because of his raging, and so he raged more. Not because he didn't want life gentler but because someone coming along after him would find it so and think it had always been that way. Their rage was against the historical injustice of their time and the way history makes such a poor umpire of life, giving one man four strikes before he's called out, but another only two.

One of the marvelous things about the woman who

lived out beyond Cedar Gap, the daughter of the stage driver, was her age. She was almost young-looking and I remarked that it seemed impossible for her father to have driven a Butterfield stage a century before.

"I'm sixty," she said, "and he was an old man when I was born. Mother was twenty-six years younger than he was. I remember him always like the picture there, with a beard, and being as old as other kids' grandpas. He died in 1914 when I was nearly sixteen, so I saw a lot of him. He was a good daddy."

Her father's name was George Wilson Nichols and he had a brother, Green, who was older and who also drove a stage. She said she had heard them talk about driving from Fort Belknap through to Robert Lee (a present-day town near the Colorado River station), and about the wild mule teams. That was why she thought her father, or his brother, was surely the Nichols who carried Ormsby.

"Once Daddy and a conductor found a Negro slave hung in an elm tree out by Mulberry Canyon [Mountain Pass]," she told me, trying to remember all the things the old man had tried to tell his young daughter. "They never knew who done it, but it wasn't the Indians. He said a man would have to be mighty mad to hang his own slave. They were worth so much money."

George Nichols joined the Confederate Army when the Butterfield stage line quit running through Texas, and after that war he spent a few years in the Indian Nation. But West Texas was still in him and in 1873 he came back out to where he had driven the stage. He camped at Burrhead Spring, on the southern slope of the Divide, south of Abilene (there's a television transmitter tower there now), and decided it was as good a place as any to put down roots. The farm his daughter was living on was within rock-chunking distance of the old spring site, but the spring is gone now. Nichols must have continued to do some freighting, for he used to tell her of the endless rows of buffalo hides—flint hides before they had been tanned—piled, awaiting shipment at Fort Griffin. And when the country began to settle up, six or seven years after he had settled at Burrhead Spring, Nichols helped lay out the streets of Abilene and Coleman.

A man could feel like a giant, being involved in all things, having to do with all history, in a place like the frontier of West Texas. And that attitude persisted for another couple of generations, and underlies much of the way the region makes up its individual mind now.

That was not the end of my twentieth-century Butterfield stage connections. Another woman called me to say that her grandfather had been a driver for John Butterfield and that his daughter, her mother, was alive and remembered quite well the things he had told her, this being, to the end of his days, the most adventuresome thing in his life, this driving the stage west. But this daughter of the Butterfield was nearing the century mark herself and in a rest home when I went to see her. A bright and wise little lady, yet very tired and very deaf.

"You'll have to get down right close for her to hear," a nurse told me, "and you'll have to speak right up."

I tried talking loudly but the nurse shook her head. "You're not loud enough," and she spoke to the old lady, "Mrs. Tucker, you got company," really putting her lungs into it. Then, when I had established a smiling, shouting communication with Mrs. Tucker, the nurse had to instruct me again: "She wants you to get down where she can talk to you."

There was nothing for me to do but get down on my knees and put my ear almost in the little old lady's face; so this I did, and we found it a workable enough arrangement.

She had heard her daddy tell about sitting up on one corner of the powder house at Fort Phantom Hill, watching for the glint, far in the west, which could only mean a stagecoach or something else from what we call civilization, for an Indian would never think of boldly flashing his way across those plains. Her father could see the dust, then hear the bugle, and he would hop down and alert the stationkeeper.

"They played a bugle, he told me," the old woman said, and I told her, yes, part of the equipment of the stage was a brass bugle so that the conductor could sound his horn while still many miles away.

Her father, Sam Nason, had been born in 1832 in Canada and was a French-Canadian. That fits history, too, a Canadian brought to Texas by a Utica, N.Y. businessman, to set out on the most colorful enterprise in Western history as a business venture. And if one or two or a dozen of his men stayed in West Texas, it was to be expected—"the lure of the West" is explanation enough.

She had been born Mary Ann Nason at the place where Denison stands today. "It was just off in the woods then," she said. What it was, of course, was Colbert's Ferry where her father drove from. His run was from there to Fort Chadbourne (the first division of the line in Texas), but he also drove all the way to and from California from time to time. Coming east from Los Angeles one trip (the City of the Angels being frontier also, then) Indians wounded one of the outriders so badly that Sam Nason had to lead him muleback for ninety-seven miles to medical help.

After the stage quit running Nason moved his family to Montague County in the lonely upper tier of North Texas counties along the Red River. The Indians were raiding there constantly, and she said she had had to flee them on several occasions when she was a girl, but one time remained in her mind with a kind of ever-fresh horror.

She and her mother and two sisters were in the cabin when the Indians approached. The mother and girls fled, but in different directions, and Mary Ann found herself with a younger sister, crouching in the creek, hiding among the cattails. The younger sister began to cry and little Mary Ann put her hand over the little sister's mouth to stop the sound, and they watched through the cattails as the Indians plundered the cabin, she holding herself low among the tall reeds, keeping her sister down and choked off, but terrified that her sobs would break out at any instant. All she could see, she said, was the feather one Indian wore in his hair. She watched it move across her horizon, a mindless, disembodied thing, now going into the cabin, then dropping out of sight, then popping up again. Then the flames of the cabin were leaping up into the sky and the cries of the Indians masked the crying of her little sister, as the redmen herded the livestock off toward Oklahoma. And long after they were gone the two little girls were crouching in among the marshy reeds, afraid to move, believing their mother and their other sisters had been killed. Later, safe in each other's arms, the mother told them they had thought the same thing about Mary Ann and the little sister. Then the mother had spanked the little sister who cried, because she had to be taught better than to make noise, to cry from fear, to sob aloud, no matter why, when it was a matter of life and death, knowing the punishment was kindness in experience.

As she talked to me, the old woman held my hand, unconsciously pressing it, so lightly, while she described the life of that other age. I held in my hands the reins of the six-mule hitch; the fear she felt among the cattails became my fear, and as she told what she remembered, I remembered them, too, seeing more than she said, hearing more than she spoke. My face was near her face and as the old, worn voice whispered out its memories, I could smell the sweet odor of age, the antiquity of human skin that cannot be duplicated by scent or ointment. The echo of the bugle began ringing in my ears, the cry of the Indians, and the terrified sounds of the livestock, or maybe it was the shouting I had done to communicate with her. I thought, where else are two worlds so wide in time and so close in blood? There are old people in great numbers across the land, but which of them has seen Indians sacking his home or crouched in horror, too young to think by anything but instincts learned from observation?

Mrs. Tucker said she recalled hearing her father speak of a Nichols as a driver and said they had worked together frequently. Sam Nason had been a very genial man, famous for his Irish songs, sung in Erse or some other Gaelic dialect; and when the family moved from Montague to Coryell County the people there used to keep him up sometimes, singing all night.

There was another coincidence about the Butterfield survivors. Both the daughter of Nichols and the granddaughter of Sam Nason had lived in a little south Taylor County town named Tuscola, where Nason's granddaughter and her husband had run a store. The two women had known each other quite well for several years, but until I wrote about them neither had known the other was descended from a Butterfield stage driver.

BEYOND FORT CHADBOURNE the Butterfield trail extended through West Texas in a long crescent from the Colorado River near San Angelo to the Pecos River above McCamey. Today the old station sites are seldom visited and many of the remains are in the midst of huge ranches whose owners often as not do not recognize what the remains are—if there are any remains.

Crossing this lonely, wide-openness, Ormsby was struck again and again by the amount of animal life present and the heavy matting of grass that parted beneath the wheels of the celerity wagon. He writes of the Spanish dagger, odd cactus plants, bear grass and some other flora he considered useful, which isn't. But he saw herds of antelope, plenty of birds such as quail, snipe, plover and prairie chickens, and like so many visitors, he simply couldn't believe they could be in the Great American Desert.

"It seemed impossible that so much life could exist without a constant, never-failing supply of water," he wrote for his New York readers. And it took a long time for the settlers to discover how you live in such a land, and as witnessed before in the predictions of Dr. Webb, not everyone yet believes you can. It is a country with an attraction only for the loving eye. Perhaps this is the phenomenon of homeland, but it does not explain the magnetic pull which harsh but dangerous beauty exerted on men who had known better and more lovely country.

I think, on my part, it is a matter of the individual; the plunging into the living of one's own emotions, for it is you who puts the beauty in West Texas and the reward is all within you. Just as a great poem exercises the art of forcing the reader to finish its beginnings and is, in itself, but the start of its reward, so is the landscape of West Texas. It is a landscape which says harsh things in violent acts, and exerts its direct supremacy over life with terrible demands on the physical composition of life. Yet it is subtle in those demands, so that to live happily in it you must furnish the love, then find the reward without help. A mysticism of geography which I find compounded by history, geology, time, and the nameless substance that lies coordinate with sky and earth which I can only term atmosphere.

I suppose the most prominent feature of West Texas landscape to me is not just the vastness of the prairies, or the extent of its plains, but the final blue backdrop of mesa, hill, or divide which frames every view. This is the difference between the rolling prairies of West Texas and the flat planes of the High Plains above the Cap Rock. The vastness and the extent are part of the High Plains, in even greater supply, but there is no boundary and nothing for the eye to achieve except distance itself. A mirage may now and then break into reality with a range of dream mountains, or on certain mornings the clouds on the near horizon may assume the shape and grandeur of the Rockies, but this unreality only emphasizes the need of the eye and the soul for some container, for sight to travel not just out, but out and back.

The particularly attractive quality of West Texas desert (as it was called for so long a time) is well expressed by another Butterfield stage rider, a Quaker, William Tallack, who traveled from California eastward on his way home to England from Australia. He came at a good time, for his passage through Texas was in June of 1860, and apparently it had been a year of spring rains and late coolness as is sometimes the delightful occasion for June.

As the stage left the Trans-Pecos area and its long stretches of admittedly desolate sand hills near the river, he wrote, with relief, "we reached a more fertile region of prairie vegetation, and traversed long undulations clothed with the deep leafage and bright blossoms of asters, red and blue verbenas, goldenrod, the milk-plant and convolvulus, the wild cherry, and with miles of sunflowers—the latter turning as with faithful glance to the great luminary from which they derive their name, and affording a lover of symbolism a beautiful emblem of spiritual and moral allegiance."

(It might be well to insert here the modern thought that sunflowers are despised by most West Texas farmers and ranchers, being taken as a pest, cattle not caring for the hairy, prickly covering of the stalks and the sharp, bitter taste of the leaves, and for dairy cattle this bitterness is passed directly into the milk.)

But Tallack continued: "Amongst this vegetation we observed herds of antelopes, several red deer [the white-tailed prairie species], many mule-eared hares [our old friend the jack rabbit], a wild turkey and several venomous, smaller creatures such as the tarantula and the long, brown centipede . . ."

Tallack also writes about the big red ants of West Texas and their wide hills which seethe with fury when stirred up. Although he does not specify that this happened, one can imagine a stationkeeper, or some other local resident, entertaining the foreign visitor by taking a stick and digging around in a red-ant bed, watching the millions of inhabitants swarm up from their underground city, looking for their tormentors, and knowing that if all those denizens of the bed were to be able to swarm over you, your fate might well be, as they say, sealed.

"After sundown," the Quaker naturalist writes, "one of the passengers exclaimed, 'Lightning bugs!' and on turning to see what these were, we found them to be fireflies [still called lightning bugs by the majority of West Texans], a number of which were gliding in beautiful curves across the stream like silently floating stars of bright green fire amongst the deepening shades of the surrounding foliage."

Tallack would have made a good West Texan. The land—its flowers, its insects, and its animals—remains gifted with the same beauty, although the antelope herds are not so numerous. But the fireflies find something on which to thrive in the cool of the evening, and if you are far enough away from the city, the coyote will talk to you, or to someone, from the edge of the horizon after dusk. And in the spring the blanket of color from the wildflowers will move up and down the gentle slopes and spot and dash against the rocks in subtle shades of harmonizing color—with the earth and the starkness—that changes tone as the clouds pass over, trailing shadows, or the wind moves among its petals with a gentle foot.

SO AS THE STAGE moved out of West Texas and crossed the Pecos River to climb to Guadalupe Pass, it plunged into a form of loneliness as severe as what it had been through, but it also entered a country where there was more to remember of people and history. Across West Texas, however, the Butterfield stage was the first work of the evident hand of civilized man. It was the outside world's first discovery of this world—a world the rest of the globe was eager to know about, for their legends and myths had created an awesome curiosity concerning this *terra incognita*. Before the coming of the Butterfield stage, civilization ended at the Brazos River, even for those two or three hundred soldiers and their families who might have lived at one or another of the West Texas posts. But after three years of twice-weekly service of the stage, the unknown could never be quite so dark. So it was a function of Columbus that John Butterfield performed, even though from afar.

The stage line continued with a remarkable record of daily reliability, changing its route beyond the Pecos River, after the first year, and adding a station or two in far West Texas for safety or economy. West Texas continued to be the most dangerous portion of the famous "Longest Stage Ride in the World," as newspapers called it. Newspapers paid an extraordinary amount of attention to the Butterfield stage, possibly because a great many newspapers were sent by stage and the reporters had occasion to meet the people running the system. The stage line also accounted for a great deal of hard news, as almost every trip brought some exciting report from the West. Searching through the files of the old newspapers of North Texas, Fort Smith, Little Rock, Saint Louis, Memphis, Chicago, and New York one finds innumerable references to word of some event being "brought by Butterfield stage."

The end of the Southern Overland Mail route came not at the hands of the Comanches or Apaches, or from lack of water and provender, or even from lack of patronage, although as a commercial venture the line subsisted mainly on its mail contract and not the passenger revenue.

The last trip through West Texas reached a confrontation with reality at Fort Chadbourne on March 12, 1861, just two weeks after Texas had seceded from the United States for her ill-fated affair with the Confederate States of America. This last trip from the west was carrying eight passengers, including Anson Mills, who had been the state surveyor who had laid out and named the townsite of El Paso (it had been called Franklin) and had erected the Butterfield station there. It is a piece of irony that Mills, who was leaving Texas to fight for the Union, despite his recent official affiliation with the state, would return a few years later to be the first commander of Fort Concho, the post located at present-day San Angelo which replaced Fort Chadbourne in the military scheme of West Texas. But on that last trip, like the rest of the passengers, Mills was racing time and events to reach the North before the hell broke loose between North and South that was clearly predictable.

A few miles west of Chadbourne the stage was halted by a band of recently commissioned Committee of Public Safety men who had been put in charge after Fort Chadbourne had been surrendered to a remarkable Texas historical character, Henry McCulloch. The band that stopped the coach was young and swaggering, dangerous because they felt high and almighty but not inclined to be very serious. The driver announced to the playful Texans that he was carrying the U. S. Mail and the mail had to go through. Mills, in his autobiography, tells how the Texas boys would grab the wheels of the stage and tell the driver he could "go on if he would," but as Mills reported, "The poor man could not, with the greatest whipping, induce the horses to proceed." Then the Texans, who may have had a little lightning juice to get them ready for the reception, demanded to know if Horace Greeley were aboard. Greeley, whose editorial views of slavery had earned him that enormous amount of Southern fury which only being right can arouse, had been on a tour of California and was said to be returning on the Butterfield stage to his New York office.

The Public Safety men closely inspected the eight faces on the stage, Greeley's famous set of throat whiskers and his pink face giving him an unmistakable trademark. But they did not find their man, so eventually the stage was allowed to move along. By virtue of the magic idea that "the mail must go through" the run reached its terminus, Tipton, Missouri, without losing mail, passengers, or steeds to the rebel forces along the way.

So that was the Butterfield trail through West Texas. Other stage lines were driven across the territory, but they were relatively short ones, between towns or military posts. Nothing ever again approached the vast scheme of John Butterfield.

Ironically, what has been best for West Texas economically has been worst for the historical remains of the stage operation: oil. Even in the remoter reaches of the trail the tread of the bulldozer has ground out the track of history. Oil-field roads, running thick as spider webs around centers of activity or drilling sites, make it impossible, even from the air, to detect those traces of the old trail which many intervening authorities reported were plainly visible in the years after the stage ran and before oil was found. Through no one's fault—for how were the drillers to know?—old foundations, chimneys, walls, have been knocked over, shoved out of the way, or scraped back to make way for drilling platforms, mud pits, or truck roads. The Butterfield trail across West Texas is better felt than seen.

14

Sandstone Sentinels

THE GRAVEYARDS of West Texas have more continuity than their counterparts in other sections. In almost any cemetery except those modern, impersonal "memorial gardens," you may find the frontier touching hands with today, the headstones lined up in rows or adjoining plots to spell out the history of a family, a town, or an era. The burial ground was the first public site marked off, and is the last remaining from dozens of lost worlds. The tide of cities receded, leaving cemeteries to mark its retreat.

Great-grandfather here, his stone remembering the beginning of that Mississippi, Alabama, or Tennessee birthplace, and by him great-grandmother, with a one- or two-line sentiment which reminds her descendants that as far as the tribe was concerned, she was where time began, for there was no memory going back to wherever they fled from to come to the frontier. (This mixture of loyalty to place as well as people remains strong.)

At their feet the sad, small mounds that were their tariff to their times, two, three, or half a dozen tiny graves with faceless names and fleeting dates. (I have seen a plot in Acton cemetery in Hood County where two full rows are required to hold the lost little children of one man's two marriages.) The frontier drew heavily on the infants, and every old graveyard offers waves of brothers and sisters, now great-aunts and uncles, who never filled their roles and were forgotten even by the ones who gave them brief life. It was an expected toll which only now and then, like a piece of foreign matter embedded deep in the body but never lost, caused a recollecting pain when the heart was turned in certain directions.

I had a man tell me, at age eighty-eight, of his wife, eighty-two, that "she never got over losin' little 'Docie . . ." a child lost sixty years before, and an even half-dozen stout sons and pretty daughters afterward.

The oldest cemeteries of West Texas have that gray, deserted corner where the burials started, nameless stones set at head and foot. Or walled graves, rising three or four feet and enclosed with stone, sometimes sealed, sometimes only other stone laid over the grave itself inside the narrow walls. Protection of the body, that was their purpose (although I suppose there was a certain stylishness to burial, also). Wild animals might dig into a new corpse, not just the coyotes, panthers, and wolves but the little burrowing creatures blindly going after something sensed rather than known. Domestic animals (although this is no description for the longhorn cattle of the frontier) were an even more present danger, pushing over a marble slab, trampling across the sacred soil where the body lay. (I was taught explicitly never to walk on a grave, and I think it was a general tenet of our society in West Texas. I cannot do it now without a tinge of near-sin.)

And yet, there is a curious kind of resentment toward burial grounds. It is as though the living wanted, somehow, to deny their debt to what was buried there and at the same time deny the necessity of their joining them. You are dead, so what have you got to brag about? Once at that Acton cemetery mentioned before, I stopped just outside the gates where a grove of tall, thick, live oaks offered shade and murmuration to me in solitude on a summer's noon. I got the few things I planned to eat—a canned soft drink, a sandwich, some tinned meats, and pickles—and set them on a wide stone table provided under the huge trees. Only as I was swallowing my last few mouthfuls of food did I notice that the stone that formed the table top had something engraved on it. With difficulty I made out the entire inscription:

SACRED TO
THE MO OF
ELIZABETH
CROCKETT WAS
BORN MAY 22 1788
DIED JAN 31 1860
AGE 72 YEARS——9 DAYS
BENEATH THIS TOMB
LAYES THE WIDOW OF
COL DAVY CROCKETT
WHO FELL AT THE ALIMO

I realized then that when the state, in 1911, had erected a tall, marble monument over Elizabeth Crockett's grave, there in the remote little Acton cemetery, the old limestone marker from the 1860's had been given the utilitarian position as a picnic table.

The men who subdued West Texas are buried through the land in dozens of now secluded graveyards, their names slowly fading from the recognition of the country, but each an excitement to the contemporary

Western historian who comes across it unexpectedly, perhaps one of the Hittson (or Hitson) boys, a Carter, a Gholson (or Golson), a Grounds or Loving. Oliver Loving, who died in New Mexico of wounds from an Indian fight, was an older man who really didn't want to be as adventuresome as he had to be when he and young Charles Goodnight were breaking the Goodnight-Loving trail through West Texas, out along the old Butterfield pathway, up into New Mexico and Colorado. Young Goodnight admired him so, felt so keenly close to the older partner, that he refused to leave his body "laid away in a foreign country," as Loving had termed it just before he died. A few months later, Goodnight had Loving's body exhumed and put in a box. He had a huge, tin casket soldered together and put the boxed body inside, packed in several inches of charcoal. The tin casket was sealed and the whole affair crated up in thick lumber. He took a wagon box off the running gear and mounted this sad burden on the wheels, to pull it back through hundreds of desert miles, this being 1868, in a desolate, dangerous journey so that Loving could repose at home in the Weatherford cemetery. They wanted an identity with the soil where they lay and sometimes their bones are what gave it its identity.

But I always feel sadder when I contemplate the unheroic and modest graves of the women, most especially the young wives. There they are, and I prefer (male-like) to think they were all pretty girls, put in the grave by a grieving young husband who had scarcely discovered the exciting wonder of living with the other sex. And their wonderful names like Rexanna, Tamsey, Purnia, Fluvanna, and Tempie. I tell you, I can come close to crying when I walk among them and read the efforts to hold something that grief said could never be lost—the headstone of a young wife in the old Dennis cemetery which says "Love Is Love Forevermore," because that was how he felt when he buried her after four years of wedded life; but then, he lies a little way away from her, beside the wife who shared his bed (according to their headstones) for fifty-five more years. But love is love forevermore in more hearts than we think, and I will not accept the notion that the frontier invariably bleached out emotions or reduced its lovers to mere partnership.

The pioneers buried them high, on hilltops, on rises, on bluffs above the river (and not always wisely in this respect, for the river eats into a burial ground sometimes, although the passage of a century may have so altered natural arrangements that their foresight cannot be faulted). They knew they couldn't run from danger anymore, and danger was an accompaniment even for the dead in those West Texas times. Somewhere the custom arose of putting seashells on the graves (and if it is wider spread than West Texas, forgive me for not knowing), and some cemeteries will have dozens of graves, even old ones from that other century, still carefully covered with shells placed in a blanket over the mound. The old Fort Phantom Hill cemetery has rows and rows of these (including one man named Autto, for us, the living, to ponder on).

But across the hard land are other graves, alone and usually unmarked save for a rock or two or a slab of wood which shows evidences of having at one time borne a legend but now gone gray and wordless. These graves are usually those of sudden death. A horse falls, a gun discharges, a fever strikes, and the body is put in the earth where it happens. There is a grave sitting right in the middle of a road a few miles south of Breckenridge, the two directions of traffic flowing around it. Its memorial is to a woman who "died in camp."

The cowboy who inspired the song "Oh, Bury Me Not on the Lone Prairie" was supposed to have been a hand with John N. Simpson's Hashknife outfit which grazed over most of upper Taylor County in the 1870's. He was mortally wounded in a fall and as the song ironically notes, his dying prayer was not heeded. There are at least three isolated graves to the north of Abilene that are claimed as his.

However, there is another kind of solitary grave, and to my mind nothing is so soulful as reading, hand-carved on the native rock, "Killed By The Indians."

We have come a good many aeons from those words, although in a few cases less than a century. But think what they imply; all the bad Western movies ground out by Hollywood, all the formulaic novels and unauthentic television series about that other world which springs to

mind with the phrase. We forget almost entirely that those were people who were "Killed By The Indians" and not folk gods who were carried off to some Valhalla, and our modern sense of fairness (or taking an equivalent view, if nothing else) tells us the Indians had a side of the history, too. Still it is a tremendous message and about as historic, I contend, as any phrase we can find in American experience. Killed by Indians where we walk or ride or, for that matter, make love. I lived for a while in a house that had been exposed to Indian attack, and I used to wonder if someone had been killed there—over by the gas range or maybe in the corner where the electric refrigerator sat, or down the hall near the bathroom, out in the ell by the deep freeze, or in a bedroom by the television set.

But the graves of Indian victims so marked and noted are fairly rare in West Texas, out beyond the Brazos River frontier at least. There were plenty of victims but there wasn't plenty of time to put down a suitable marker in that remoter casting of civilization. And after a herd or two of buffalo had passed over the spot, there was scarcely any way to come back and commemorate the grave.

Or if there was time and stone, often it was sandstone, some of which has the deceptive quality of looking as firm as granite but sloughing off in thin scales with the years and rains and freezes. Sandstone sentinels, a historian friend once called the old frontier burial markers found in those weedy, forlorn cemeteries through the middle of West Texas. Sentinels, but not too faithful, carrying now only an enticing line or so, a date for death but a haze of numbers for birth, to puzzle and tempt the eyes which would unravel the story of what lies below. But finding one inscribed with that primitive, powerful blow to civilization is worth whatever effort it takes, and so although it was a cold day (snow had been lying in a thin blanket in the morning when we arose) and not knowing the way, we determined we would go and find the grave of Phillip Reynolds, buried out beyond the fringe of our society, on a lost road where he was felled while hauling wood to the Ledbetter Salt Works a century ago.

It was a cold February day with the sun so bright you had to squint, but the wind so harsh your neck turned raw where collar just missed the hairline by a centimeter or so. The dry snow had all blown away or melted from the reaction between light and earth, but the temperature had not risen by so much as one degree and the wind was coming in from the north even harder.

Phillip Reynolds was one of those unnumbered unfortunates who populate West Texas history like pathetic ghosts, having no identity but a name on a grave or an association with some mythic event. He was young, he was not kin to the numerous other Reynolds who lived on the frontier there, and he died. But someone thought enough of young Phillip to put a stone at his feet, so he was saved being a mound of oblivion.

Since Phillip Reynolds had been headed for the Ledbetter Salt Works, Bob Nail and I decided this would be a good place to start. (The Reynolds grave was so out-of-the-way that outside help had to be called in, two historically minded young women who had visited it.)

When I was a youngster the passage through Albany was marked by three visible reminders of time and events —the courthouse clock (Abilene had nothing of such lofty magnificence to commemorate time), a sign that stretched in an arch over the road which read ALBANY HOME OF THE HEREFORD, and two huge, cast-iron kettles from the salt works which sat on one corner of the square. Later the highway was widened considerably and the motto was reduced to the size of a small service-station sign, and when Albany established a little park and outdoor museum on one side of town the kettles were moved out there.

But the salt works were of an age long before the Herefords and their sign, the wide highway, or Albany itself came along. Salt was like gold on the frontier, and settlers, Indians, and the animals—especially the deer, buffalo, and antelope—contended for the salt licks, ponds, and springs scattered across the land. There is a good deal of difference between a salt pond and merely bad water. There is plenty of bad—i.e., gyp, alkali, brackish—water in West Texas but not all of it can be rendered into usable saline. A map today which takes time to name the creeks, draws, and gullies will show as many "Salt Prongs" or "Salt Forks" as any one designation.

In the days when civilization was somewhere back around Weatherford and safety even farther east, the salt works were worth the risk it took to keep a party working there to render the gray saline crystals and send them back to the settlements. During the Civil War, which in general left West Texas virtually untouched, the salt was needed back where the fighting was going on. Thus, this spot in southern Shackelford County was probably the farthest extension of wartime industry in the Confederacy.

In that little museum the Albany people still keep the rusty metal stencil which Ledbetter used to mark his bags of salt: "25 lbs. W. H. Ledbetter^s Superfine Table

SALT." It is one of those insignificant pieces of history whose survival astounds me. First of all, one is not inclined to think of the pioneers, who were working like Nehemiah's wall builders in the Bible with one hand on their weapons, taking the trouble to weigh out, then mark their produce so commercially—"Superfine," no less. Secondly, this by-product of that antique industry is the sort of thing that ordinarily goes on the junk heap first, there being little likelihood of a future Ledbetter Salt Works. But somebody saved it for some reason (sentimentality, I would assume, having little faith in the foresight of self-appointed historians), and today it exists to confound people like me who probably spend too much time trying to figure out unnecessary motives for a society which seldom did motiveless things.

South from Albany some twelve miles, along a gravel ranch road, we came to a wide, flat field sloping north toward Salt Prong Creek. Something about it said people had been there, although there was little enough visible from the road to provoke the thought. But something was hanging in the bright, chill February sunlight which spoke of others, of busyness and men working on this land in purposes as dead and invisible as they now are.

I believe this phenomenon of "presence" works. I believe that when you come upon some spot where man was and is no more, the ground speaks. In our case, the terms were easy, and once off the road the eye found details all along the rutted pathway heading into the field. The hardscrabble field, not even mesquites to dot it, was unnaturally bare, and one could guess that man had helped nature kill off the flora that might have found footing there at one time.

The first thing I did, stepping from the driver's seat, was stoop down and scoop out of the dirt a triangular flint scraper, white with patina. Others, then, had known this salt flat and had come here long before Ledbetter to find that saline substance the hot, animal blood in us thirsts for, remembering blindly, we are told, its beginnings in the old sea. A heavy coat of patina on flint, in this particular section of West Texas, speaks of two to three thousand years at the soonest.

Above and below ground in West Texas are testimonies of the sea, for this salt spring (now dammed by the city of Albany so as not to contaminate the town water supply a few miles below) gets its salinity from deposits laid down by some ocean of primal antiquity, and below these beds, deeper in the earth and in time, is laid down the salt water on which floats the petroleum that spouts to the surface of Shackelford County and the rest of West Texas with such financially delightful frequency when man augurs his way down there. How strange but compelling is the idea that here, five hundred miles from what we call the ocean, the sea manages to exert as much influence—maybe more—on the form of living as it does on many a coastal city.

The site is silent, except for the footfall of a winter wind that comes over the little bluff to the north, unseen because there is so little grass to mark its broad footsteps. It is an uneasy accompaniment to the loneliness of our recollections of the times a century or less back, when standing here would have been a constant temptation to danger. How much of this atmosphere invades you in the new-old land of West Texas?

There are hills rising a few hundred yards to the southwest, and Axletree Creek joins the Salt Prong of Hubbard just a few yards below the city's dam. A small cemetery lies across the road to the south—the oldest graves undated on their rock markers, and rolling off to the north is a broken ridge that stands scarcely higher than a utility pole.

My patinated scraper gives evidence that the salt spring here was found early. In the annals of American civilization, however, the discovery came when Cal Greer, William King, and Vol Simonds found the place while returning to the Greer Ranch (farther down Hubbard Creek) from a cattle drive to the Concho River forks in 1861. Uncle Billy McGough says he and some other settlers went out and made salt by boiling the water in cooking vessels in 1862, but it was so dangerous (the Indians nearly always stopped at the spring) the handful of people never stayed very long. In 1863 Ledbetter moved several families out to the spring and set up his salt works.

Today there are some stone-lined pits where the big kettles sat over their fires, faint traces of something that might have been a gravity flow from the pond to the pots, and here was a wide stone corral. Occasionally the eye will find a rusty square nail around those sites where some sort of structure stood. Square nails are a beloved sight to me, for nothing makes the past so near as these simple, humble pieces of iron that lie by the thousands through the West Texas soil, but brought out here at great price and sweat by the pioneers to whom a lumber house, and one that used nails, was a luxury. I have developed a sixth sense or a third eye for square nails and I have the happy knack of finding them in the most unlikely places—but this personal attribute (as I like to interpret it) is not altogether germane to our narrative, I suppose.

The pond from which the brine was taken is rock-bottomed and clear but the salt has created a miniature Dead Sea and the water has a curious brown tint. I would guess that fewer than a dozen people come here in a year's time, outside the rancher and his crew who work these holdings. Many of the scattered inhabitants know little or nothing of the Salt Prong's history.

The thought that this spot, so open, removed, and pleasant (if one disregarded the instance of the cold wind) was worth braving death to hold, is hard to accept now. Salt. There is something about it that has tinged history with blood, as though our mortal fluid were, by its salinity, attractive to violence in all similar manifestations. Texas has seen intermittent wars rage over the use, the taxing, or the fencing-in of several salt lakes. The Ledbetter site was never a part of such intertribal fighting, but it led to death in its time, not just Phillip Reynolds's killing and scalping but that of others who intended making the brine pools their destination.

I knelt down to sample the waters, and sipping from my cupped hand, caught a fleeting burst of flavor. In so doing, I tilted my head until only the very crest of the bluff and ridge to the north were still in view. I gained one of those precious moments when the world and all that is drops away, taking time along too, and leaving me alone, suspended above and beyond the reality and the effects of a ticking clock on my wrist. I regained history, although I couldn't tell you which era or what particular piece of it I recaptured, but this taste of salt water had for me the same effect as M. Proust's madeleine had on him when one bite caused him to remember things past to the extent of seven volumes.

The rest of my companions were decent enough not to inquire as to the ecstatic beam which, I am sure, wreathed my face; but one of the ladies did point out, in the most delicate way, that cattle had obviously intruded into the area where I sipped. I chose to accept the cleansing power of Mother Earth over any foreign agent. My history was only accentuated by the symbiotic compounding of cattle.

THE ROAD that came to the salt works from the southwest—the one Phillip Reynolds had been traveling—has long since been fenced, pastured, and mesquited to death. So we could not go down that salt trail and skirt the slope of the hill that jutted out onto the plain in that direction. We must go back to the straight line of civilization; the fence row and the highway were the only trail our low-bellied metallic horse could traverse.

A few miles of pavement going south and we turned across a cattle guard into a deserted downhill pasture. It might be good to describe a cattle guard, for their presence in the range country is so constant that they form an unalterable part of the landscape. (I have even found a landing strip over in Palo Pinto County with a cattle guard at one end.) Large animals cannot gait themselves so as to be able to put each of their feet on widely spaced supports. Therefore, where ranchers have need to build an access—one that will be used too much to have a wire gate or something you have to get out and open or close —they will construct a cattle guard, using pipes or rails set over a pit with four or five inches of space between the pipes. That way a wheeled vehicle can pass over them without the slightest trouble, or a man can easily walk, but a cow will get a hoof hung and retreat. Deer can jump across cattle guards which are six or eight feet wide in most cases, but then deer can jump a fairly tall goat-wire fence, too. But Hereford cattle would be hard put to lift themselves over a city curb, being bred blocky, as they say, meaning as square and full of usable meat as possible.

One side of the field we turned into was thick with

mesquite scrub, after we crossed the cattle guard. There is high nobility to a twisted mesquite which has braved the winds for a few decades, but a field full of brush and choking undergrowth is a tormenting sight because it is a sign of desertion, of surrender or laziness. Even to the asphalt breed, a well-kept, cleared pasture is a thing of beauty, rolling away from its tight fences in long, grassy swells, without the bloody red gashes of erosion or the sick green blotches of cactus and the needle jungle of mesquite which take over unloved land. Prior use of land for crops or pasture seems to leave it more vulnerable to the fierce, wild-growing things. Old-timers say that a pasture of native grass, left in virgin condition, will resist being taken over by their infestations, whereas a plowed field or one seeded to imported strains, like coastal Bermuda grass or blue panic, must be protected and coddled or it will be overrun in a matter of months. This may be true or it may be nostalgia for the strength which old-timers customarily associate with anything that was, rather than things as they are. I like the thought, regardless.

Although my generation is of the city and our pleasures are socialized and even sophisticated (I despise the word), I like to talk to men who love the land with simple affection and regard for its moods and characteristics. Land can be downright human in its variance, in its changeability and perversity. The easiest example of this might be those all of us know who have a green thumb—people for whom the very earth responds. I am certain this is not just expertness in those people. My own unfortunate trait is just the opposite. A brown thumb, if that isn't too grim.

Ask any farmer or stockman who has had a certain field, a ridge, or a piece of well-defined land which resists him, his plows, and his seeds. Or, in the ranch country, there are pastures whose grasses seem to put more fat on the cattle than adjoining strips.

Sections of land will act like individuals. Some will be streaked with poor soil or boil with rocks, for no apparent geological reason. And some will get more moisture or less. This is a true thing, and anyone depending on the soil for a living in West Texas will point out to you in witness this business of rain favoring or avoiding special places, some no bigger than an acre, some large enough to have acquired a geographical name.

I don't know about the rest of the United States but I would guess this to be especially true of prairie lands or lands lying among broken hills and uneven elevations. There is a graphic demonstration of this moisture-seeking and moisture-rejecting geography near Abilene. When the U.S. Weather Bureau moved its offices from downtown on North First Street, after forty years in that location, it went out east of town to the municipal airport. Old editor Frank Grimes, who spent a lot of time and ink worrying about weather and rainfall, despaired of Abilene's moisture statistics. "We've called that place 'Dry Knob' since I came to town," he said. And sure enough, rainfall totals began to drop, although the change of location only amounted to four or five miles.

Rain often seems to stop abruptly a few miles east of Merkel where the 100th meridian crosses Interstate Highway 20. I do not propose to sound medieval, but driving along, one may almost distinguish the edge of the rain as though cut with a knife. On the other hand, northwest of Abilene, in a sort of half moon of territory, rain seems to average as much as three inches more per year than falls in the city itself—a considerable difference when you realize that the normal annual rainfall for Taylor County comes to less than twenty-one inches.

In Coleman County there is a field which can be seen from the highway in beautiful summer-time green, drought or no. An old native told me that particular field, in a phenomenon conforming to the fence lines, gets a good shower at every crucial juncture of the calendar and the crop. And once, he vowed, the fence was changed by some twenty paces or so to allow the state to straighten out a curve in the highway, and the rainfall adjusted nicely to the new boundary. That latter twist could be a leg-pull, but it was done in masterly pattern, for the old-timer never moved a muscle as he told it.

Some lands respond to irrigation with a magical green face, while another plot, across a narrow road, or maybe just through the strands of a barb-wire fence, will not assume fertility, pour the liquid fertilizer to it as you will. Geology accounts for some such freakish soil reac-

tions, of course. Coming east from Crosbyton, farther northwest, there is a dramatic spot where the Cap Rock breaks off so sharply that a field on top, irrigated, runs right up to the fence where, in a matter of a foot or two, things drop off to sterility and desert. Sighting down that fence is like viewing someone around the edge of a mirror—two unbelievably split faces.

Chemistry can run in narrow bands and slices through the soil, and old riverbeds, laid down too far back to leave surface traces, can erupt with sand and rocks (some experts say the Jones County shinnery was created in the vastness of time by the shifting bed of the Clear Fork with its sands). But there are more mysterious manifestations. . . .

Plowmen (what an archaic sound the word has to a city dweller) know that along one row stones will break the points of cultivators and harrows, while an adjacent row will be soft loam, mellow, and chocolaty. A farmer who used to raise cotton west of Anson, where rich, almost flat land gives agriculture a big edge over cattle, says there was a piece of acreage along the northern quarter of one of his sections where his tractor radio refused to "act right at all." (Tractors with radios? That's many years old; now the West Texas agricultural wrinkle is air-conditioned cabs on its tractors, cotton pickers, combines, and other large implements. As a matter of fact, that's getting to be old hat, too.)

Who says the very ground we walk on isn't reacting to our tread—or that it can't act on us?

ALL OVER West Texas you will find deserted farm and ranch houses. Usually they are modest in size, one story of frame with a chimney at one end made of brick or possibly frontier stonework. The world is moving to town—in West Texas, but everywhere else, too.

Few of these deserted farmhouses were large and manorial like the one that stood on the trail to Phillip Reynolds's grave. It was a tall, fourteen-foot-ceilinged, two-story home with fancy mantels over its half a dozen fireplaces and a long wing running back from the main structure which enclosed a well. It had been a ranch headquarters, a baronial domain set up in the late years of the seventies. But something had happened: bad land, bad breeds of livestock or sons, bad investments, and the domain had shrunk, then been deserted. Now (after we made our trip to the grave) it has been pulled down. But it had a wilderness magnificence seldom come on in this part of the world.

This is hawk country, also coyote country. There is enough open space for the big birds to sweep across without giving their prey too much coverage, and not too many cross-fences running through the pastures to cause a hawk's flight to become erratic. The coyotes are hard to find, except for their death on the highway, but you can hear them yipping their sharp bark on dark nights.

We drove quite a way without finding any familiar landmarks, taking to foot, eventually, when the ruts petered out. The old-timers must have been right about this part of Shackelford County, at least, in saying there was no mesquite when the land was young. No road, not even a wagon trace, could have been pushed through the thickets.

When we found the grave it was mainly because the field where it was had been chained and the trees knocked down. At first I was fearful that the gravestone might have gone with the mesquite (bulldozer drivers aren't paid to be archaeologists, I suppose), but a bigger tree has grown up through the years to mark the grave and protect it.

It was almost dusk when we found it. The hills were very close behind us, and the shadows had already reached out to overtake the spot. The stone was leaning forward—a fact which may have helped preserve its lettering—and the grave itself was heaped up with big rocks. The loneliness of the spot, the cold, windy shadows, the backdrop of low hills immediately on our west, gave it a suitably remote and timeless air.

The inscription was of rough-cut letters, unpunctuated and untrained, cut into the sandstone so long ago that soft green lichen was edging onto it and flakes were beginning to pull away.

PHILLIP H REY
NOLDS WAS BO
RN FEB THE 17
1843 AND WAS KILL
ED BY THE INDIANS
JULY 17 1865

The mesquites and the scrub oaks were set among the rough, rocky washes and gullies that surrounded us, for this was grazing land, not pasture or field. In fact, in a hollow just a few yards from the grave we found the carcass of a cow that had died trying to give birth to a calf, which was still protruding from her body. The carrion vultures and others had started their job. For a rancher not to find a dead cow for so long a time means she has died in a spot notable for its hidden properties. Thus with death, of man or beast.

One of the women who had led us to the place asked if I was satisfied with what we had found after the work it had taken to find it, and I said, half in and only half out of the nineteenth century, that it was a good place for a man to have been killed by the Indians.

15

So All the Generations

THEY WERE of that blood called Scotch-Irish, my mother's family, but the Scot completely dominated the Irish tint, if any there was.

Scotch-Irish, historically, is that name given those hard-bitten Presbyterians shipped to Northern Ireland in the sixteenth century to make sure the Papists of the south didn't drive out all elements of Protestant English rule. In the United States the application of the name has become generalized, but it is still a fit specific, and in our minds the image shapes itself at the mention.

One wonders how many of the historic stress-points of American society can be laid to this undigestible lump in the belly of the body politic which nevertheless could not have survived without it. High-strung, hot-headed, and brave; obstinate, opinionated, and moralistic, the Scotch-Irish have devoted perfervid loyalty to whatever cause they have taken up, and are the worst and yet the best of Anglo-Saxon democratic inheritance. Stubborn, reckless, independent, and constantly restless, they make bad fathers, good hell-fire preachers, and the most cantankerous followers any authority was ever offered control of.

Texas was the natural destination for their numbers as soon as it was open for them to migrate toward. Mexico's fatal mistake involving her northmost province was allowing Stephen F. Austin to settle three hundred or so of the strain there in 1821.

But their background, ethics, and philosophy fitted the settlement of new, remote, demanding lands. Danger and deprivation were chosen accessories of their lives, their scant letters and rare personal diaries show; and nothing drove those Scotch-Irish pioneers to penitential remorse like comfort, ease, and a plenitude of staples. (Even today the breed mustn't be given too much: too much of goods, too much power, too much love. They are not wise about abundance. Their genes go back to want and their wisdom is in the allocation of the spoonful, not the prodigalities of the peck.) Coupled with their uncomfortable spirit were fatalism and intransigence, which made them acceptable mates only to their own kind and equipped them well for privation and hazard.

So they came to Texas. There may be some drop or two of what they called "Northern" blood in our veins; some ancestor who made it to Texas by way of New York or Pennsylvania and not from Georgia, Alabama, or Tennessee, but I have never been told of the fact. The Coles, Craigheads, Dockrays, Poes, Suttons, Hutchisons, Woods of our line were Southern by geography and emotion. However, their Southern background was poor, not plantation. Although my great-grandmother, who came out of the Civil War era and helped rear me, could think of no stronger term of derogation than "Yankee," there was never in her that blind Southern fury that swept every logical or historical barrier before it, such as characterized the redneck. Religion, for all its hot personal implications, kept my family cooler. They came early under the strict legality of Alexander Campbell's purified, simplified Christianity which operated like the balances of a justice court. As one rather unusual inheritance of this

universal fairness, I grew up forbidden to pronounce the word "nigger" in my home, although all around us it was a common, daily noun. Campbellite morality demanded the recognition of reality, and my grandmother Cole assured me that the Negro was just as good as anyone else in God's sight because God had made him, too. "Just like you," was the phrase she used when trying to drill into my head the level at which God held all his creatures in His view. Not only that, but she instilled in me the historical idea that the South lost the Civil War because the South had been in the wrong, fighting for slavery. She was no sociological crusader, and she never attempted to convert others to her racial views, but I must witness for this kind and sympathetic woman that never in her household—a plain enough, ordinarily educated, lower middle-class family—did I ever know anyone to take another, more traditionally Southern view; and the mere fact that a man or woman was a Negro had no bearing on any question concerning their suitability for fair, equal, human acceptance. I would not try to make of her some kind of heroine, either, or a woman who stood up to community emotions. It is just that this deep sense of fairness and reality were so unusual for the time and the place that I have often wondered just how it came about. It almost had to be autogenetic, something growing out of her reading or listening, for she had no formal training that might have created this spark of philosophical awareness.

But Alexander Campbell's message of God-fear came at just the right point in family history to inflict everyone of my past with a zeal for righteousness and a conviction of guilt, with the confident expectation of doom. This same kind and loving grandmother never saw the bright side of any tomorrow, and most of her immediate kin far exceeded her in dismal discernment. How many hundreds of times have I heard the sound of the old hymn, "Almost Persuaded," with its slow drag of impossibility: "Almost will not prevail, almost is but to fail . . . sad, sad, that bitter wail . . . almost—but lost." It was the theme song of my childhood worship, the constant invitation used to call sinners away from the lip of hell, yet always hinting they would never make it. The God they worshipped showed His love by never making any exceptions.

So All the Generations

THERE IS A STORY in the family which may be mythical, although I cannot believe there were any myths allowed in the Dockray clan. It is about my great-grandmother's grandfather Poe, and it exemplifies not just my own bloodline's adamantine tendency but that of a whole social era.

Grandpaw Poe's sons, and maybe a son-in-law or two, decided on a buffalo hunt one fall when the food situation was bad around the San Saba frontier in central Texas. This was before the Civil War, sometime in the 1850's, when West Texas was not even named that, when only a few, scattered federal troops represented civilization in the whole enormous area.

A buffalo hunt was not the usual thing for these men on the frontier at that time, because the buffalo had withdrawn from the surrounding territory several years before in that mysterious way the great beasts had of readjusting their cycles of migration and feeding. The people of the tiny settlement of Dallas, for example, had not seen a buffalo east of the Trinity River since 1846, and Dallas was still considered thrust out pretty far from civilization.

But the Poe boys decided on a hunt into West Texas, more than a hundred miles away to the northwest, possibly trailing up to the very same prairies where their descendants would put down roots a few decades later. They were going to travel light and travel swiftly, getting some meat and a few hides before the Comanche could find them out on that prairie sea.

But they reckoned without their father, Grandpaw Poe. An old man, he was not fit for winter traveling or for buffalo hunting, and certainly not for West Texas and the Indians and all the other possibilities of that country.

But, Scotch-Irish, he said he was going. The family tale does not say what his reasons were, but they must have been dear ones. Maybe he thought his grown sons couldn't be trusted to get back. Maybe there was something about the *terra incognita* of West Texas he wanted to see, curiosity accounting for at least half the pioneer motive. Or a final try at hunting, perhaps, by a man who had lived by his hunting rifle all his life, always moving west until age trapped him and civilization caught him on its edge.

Of course, I think I have seen the old man re-created in many of his come-afters, although he died more than seventy-five years before I was born. And I say he said he was going simply because everybody else said he shouldn't. At any rate, nobody could argue him out of it, and so the sons and the sons-in-law gave up and said all right, but for God's sake, Papa, take a wagon and ride in it. This he did, using as his defense the fact that the buffalo, if found, would make a tremendous pile of meat and hide.

So they saddled up, and harnessed up, and buttoned up (because I think it was November or December), and headed up toward the West Texas hunting grounds. Naturally, the old man discovered that hardheadedness and old experience are unsuitable substitutes for youth and strength when it comes to facing extreme physical rigors.

Some few days after the hunting party had left the San Saba farm the air turned blue with cold, the sunshine turned bleak, the temperature at nights dropped below freezing, the hard, north wind ate at their skin, and the land became unfriendly, rough, and dry. Having arrived in West Texas, Grandpaw Poe announced at this point he was turning around and going back home.

We can imagine what kind of furor this caused. The

Poe sons were not able to challenge the old patriarch, for the clan spirit was not scrubbed from their blood by a mere two or three centuries away from their ancestral land. Nor were they able to spill out their wrath properly over the hardheaded old fool's noggin the way a son might do a foolish father today. There was a godliness there that resembled all too much the great Jehovah. So they chewed their mustaches and argued every kind of logic they could think up, from personal safety to prior obligation. But, being his sons, I expect they knew from the beginning their pleas would not work, so they made the best of the situation. They insisted the old man take the wagon and a team back with him although he had asked merely that he be given the poorest horse.

He left them one morning and they reluctantly continued north, driving deep into Taylor County and the region around the headwaters of the Clear Fork, onto the buffalo plains.

The first night going back, the old man hobbled the wagon team and camped. It turned even colder with a blue norther sweeping down on him during the night, so he pulled out early so as to be moving toward the settlements in as much warmth as the daylight sun afforded. Somehow, in leaving, he overlooked his grub box, and when he stopped that night there was nothing to eat. And sometime during the next day he came down with a cold and began running a fever, and maybe this caused him to get light-headed, or maybe it was just age laying a typical ambush, but hungry and giddy, he didn't hobble his horses, and the next morning he found himself afoot—the ultimate misfortune of the frontier.

We may presume that the old man recognized at last what was about to happen to him because he was a lifetime product of the American frontier and its lessons must have penetrated his old mind. He had only a short time to survive unless he reversed the odds in immediate fashion.

He set out to find the horses, following their tracks even as his senses reeled from sickness, hunger, and the pain of conditions. But the horses were not to be found, and he didn't know whether they had run off with a herd of the wild mustangs that ranged that land or had been picked up by Indians. The whole idea of him not hobbling the team is hard to swallow, for his life and all the lives of everyone he knew had been suspended from that thin, fragile human necessity of never forgetting.

He spent the day, or a good part of it, wandering until, finally, he was himself lost, no food, a sickness eating at his bones and his brain, with only the stinging, digging winds to direct him. Sometime during his feverish ordeal he crawled into a cave along a cliff that swung a limestone back to the wind, and he collapsed. The fever climbed higher until he was out of his head, weaponless, powerless, defenseless, in a place and at a time when any of these was disastrous.

But the cave was not unoccupied, and in keeping with the succession of bad luck, the other occupants were rabid skunks—the legend says there was a whole colony of them. One would have been enough, of course. But rabid skunks were not uncommon in the wilds (and are not now), so we may presume this to be true, I think.

Meanwhile, the hunters had not done much better than their father. Buffalo were not to be found, and none of them could quite put from his mind the vision of that stubborn old man wandering back toward San Saba, with a fresh norther at his back, across a hundred miles or more of barren land, and no guide but his instincts—which had functioned so beautifully until age had twisted them into a net instead of a guide rope.

At the end of the first day after his departure from the hunting party the youngest son finally announced he could stand it no longer and he was going to backtrack on the old man and catch up with him. With a little consultation the whole hunt decided to return home, finding Grandpaw Poe in between.

They rode with the terrible cold urging them from the rear, not even the afternoons getting above freezing temperatures, the rare creeks and waterholes being their gauges, and the night bitter with dust and icy wind.

First they found the food box, torn open and everything edible devoured by the vultures, coyotes, or Indians, or all three. Then, pushing their horses, now in fear and a conviction that God would punish them for what they had let themselves be talked into doing by the very person it was done against, they found the wagon. It was horseless, of course, and the signs leading from it disappeared. So they spread out to search for him according to a rough plan, figuring his old steps could not have dragged him many miles from the wagon. At dusk, the cold sun's rays forming a sudden shadow on the limestone bluff to indicate the cave mouth, they found him. The young one is said to have been the discoverer. The skunks were at him—the old man—but he didn't know it. Face down, his long beard poking from under him, his blanket roll halfway under him, he lay unconscious. The animals had chewed his extremities. The boys thought he was dead when they gathered in the cave after the youngest's gunshot signal had ended the searching. They drove off the skunks (theirs is the witness both as to numbers and madness of the animals), then made him a pallet in the wagon, to which they had hitched two saddle horses, and drove their gentle, slow way back to San Saba County and the ghastly certainty.

The old man was delirious, either from the skunks, the lack of food, the fever, or the cold. He roamed his mind out loud, giving them strange orders and preaching to them sermons on times and events they had never witnessed. His old mind, chewed with as keen a tooth as had gnawed his fingers, his ears, and his nose, was living somewhere and sometime else. The sons rode silently, none of them wishing to open his mouth and assume some extra portion of the responsibility for what had happened, yet none wanting to say aloud, "See? See what you have done? If you had listened to me . . ." They admitted this, later, one or two of them. It is easy to imagine the state of the party when at last it raised the cabins and farms of civilization.

He died, Grandpaw Poe, a few weeks later. His end has been described as one of torture and terror, for he regained consciousness (and told his story) even if he never quite recaptured his sanity. But he knew what was before him and he dreaded meeting the inevitable, they said.

Time gets telescoped in the telling of this story (I heard it from my grandmother, his great-granddaughter) and it may cover more days than are here outlined. But my grandmother, telling me the tale, could not seem to blame the old man for the thing that I felt killed him, his obstinacy, his pig-headedness. She seemed to think he had the right to hold this determined attitude, either because she thought stubbornness was natural, therefore God-given, or because he, being an old man and wise in most other ways, had earned some dispensation in those weaknesses he did have. She even implied he had a right to die the way he did, although death was always held to be somewhat sinful on the frontier, I think. It was impractical and a waste. But a man who knew what he wanted, he had that certain right to reach for it.

WE WOULD CALL the lives of my ancestors tragic, reading the bare kind of things that are left to us now about them. I am sure they were not unhappy, except in a sudden way. Tragedy, grief, loss were all a more integral part of living for them than I would accept now. My great-grandmother's life serves as an example of this going from one dark event to the next. Her mother was Paralee Poe, Grandpaw Poe's youngest daughter. Paralee married Sam Dockray (the name was spelled four or five ways), and the tribe he came from was as tough, firm, and hard as the name sounds. Paralee and Sam had two sons, then a daughter, Mary Catherine. She was born in 1861 but never knew her mother because one night when the baby girl was six months old, Paralee Poe Dockray died in her sleep, and the next morning they found her with the baby nursing the cold breast. The cold milk of life was that child's inheritance and there was nothing soft or frivolous about her. She got married at age sixteen to Lytle Craighead, a gentler man than any other in my bloodstream, and began her lifelong career of giving orders to males. She and her young husband moved to the West Texas frontier of Eastland County after her first baby (my grandmother) had been born. Lytle's older brother, Jim, wanted him to come out to that land of milk and honey—although one family legend has it that Jim had gotten involved in the activities of the White Caps, a night-riding group, and wanted more blood-kin near him for protection. Once on the frontier, however, my great-grandmother wasn't very happy with her lot. The young couple moved into a log cabin near what is now Carbon, and one day Mary Catherine was hanging out clothes to dry while a baby daughter, Leeta, was playing on a blanket near the cabin. The mother looked up to see a panther between her and the baby, and without hesitation she ran to the wood pile, grabbed the ax, and killed the beast. I think she must have been softer then, almost a girl, although a wife for four or five years, because she immediately ran into the cabin with her children, after killing the panther, bolted the door and spent the rest of the day crying, refusing to let her baffled husband in when he came back from plowing. She blamed him for taking her to that awful country.

By 1884 the drought had made it impossible for them to keep their own place and Lytle got a job digging wells for a rancher named Warner, who offered to let them live in an old dugout which had been his first headquarters a few years before, in Comanche days. Mary Catherine cautiously entered the half-cave, half-house which was dug into the side of a hill, and discovered that it had become a den for rattlesnakes. She was getting tougher, I suppose, because she is said to have been the one who killed the snakes.

Lytle Craighead must have been a man out of joint with his time. He came from a more educated Sutton inheritance—some of his uncles were professors and doctors. My grandmother (who was nine years old when he died) said he wanted to be a schoolteacher and tried to write poetry at times. This is a damning revelation about a young man attempting to keep a growing family on that ragged edge of West Texas, but I cannot help but love his memory as much as any of that nameless line of ghosts that still walks in my veins. Whatever his weaknesses or his virtues, he was probably the wrong man for Mary Catherine Dockray, for she came of tougher root-stock and hadn't the patience to be mated with an artist—or a dreamer, a word she used throughout life to discredit the males around her who could not perform to her standards. Once she got mad at Lytle because he didn't move quickly enough at her request, and she wrestled a huge barrel of flour from one corner of her kitchen to another. The enormous, impatient effort was too much for her condition and she lost a set of twins, born prematurely that night. Did she blame herself or her husband?

But she loved him, maybe for the very things that frustrated the frontier energy of her soul. He was the only man in all her eighty-five years who brought a romantic word of recollection to her lips, and only a grandson and a great-grandson (not me) later found the carefully guarded soft spots in her heart that hardship left in such scarcity. She and Lytle had six children, but only my grandmother survived past the seventh year. The drought eventually drove Lytle back from West Texas, and he can only be called a failure, insofar as his role as provider and family leader were concerned. But he played the fiddle for her and maybe he even wrote her poetry. And whatever he turned out not to be, there was one thing he was: he was the first—the first love and the first, fearful passion; of whose power she felt the hint but could not understand and could not believe was allowed the male and female of this human race. She learned it just a bit too soon to have had all remembrance driven from her by the stern society around her, but she willed the fear of it to her daughter, and it passed to other daughters, the prospect of love that it is more dangerous than trustworthy, more treacherous than its rewards merit, that it verges on shame if it causes the heart to beat up, the voice to sing or the feet to dance. When the man she loved turned weak (those men of her childhood had not loved, but they had been strong) and therefore unreliable, she decided there was no use for the grander passions in the rougher, firmer ways of life.

SHE WAS STILL in her twenties when Lytle Craighead died. She took her three surviving children back to her father's house in Bell County. Sam Dockray had come out of the Confederate Army and married Martha Wood and they had had seven children, several of whom were still living at home, so four more mouths were too many to feed for long. Her family saw only one solution to the young widow's problem and that was for her to marry a man with enough money to support a ready-made family. Such men were scarce in that narrow society and their choice was Campbell Longley, a bearded old man of seventy-three, who had been widowered a few months before.

Can we imagine what it meant to have the care of three little children in a poor society, and to be young and knowing that you must sell yourself to survive? I suppose it was nothing new, that it must have happened frequently at a time when women had little or no way to make a living except to be someone's wife. My grandmother, talking about her mother's past, said the Dockrays thought old Cam Longley was rich. He had been a boy soldier in the Texas Revolution, joining Sam Houston at San Jacinto, and thus had been given a large (by today's standards) grant of land for his services. He was better known, however, for being the father of William Preston (Bill) Longley, that dark and bloody gunman of the Texas Reconstruction era, who is reputed to have killed thirty-two men before he was finally hanged for keeps the second time. The first attempt had been bungled, or bribed off.

My grandmother probably wasn't fair to the memory of Cam Longley or her Dockray kin, either. Seventy years later she still charged the Dockrays with virtually pandering off their daughter and sister, going to the old man and subtly reminding him how sweet a warm, young woman could be in the bed. His own grown sons and daughters fought the idea of his remarrying with dismay and bitterness. But he was a vigorous, decisive man and memory heated his veins and he got his new wife not many months after her widowhood had begun.

The first thing he tried to talk Mary Catherine into (her daughter said) was sending off her children to an orphan's home. She refused and, the family legend whispers, he tried to poison them. Whatever the cause, two of them died of a vague fever; Leeta, not long after the marriage, and then little Newton, in whom the fires raged for four days and nights while his mother sat mopping him with wet rags. But on the fourth day the boy's eyes burst from his head, the fluid ran out of them, and the cords held the husks of them on his cheeks for two more weeks before he, too, died. My grandmother, a girl who stayed in the oil lamp shadows, fearful and silent, remembered the scene (with horror if not accuracy) all her life.

Mary Catherine left the old man then without ever having slept with him, my grandmother said, although I doubt this. In fact, there is another half-hint, half-story that the young widow had in fact entered into the marriage with the understanding that Cam Longley was too old to want to perform those physical functions of the marriage bed, and that part of her fury toward him came when she discovered how erroneous this assumption was.

I have never seen a good early photograph of my great-grandmother—she was in her sixties when I was born—but she must have been attractive, because her first marriage had been at age sixteen and then with her second, despite her running off from him, the old man came to re-woo his reluctant wife. This second wooing she resisted the pressure of her family to go back to him unconditionally. She told him she wouldn't live with him until he had built her a new house of her own so she wouldn't have to live in the one his first wife had kept. He gave in and, against the opposition of his children, raised the new home on the Lampasas River. She went back to him then, and Longley's son Jim and a grandson moved in with them. It was a bad time. Mary Catherine's brother, John, feeling some late responsibility for his sister, and also hearing that she was being shabbily treated by the Longleys, sent word that should anything happen to her or should she be forced into some relationship she detested, he would ford the river and come gun in hand to straighten things out. Notorious as the Longley name was (although outside Bill the family was known as God-fearing and honest), the Dockray reputation was more than matching in the matter of fierce enmity. John was a big man in size and daring, and my grandmother says she stood around, in that torn household beside the Lampasas, and watched Jim Longley mold bullets so that if John made good his threat the father, son and grandson could battle him off.

Nobody talked about Bill Longley, my grandmother said, but to the people of Bell and Lee counties he was still alive. Because he had cheated death from the rope one time, it was popularly felt that his second hanging could not have been real. There were stories of how a special silver throat piece had been fashioned so that the rope would not choke him to death, or that a shoulder and chest harness had taken the terror out of the gallows' fall, or that the carcass of a hog had been substituted for Bill Longley and buried under his name while he fled south with the connivance of the sheriff. My grandmother saw letters supposedly from Bill in his South American hiding place, but she said the old man had had the letters written to help ease the sorrow of Bill's mother. These letters came even after Cam married Mary Catherine and he showed them to her. Cam had a girl who had married a Mormon (though he and his family were firm Campbellites), and this daughter included Bill's purported letters in her own from Utah when she wrote home. (Years later my grandmother met a woman in Abilene whose father was one of the doctors who pronounced Bill Longley dead when he was hanged, and neither my grandmother nor her Abilene friend had the slightest doubt that his final hanging was effective.)

The unnatural union of a seventy-five-year-old man and a twenty-eight-year-old woman could not be firmed, and Mary Catherine left him for good after their stormy time of some three years together. The old man lived on for nearly twenty more years. It is ironic that from this marriage that was so little a marriage, she eventually gained not only more fame but what was, to her, a measure of financial return. In 1936, as Texas was preparing to celebrate its centennial of independence from Mexico, it was discovered that there were still three women alive who were widows of old Texian warriors and she, Mary Catherine Longley (she went by his name the rest of her life), was one of them. They were brought to Dallas, the site of the Centennial Exposition, and a day was set aside in their honor while the governor, the military, and the whole state did honor to them. My great-grandmother eventually lived to be the last surviving widow of the Texas Revolution and drew a modest pension of twelve dollars per month, as I remember, from the State of Texas for her late husband's services to the Republic of Texas. She was quite proud of this income and referred to it, rather too constantly in the hearing of the rest of the family, as "my money," as though someone were planning to somehow subvert her holdings. I have often wondered why she kept her Longley name for nearly sixty years.

There is also another footnote to her history. In later years she and my grandmother were contacted by some of old Cam's survivors and made friends with them—those stepsons who were older than she was.

Hers was a tough philosophy, I suppose; a philosophy of take what is offered and evaluate few things on the balances of pleasure and happiness. Cam Longley, for all his age and his bedtime notions, his beard, and his meanness, gave her salvation at a point in her life when no one else would. And in later years, when she was known to her church ladies as Granny Longley, the name seemed natural. I could no more think of her as Granny Craighead than I could accept something else for my own name. In fact, I cannot keep from thinking of myself as a Longley, even though there is not a drop of Longley blood in me, because she had such a part in raising me to manhood with the Longley name always there written or spoken.

THERE WAS A GENERATION that ended with the frontier's end although the people of the generation lived on for another fifty or sixty years or more. My great-grandmother was one of them. Born and raised on the raw edge of civilization, she could, by the age of fourteen (when she was considered seriously ready for marriage), make the cloth for anyone's clothes, create food from any raw, natural source, make her own soap, invent household tools from nature, and practice several arts of healing, surgery, and therapy. These were the virtues, the criteria, the necessities of womanhood, and items to which beauty, emotional impact, and artistry bowed. This was what being a good wife, mother, and woman meant.

Yet within a decade, from 1880 to 1890, these things changed so abruptly and so structurally that a great many people of the time—especially the women—were thrown into a kind of cultural shock from which they never regained social or moral orientation. This emphatic change and its dislodgments remain, of course, to haunt the foundations of Texas society. What the women, such as my great-grandmother, had been taught was the essential quality of Womanhood became not just old-fashioned but foolish. Making your own soap, for example, was not only a waste of time but resulted in a less satisfactory product. You were being silly and refusing to help your family if you continued doing it. Therefore, my great-grandmother, although still a young woman when the change swept over them (and it can be, roughly, based on the building of the railroads through West Texas), was never able to adjust her life, although she lived sixty years longer. Her skills became useless and unneeded, but she could not divorce them and their virtues from her values of life. The unprecedented alteration of living, brought about by the introduction of electric lights, the telephone, mercantile retail establishments, self-powered vehicles, and household appliances, was too much for her. Consequently, she regarded them as a threat, as evil in themselves and a trap to destroy her womanhood and the reliability thereof.

She never really learned to use any of them, and she never even tried to adjust her views. The telephone was an instrument for which she had a particular suspicion. Even with the introduction of the cradle headset (which was in the 1930's) she retained her vast antipathy for talking on the telephone. She showed this by reversing the ends of the headset, speaking into the earpiece, and listening, or attempting to, by means of the amplified end. Showing her her mistake did no good (remember that this is Grandpaw Poe's granddaughter), and she insisted it was the nature of the machine rather than her inability to accommodate to it that was the flaw.

She retrogressed, in her seventies. She began to make her own soap first. She had me gather up the proper kind of ashes, then she built her own hopper and thus made her own lye by pouring water through the ashes in it. The soap was made from cooking fat and lard and it was light brown in color and developed a tough rind after being cut into bars. Needless to say, its essential ingredient being uncontrolled lye, it was stout stuff, almost too effective and unthinkable for human skin—except that it had been the soap which cleansed her own human skin most of those early years, therefore the fault was in our skin and not the soap. (The comparative cost of her soap and Oxydol was something of which we did not speak, but it was all in Oxydol's favor.)

She also grew discontented—guilty is the best word, but her discontent never came out as guilt—with the electric iron, and after my Uncle Stub had found an old charcoal iron somewhere on Abilene's South Side, she took to using it for her personal laundry. Here again, there was no comparison in the matter of convenience, efficiency, or cost—the facts were all on the side of electricity—but her contentment at again having a charcoal iron in her hands was probably worth the price.

Granny also made her own yard brooms from the broom weed which was easily found within a block or two of our house. A yard broom dates from those days when bermuda or other cultivated grasses was unknown, and around the cabin there was nothing but hard dirt which was kept clean by sweeping. A bundle of broom weed (which is a tough vegetation that grows up into a clump about two feet high on a single stem) tied around a long stick or an old mop handle did make a suitable broom, but not nearly so useful as the machine-sewn straw broom that was selling at that particular Depression time for about ten cents. Only the fact that she had a young and energetic great-grandson to cooperate with her frontierism kept Granny's projects from soaring into astronomical price figures.

But the final purpose of all this retrogression was not from the spur of economics, poor as we were, but a need to regain what had been a moral position: truly worthy people made their own items, made their own decisions, made their own ways, made (or destroyed) their own lives independently of the rest of society. Thrown out on the frontier, even if a tiny trading post might be only a day's ride or so away, virtue resided in your ability to create to meet needs. Doing things. Thus, Texas today is cursed with this philosophy of the doer as contrasted with the planner, the thinker, the teacher, the moralist in a philosophical way. God helped the man who helped himself; them as can does, them as can't teaches; if you're so damn smart, why ain't you rich? My great-grandmother was not an unfeeling person and was not a materialist insofar as her life-aims were visible to her. But she was so conditioned to the sacredness of productivity, the necessity for sweat in one's labor, the suspect quality of ease, that the total immediate motivation of her acts appeared to be that of a hardhearted, greedy, petty, and mean individual. Fortunately, there were so many like her, these relicts and derelicts of the frontier, that she was far from unique, so I never particularized my dismay on her or felt that her constantly expressed piety was hypocrisy. Just as she would not let her social brother keep her, neither would she attempt to keep her public brother. There was a popular comic panel appearing in many newspapers of that time which was titled "Born Thirty Years Too Soon." In Granny's case, and her whole generation's, it was born sixty years too late. They spent their first twenty-five years or so getting rigid and imperative rules drilled into them, not only for survival but as moral foundations; then for the next sixty or so, depending on how long they lived, they faced the baffling hurricane of change, seeing all their constants shredded by the technical revolution that became to them the degradation of the world.

MY MOTHER'S FAMILY passed on, as its mark, a thin mouth and a narrow upper lip. It makes the one who bears it look like a cold and unresponsive person, on sight, and in fact it operates to turn them into what they look like, because people hesitate to test the physiological legend that thin lips mean cold hearts, and such. Yet I have never found a warmer and more responsive person than my grandmother, Maude Elfie Craighead, who married Ambrose Hutchison Cole and added red hair and wild irresponsibility to contest the dedicated ferocity of our other bloodlines.

I shall not write a great deal about this grandmother who was, in fact, a mother to me because this document is not a story of my life but an exploration of what a region did to me, directly and indirectly. Therefore, because the region of West Texas added, shaped, turned, and tormented my great-grandmother a great deal more than it did her daughter, I have written longer of the older woman who, while influential, was never at all so completely the artist of my future as was my grandmother.

My grandmother fought West Texas. When her father died and her mother remained in the central part of the state to survive, my grandmother turned her back on what was still the frontier and looked east. Adventures she had—she was one of the survivors of the Galveston hurricane of 1900 which was the greatest natural disaster in American history—and achievements she gained, but she went to the woods and damps of Beaumont and the country around there, and for more than thirty years never gave West Texas a thought except to shudder at her memory.

But fate had destined our blood to West Texas, and in 1920 when her son got out of the Navy and World War I, he went to the ancestral stomping grounds, and when her husband, my grandfather, grew too ill to support the family, she reluctantly packed everything and everybody and went back to West Texas, too.

She tried many ways to make money, succeeding mildly in them but never having the competitive soul which drives one past commercial survival to something bigger. Her florist shop was popular and so was she, she so obviously loved what she sold. She operated a hat shop which was the kind of soft, pretty store that never used fashion's iron bar to pry sales from customers. Eventually she gave each of these up because what she was at heart ate at her day and night. She was an artist—an artist of colors and an artist of words. I was too young to have been intimate with details behind the bone fate finally threw her, but I am still glad for it. She was given a job in the Abilene Carnegie Library and in a few years became the head librarian, a job she kept for twenty years. I never knew the time when the library was not my home, or when books were not a topic of our daily bread, the written word was not held with the same care and respect with which a master carpenter holds and guards his saws, levels, squares, and edged tools.

This tall, red-brick, tile-roofed building sat on a

downtown corner of Abilene and in a concrete way was the oasis for intellect in the city. My grandmother had no college degree (although once in a burst of rare insight, her mother had offered to slave out as a washerwoman to raise tuition to Kidd-Key College, a private female institution of the time), but she had that which so many degree-holders lack: a genuine love and response for creativity. She became the center of all the longing, bitter, nervous, pathetic, but emotionally striving movements in that part of West Texas. How many poets, short-story writers, and novelists wrote because they had met her, I would not guess, but with three colleges in Abilene, her contacts with aspiring ambition were multitude. And she believed in her boys (she was partial, always, to the males, although she had two daughters and only one son) and told them they must keep at it, and that they were Given a Gift, and that they had Something to Say.

She encouraged them because she loved them, and as a critic, I am not sure where her competency lay. She liked sweet stories, not so saccharine as Grace Livingston Hill's, perhaps, but certainly not like "that trashy old Hemingway." But here again, she showed a tolerance beyond explanation in that when one of "her boys" brought her a story full of four-letter words and the kind of earthy reality that writing age was laboring so painfully to produce, she read it with an eye to its genius and not to her own morality. When my time came to taste the tingling fruits of literary sex, there were but two books she forbade me to read, putting them in her lockup, a dusty little closet located under the stairway that led up to the children's library. These books were Erskine Caldwell's *God's Little Acre* and one called *Concert Pitch,* whose author I have forgotten; indeed, I never learned anything about the book except I once heard my mother remark to my grandmother that the title "should be spelled with a B," a reference whose implications escaped me then. I waited years to get my hands on a copy of *God's Little Acre*, and it became the first volume I read in the Great Lakes Naval Station library when I finally got safely away from home and West Texas. I was not disappointed with it, although half expecting to be caught while reading the Will Thompson chapter. *Concert Pitch* has eluded me thus far.

Even in a small West Texas town such as Abilene in the twenties and thirties there are lost but talented souls who feed on a manna that does not come down on any Pentateuchal schedule, and the library drew them as magnet and sanctuary. Houston Heitchew was a tall, thin young man (a great-grandson of Sam Houston), and very learned, who tried in vain to scrub the West Texas drawl out of my young voice, keeping me, one summer afternoon, pronouncing the name of the founder of Pennsylvania hour after hour, "Pehnn . . . Pehnn . . ." after he heard me drawl out "Pin" for the name. My payment for scholarly activity was a lime Coke (the first I ever drank) at the Greyhound bus station soda fountain. Houston, alas (why isn't there another word to use for true despair?), was a lost soul of truly deep erudition, doomed to blossom and die, sniffed only rarely by equal genius on our West Texas desert air. His ancestral association not just with the heroic General Sam but with early Abilene days (his grandmother, the general's daughter, had been the first postmistress) was the only thing that kept him from being ridiculed and scorned by his fellow citizens, for he was as outspoken about other people's flaws of learning, speech, or grammar as he was about his more literary opinions. Worthy of the keenest kind of competition he could have found, Houston came to an unexpected and tragic end at a young man's age by his own hand without having ever tested his scholarly equipment on anything but Abilene.

Eddie Anderson, a reporter on the Abilene *Morning News,* was our author in residence at the library, for he was working on The Novel. Eventually he wrote The Novel and for a while he looked like he might join Steinbeck and the others who were discovering a deep, sad America for us, but now I search in vain for copies of *Hungry Men* and *Thieves Like Us.* And Francis Finberg put out a poetry journal called *Harlequinade;* and two old sisters spent eight or nine hours a day writing constantly in small, blue notebooks for years, and when my grandmother inadvertently found one and read it, she discovered the sisters were copying down, an entry at a time, the *Encyclopaedia Britannica.* And Judge Bentham, who was no judge at all but a tiny little man who sat around on park benches and talked learned nonsense, used to come in every morning in his threadbare gray herringbone overcoat (summer and winter) with newspapers in the soles of his shoes, demanding to be told just why the Abilene Carnegie Library didn't subscribe to the *Wall Street Journal* so he could keep up with his stock holdings. After a couple of years my grandmother did subscribe and Judge Bentham was as good as his word and devoured every line of what was at that time the dullest, most indecipherable publication available for anyone not deeply in the market—as Judge Bentham never was, of course.

The library to her was a special place, guarded with special attitudes and splendid in its flexibility. I don't suppose my grandmother ever disbelieved in anyone. Once, reading Thornton Wilder's novel about a traveling book-salesman, *Heaven's My Destination,* she came on a chapter which had several narrative references to Abilene and one long passage about how the anti-hero of the book, George Brush, had come into the Abilene Carnegie Library, taken down the *Encyclopaedia Britannica* (using a volume not drafted on by one of the sisters, I presume) and by the entry on Napoleon Bonaparte had written in the margin, "I am a great man, too. But for good."

My grandmother ran immediately to the reference room, took down the volume containing NAP-, and was dismayed to find nothing written or erased in the margin. She then thought that a couple of years before she had been allowed to buy a new set of *Britannica* and had been able to prevail on the board to let her give the old one to the Negro library of Abilene instead of letting some board member's son-in-law or nephew have it. My grandmother called the Negro librarian and had her look up NAP-, but Thornton Wilder had played her false. He had made the whole thing up. Her disappointment was not in Wilder's having written it but in his having never done it; to her it seemed so appropriate a thing for a writer to have done as a gesture toward fate.

She would not be a good librarian today, and I would be the first to admit it. The growing demands of the library-science schools and training hurt her because she sensed that every young, well-trained girl with a library-science degree whom she brought into the library was looking down her nose at her because she lacked formal training which extended past the Dewey Decimal System. But my grandmother was perfect for her time and her place. She matched the minds with the words, and if she inspired dozens of writers, artists, and poets, she must have opened a new country to thousands of others whose only talent was to read. She knew what her books contained and she had that motherly knack for directing her customers to just the right bins. Information retrieval, audio-visual departments, stereo loan services were things she never had to face but couldn't have handled had they come in her time. But somewhere in her prairie mold, somewhere in the bank of genes which reached back into dark time for their father, was the native seed of intellectual dependence which saw the world not as a place to get, but as a place to give. The spark skipped many generations—so many that I am not able to find its duplicate in the ages of ours that I know. I just thank God, if I may be forgiven a certain sentimentality at this point, that it flamed to life so near mine.

THE TREE-SHADED, wide-eaved old Carnegie Library was torn down many years ago and one of our stark glass and concrete boxes (no trees allowed near) erected in its place. Even the name was dropped, Andrew Carnegie's gift having been observed for fifty years, as per contract, and it became the Abilene Public Library. (Carnegie, for all his money, could have remained much more immortal in most of his Texas towns, at least, if he had founded a local bank or been a weak-minded mayor.) A large staff works in air-conditioned competency there, and even city hall, which used to balk at a $1,200 a year book budget, seems cognizant of the need of the city's image for such a civilized place—although I don't want to give city hall too much credit; only a few years ago the library was closed two days a week to save money.

But when I go to the "new" library, I am overwhelmed with nostalgia as I am in no other spot from my beginning. I cannot stay long without wanting the old back. It was so perfect in its setting, so declarative of its intent, so persuasive of its purpose. I am inclined to preserve rather than erect new, I will admit, but most of the time I can rectify public need and my own wishes. Except here. The destruction of the Abilene Emergency Hospital was painless to me, except in a slight historical way, and when some new owner moved my grandmother's house at 3118 South Seventh Street away, I didn't flinch. I can still go by the duplex on Vine Street, or the cottage on Sammons Avenue without worrying about who owns them now or what takes place within the walls that confined parts of my boyhood. Downtown Abilene was scoured of all historical interest late in the fifties, in a costly program (which proved to be misguided) that widened the already wide streets, tore down all the old original town, and erased any landmarks or architectural beauty that had survived their frontier beginnings. But this, too, proved not so traumatic as I might have thought, going back and seeing the unfamiliar, rather dull, and definitely dead downtown. It is so changed and so without charm that I cannot relate the "was" with the "is," therefore, I am unattached.

But the loss of the old Carnegie Library building is still hurtful, and I can replace every red brick, put back every roof tile and deep, wide window in my mind. From the low spot where the original water-supply cistern had been to the cellar door, from the unused coal chute to the cornerstone at the southeast corner, from the red dirt of the unfinished basement to the old auditorium on the second floor with its midnight-blue velvet curtains, I can re-erect the place with much more precision than I can recall the parts of anything that has replaced it.

And all the people who were in it through those years. Mr. H. Lilius—Hjalmer being too hard for West Texas to pronounce, so he went by only "H"—the old Swede who was the first custodian. He had come to Eagle Cove colony in the Abilene country before there was an

Abilene, and I can hear his accented voice as he worked his brush in the hot glue pot, rebinding books or putting new spine strips on them, dipping a pen in thick, white ink and lettering the titles and Dewey Decimal System numbers on them, telling about what it had been like. Once a baby child of his died, and he had to make a coffin. Then, as he finished the coffin, a band of Comanches appeared and began circling his cabin, one of the rare log cabins in that part of West Texas. Until he finally went out with the dead child in its box, and knowing no tongue to communicate with them (not even English, for he was too new to America), he lifted it up in his arms and held it for them to see. And they rode off leaving him unmolested, seeming to sense what he held.

And all the pretty young women who worked there (for it was more than just socially acceptable to work at the library), Emily and Gladys and Ruth and Helen—grandmothers now, themselves. And Miss Anne, the night and Sunday librarian (it was years before I realized she had a last name, Shelton) who worked there longer than anyone did, even my grandmother, but whose sole literary fare was mystery stories. Plus a dozen others whose names I can recall along with some memories not so pleasant (for there was bickering and there were those lazy and incompetent ones, too), and there was, looming over my childhood memories like an unscalable peak, the Board. It met once a month in the reference room and was composed, for the most part, of dowager ladies. The library had been founded by the women's clubs, and their petition had been what moved Andrew Carnegie (or his secretary) to dispense the modest sum (by today's standards) it took to build the structure. So the Carnegie Library, while nominally a municipal function, was controlled by this semiprivate group. Because my grandmother was not a strongly assertive woman, and during the Depression was so grateful for a job that she accepted several deep wage cuts without a protest, the Board held (in her mind) power of life and death over her, renewable every third Thursday of the month. She died a thousand deaths the four days prior to those meetings, convinced each month she would be fired. (Male voices used to call my grandmother on the phone, during those dismal economic times, and rebuke her for "taking money away from a man" because she was a woman holding a magnificent eighty-dollar-per-month job. If they had known, she was more than half the time supporting two other families on that salary.) I could recite every name from that awesome Board, except that after I became an adult I discovered they were not nearly so fierce and unyielding as I had grown up thinking; and when I met Mrs. McDaniel (who had been elected permanent president of the Board) years later, and she was approaching ninety, she turned out to be a perfectly wonderful old lady with a marvelously youthful view of life and a matching memory, full of stories about frontier Abilene and her father, Colonel Parker, who weighed more than three hundred pounds but was a dandy, and reportedly had built (of zinc and rosewood) the first bathtub in town. She showed me a clipping from the Abilene *Reporter* of her wedding, which had taken place in 1891; and Clarence Dillon, who became the renowned financier, was her flower boy.

How could I have wanted for a roomier boyhood mansion than a Carnegie Library?

MY MOTHER MET my father as she was crossing a footbridge in front of the old Abilene High School. She said she thought, at that first meeting, he was the biggest show-off she had ever seen. I am sure that if she could have been interviewed on the last day of her life, after forty-two years of marriage to him, she would have said the same thing.

My mother inherited all the wrong parts of her past to ever be unconcernedly happy. From her grandmother, Mary Catherine, she got a dour and pessimistic outlook as well as an inability to accept physical love or emotions as a normal part of life. Secretly romantic, she could never equate affection—especially on the part of her husband—with true love. She wanted to hold people close to her but not touch them.

She was an intelligent woman who learned quickly almost anything she set out to do, but she mistrusted the intellect and contemplation. She was a puritan whose salvation was labor, and the only warmth God allowed men and women was the flush of hard work, the sweat of enterprise. Yet work, too, was a curse. It took her years to accept the fact that a man could love his occupation and not be doing something sinful. You were not supposed to enjoy a job. It was a matter of doing your best and making the most—but not dedicating yourself to what you were doing. She was amazed that her oldest son, by doing nothing more strenuous with his hands than poking his fingers at a keyboard, not only survived but was welcomed in polite society—a social situation she considered reserved for ministers and CPA's.

She and my father married on their birthdays—they were both born on August 24. It was her sixteenth and his twentieth year. If it were not so foreign to the woman I knew, I would attribute this romantic deliberation to romance—this joining their common birthdates into a marriage. (Later they had a son, my only brother, David, born on the same date.)

I was born a few months after my mother's seventeenth birthday. It seemed to me, of course, the ordinary thing to have such a young mother, and when I started to school I wondered why all the other mothers at PTA meetings were so elderly. The farther along I got in school the more bewildered my teachers were to come face to face with this girl who said she was the mother of this lanky, intensely inquisitive boy. She had quit school in her first year of high school and rued it the rest of her life, inclining to blame my father for her foolish decision, although admitting she did it to get from under the domination of her older brother. But even without a high-school education, she appreciated certain accomplishments; she had me repeating "The Owl and the Pussy Cat" at age two from memory and she never tried to stop me from reading what I chose, when I got into the book world.

She was innately quick-witted (not witty, however, because humor left her totally unmoved unless it was slapstick or housewives describing their husbands' discomforts) and was a genius at basic financing. My father, who suffered more from this talent than anyone else, although none of us escaped, used to say she could squeeze a nickel (of that era) "until the Indian was riding the buffalo and the buffalo was down to a jackass." Saving money, both as an economy and as an investment, was a frenzy with her. The rate of interest was unimportant, only the balance in her name made sense.

Her views of sex were straight from the frontier by way of a Campbellite brush arbor. Interest between the sexes was something to be endured for a purpose, and it had no more to do with love than lipstick did with kissing. When I started going with girls and proved not to have this archaic slant on the male-female relationship, she told me, in a matter-of-fact way, that she certainly hoped I knew what I was doing, enjoying things like that, because she never had seen any point to it.

But she was a good mother, warmer than I have drawn and more generous than one might suppose. She weighed everything, it is true, but she was content with little in return. Her main drawbacks as a person were from the circumstances of her life, I am convinced. Had she not quit school and married so young, had she not been born and rigorously reared in strict religious fundamentalism, had she lived in some other part of the country, had she been the daughter of a wealthy family, had she not married my father—the list is long and maybe beside the point, but I feel she could and probably would have been a female for the history books. Within limits, for she could never have been a Mata Hari or a Madame de Pompadour, but with reasonable chance, for she knew how to use whatever she had, whether materials at hand or spiritual and mental resources, and she had a zeal for order and control.

My father was her cross, when he could just as easily have been made her slave, for he was a man whose life was dedicated to pleasing women. Poor man, his wife, whom he was legally dedicated to pleasing, could not ever be pleased with anything he did. Christmas morning was a constancy of tears and recriminations that he had spent too much on her, got the wrong size, or bought something too frivolous—that is, too feminine—for her to conscientiously wear. And if he dared venture to please some other woman (which he constantly tried) her suspicions and alarms were set to jangling. He had no daughters, which was probably an act of God after due consideration, and all he was alloted for his granddaughter was two years, but he strove hard to make up for the lost chances in that time.

His family had not come to West Texas until the frontier was gone past and the settling was over, which is why I have said little of that side of my family past. But there were traits in them that would have made wonderful frontiersmen—a recklessness in the face of danger of any kind, physical or spiritual, a dogged loyalty to a friend or leader, generosity so far beyond the demands of Christian duty or obligation that among people who knew them it was a warm legend, and a high and unrestrained gusto for laughter and the joke. Jim Hopkins, an acquaintance, once combined the latter two qualities by going in to my father's little picture-framing shop one afternoon and asking him for his shirt.

"Carl," he said worriedly, "I've got to have a shirt like the one you've got on, and I've got to have it quick." My father looked more puzzled than hesitant, but Jim (who was also a man of unbounded humor at any time) hurried him up, "Come on, Carl. I can't answer questions. I've got to have that shirt." By the time he finished talking, my father was unbuttoning his collar, taking off the work apron he wore, and stripping his torso. Jim Hopkins actually let him get it all the way off before he burst into laughter and ran out to report it.

But people liked my father for this kind of unquestioning openhandedness. As Jim pointed out in telling the story to me, if he had been a complete stranger, "Old Carl would have come out of that shirt just as quick."

My father was capable of losing his temper, however, especially when he was younger. He, too, dropped out of high school because he felt put upon at home. He got a job driving an ice wagon and if my mother hadn't put ambition in him would probably have endured as long as iceboxes did, for the housewives to whom he delivered loved him above all other service men. (Forty years later he could drive down the older streets of Abilene and tell me exactly what kind of ice chest each house had had and how much ice each one took.)

Except for marrying my mother, my father would

probably have gone to hell in a hack, as West Texas said. He had no restraints against persuasion except stubbornness. Yet he was able to exercise a marvelous kind of self-control when he got interested in doing so. When I was a teen-aged boy he walked in one day with a half-empty package of Lucky Strike cigarettes and announced he was through smoking. The pack lay on top of his bureau for nearly a year before my mother threw it away and I do not believe he ever took another puff of a cigarette—a matter of nearly thirty years. Another time, much later in life, he was told that he needed to lose weight, and he promptly quit eating and slimmed down by twenty pounds, not on a diet or through controlled regimen but just by not eating. But these applications of self-control didn't work when it came to a friend's hard-luck story or a smile or tear from a woman. My mother never did know the true state of his finances because he had a quiet deviousness about money that defied even her steel-trap economy. I wish he could have made several thousand dollars some year (I don't believe he ever topped the $4,500 mark). I would like to have seen him confound the Internal Revenue Service. Having confounded Johnny Marie Greene for so long, Uncle Sam's agents would have been scarcely any obstacle at all to his confusing reactions to direct questions about his cash.

But the senses battled continually with a set of artificial morals clamped over him while he was too young to reason or humanize his way out. He considered himself a true sinner because of the things he allowed in his heart. As a boy I could never understand his sad degradation of himself; as a man I knew why but could not accept it. He confused the deed with the thought, and he took the New Testament literally when it warned about lusting in the heart being the same thing as performing the act. He could not grasp the subtlety implied by this approach, and he let hypocritical men (who were in reality the targets for that verse) treat him as being lesser than they were because he had the openness to expose his flaws. This, of course, was in keeping with both West Texas and the level of society on which he lived all his life. He was a captive of an inhuman system which punished a man for existing, more than it punished him for actually breaking the code.

His goodness was not spectacular, his flaws were visible from some distance, his mind was excellent but untrained and untamed, and his weaknesses were vast and constant. But at his death hundreds of persons whom I did not know and whose acquaintance with him was limited to a few business encounters, told me he was the most likable man they had ever met on short terms—although the more candid ones added that meeting him was never a thing of short terms because he was also the biggest talker they had ever met. I have often wished I could have known my father as a friend rather than just a father.

So THOSE are the ropes of blood and human time that reach down and up and back into unknown territories of inheritance for me. That they came to West Texas and there met events in their way is, I contend, more than a coincidence of history. It has happened before in other places and to other people, but I am examining one place and one person.

Something is held in common by all of us, going beyond where we stand, going above what we are composed of, compacting all our histories into any human history. The events and changes of our lives are only the surface for the deeper human history that is held in common and that has operated in each of us in identical ways. The medicine bottle serves as illustration, with its ninety-five per cent inert vehicle, even in the most powerful antibiotic, and its two or three per cent active ingredient that makes it different, powerful, effective, or dangerous. We all share the vehicle, whether we are one kind of human or another. In a sense, we all share fathers and mothers, we share pasts and places. Only the future is different for every man, and it is different only in his hopes or wishes.

16

Bring Me to . . .

It is a cold, lonesome day outside the motel window. I am alone and very near the end of my journey, here in this room that is neither mine nor the next traveler's, this room that is reproduced in a hundred thousand other rooms for hire. It is a minimum world, put together as much as possible to keep the mind and body from unwanted response.

The landscape matches the room's disinterested qualities. To the north, beyond the highway and railroad tracks, are low, unidentified warehouses, hiding among their sandy brown surroundings. Looking south, through the parted curtains over the picture window, there is a monotony of colorless residency, sun-bleached houses whose pale walls and roofs insinuate the neutrality they shelter.

This is the edge of Abilene, the edge of every Southwestern town. Even the name of the motel is anonymous in its countless repetition in uncounted places. Remembering is almost cut off by sameness, but not quite, for even as I stand and stare into the uneventful distance, I search the past involuntarily, and find some part of me that is on every acre of this country. This spot, I tell myself, wedged uncomfortably between two wide, swift highways, compounded about by faceless suburban fences, was once part of the Maker brothers' airport. From a north-south runway, which must have extended very near to where the motel stands, I took off on my first airplane flight. This instant identification comes wherever I am in West Texas. It is not simple nostalgia, it is constant reorientation, an assurance, perhaps, that I am not lost or dead.

I feel that the important thing is not so much to know a city or a region, nor even to understand the people in it or react to its history. The important thing is to find all of them in you. If you can thus explain to yourself the causes of an anxiety, the basis for a decision, if you can form a solid understanding beneath your life, no matter what kind of tossing back and forth that life takes, then you may have gained a double birthright that transcends the inheritance of goods or of gentility. Perhaps it is because I had less of these to inherit that I must find an inheritance in the land, its climates, seasons, flowers, beliefs, and its people—especially its people and what they have done on it and what it has done to them.

There are persons in whom this regional relationship is unnecessary, I suppose; persons who, by a wandering or unstable history, have come to put their continuum in the tribe or some moral tradition. For other individuals there are family histories so strong and exclusive that geography is created or destroyed by the presence or absence of their blood-kin.

And there are fewer and fewer persons who must go back, as I have done, to find something in a region and all its associations. The point in doing so may well be questioned today. Not only can one not go home again, in the social sense, but there are fewer and fewer natives left to make the return trip. We identify with our ambitions; we function with our chosen class. We still use the phrase "the outside world" in a social sense, but in reality it has an increasingly diminishing meaning. West Texas is one of the few places where it still retains some salt.

IN THE MOTEL coffee shop someone waits for me to join him, an old friend who remained in West Texas when I left. Once, long before, when I was reluctant to turn loose of the past and my love for this land, he had urged me to break away. His argument was not against West Texas or the people and their mores, but against my binding myself to this place and these doctrines. But he could not take his own advice, even though we knew he was speaking to himself as much as to me when he was assembling his reasons. So he had stayed, tied by certain roots I did not share, under bond to commitments from which I was free. In staying he gave up his chance at the dice. He needed a broader world of men, he needed tolerance for personality, he needed freedom of experimentation. These things are hard to find under the West Texas tradition. You may be born with them or, in even fewer cases, you may create alternatives to them which function as the other side of the coin, but mainly you fly in the face of happiness when you persist in the unorthodoxy implied in these acts. He stayed and now I knew, walking across the wind-swept open courtyard between my room and the restaurant, we would have to talk of two worlds, and mine would be of little importance to him, while his would be sad history to me.

But I did not come back to West Texas to discover failure or to congratulate time for delivering me. I did not examine the past just to find what flaws I might have escaped or to bolster my life's intentions. I came to find myself, or that part of me that seemed to be missing or undefined after I had made my own changes of time and place. What is this thing of finding oneself? Why need to seek to know?

I would lay it to that vast insecurity that is within each of us as humans. What we cannot know we will mythify in our long search for identity. Learning the ways of nature, the ways of men, and the ways of our past creates in us a harmony that reveals our own ways to us. And perhaps, in the end, its real value is not only to make us do what we have to do in life but to understand that we are going to have to do it. If nothing else, learning to know ourselves through where and when and who we have been teaches us to endure our share of the common iniquity, because we discover how very much of it everyone else is sharing.

THE LAST FEW MILES, now, to the heart of something that will have to end questing.

From the motel I drive on an old-new street that, for me, cuts time into many pieces. It is called South First, and from my birth it has been part of the road home or the road out. Going into downtown Abilene it crosses Elm Creek, at the spot where Will Watson took me, sixty-five years later, to show me the location of a vanished brickyard where he worked in the 1890's off-loading brick. When we got out of the car to walk along the creek bank we found, miraculously preserved, row on row of those old handmade bricks which had survived the decades after the kilns and yard were abandoned. (Two weeks after our discovery a bulldozer ended the sixty-five-year miracle in one swift scoop, preparing that piece of soil to receive a pancake house.)

Some buildings seem to survive because they are so worthless. Farther on the road to town is still standing a sheet-iron structure that housed a wrecking yard in the thirties, and one Sunday as we started for a pleasure drive in the 1928 Nash my family owned, Aunt Gerty and I discovered the gearshift lever had simply pulled itself up by the roots from the floorboards. My aunt is not the female mechanic type, but finding herself with a gearshift assembly in hand, the broken piece in plain sight, a car that wouldn't move, and a disappointed young nephew, she decided on the drastic maneuver of taking our imperfect contrivance to a wrecking yard and seeing if someone couldn't replace it. We walked from South Seventh down to South First and found this little place open, which was not unusual in the thirties when everyone was willing to stay open on Sunday if it meant a chance sale. The operator searched among the wrecked, scrapped, and always dilapidated automobile carcasses, and came up with a shift which, while not from a Nash, appeared to have the same mechanical characteristics. We took it back home, agreeing to pay for it if it would fit, and my delicate little aunty unbolted the plates, repositioned the new gearshift, tested it for efficiency, and, after an hour or less, screwed down the cover for a final fit. It worked perfectly, save for the fact that the new shift lever itself was straight and our Nash lever had been curved. For the next two or three years it worked and it was working when the car was finally traded off. I have never heard of anything else Aunt Gerty ever fixed.

As I approach downtown there is another building that survives, the W.O.W. Hall, in a large block of brick structures now in a generally dilapidated condition, but swarming with recollection.

When I was two years old my mother began playing the piano for the Woodmen Circle women's drill team. The ladies wore white uniform dresses and carried

wooden spears with gold-painted tips. The officers had billed military caps of white and bore their rank in gold lettering on wide sashes draped across their chests from one shoulder. Everything was done quite seriously, and smiling in ranks during drill was taken as a sign of moral giddiness. My own sash read MASCOT, and in one of those long, narrow, group photographs made with a slowly rotating camera, you can spot me at the very end of the front row, looking curious but uncomfortable in my little, white satin pants which, in all the excitement, I have obviously wet.

The drill team practiced in a long, drafty upstairs hall in this brick building on South First. The hall was used by several other organizations during the week, and

I remember the Ku Klux Klan insignia usually was left in place behind the podium. My grandmother, who was a drill captain, always wrestled it off in a corner out of sight because she didn't approve of the KKK, remembering the White Cap night-riders of her girlhood. (The KKK died quickly in Abilene in its 1920's revival, killed by the courage of Editor Frank Grimes.) In later years I was dejected to discover the Woodmen Circle was primarily a scheme to sell life insurance. I had truly thought it was on a level with church.

Beneath the drill hall was located the Laughter Funeral Parlor. I could not understand the amazed response from travelers (South First was the main east-west highway through Abilene) who saw the sign. Even Robert Ripley used the Laughter Funeral Parlor name in *Believe It or Not*. I took it for granted everyone realized it was pronounced *Law*-ter and had nothing to do with mirth.

The bus station was also under the drill hall, and the concept of adventure was born in me when I went up the side stairs and was able to look down on the heavy, square-radiatored buses with the piles of luggage strapped to their tops, black leather seats for the passengers, an imitation observation deck on the rear end, and two spare tires mounted beside the engine. I learned to read a few of the destination signs on the buses and gained an imperishable interest in geography from those drill-hall visits. (For some reason, however, my true affections and my historical interests have always been wrapped up in railroads—which is a poor way to repay the Sunset Stages and West Texas Coach Lines, I suppose.)

On the street behind the bus station and the drill hall was J. E. Taylor's wagon yard. Country people still traveled in wagons a good deal, and many farm families parked the wagon and team in the yards all day Saturday when they came into town to do their weekly or monthly shopping. There was even some inter-city travel by wagon and team, and it was exciting, but not at all uncommon, to see a covered wagon or two pulling out South First early in the morning, headed for New Mexico or some remote, far West Texas ranch. Abilene had at least one other accommodation that I remember well, the O.K. Wagon Yard at North Fourth and Pine. I suffered precocious remorse (because a five-year-old shouldn't have that sense of historical loss, I flatter my memory) when it was torn down later in the twenties so that Conrad Hilton, then purely a Texas operator, could erect a hotel on the site.

Animal power was very important in the Abilene of that day, although I had to remind myself of this by reading a few yellow issues of the *Reporter* and the *Morning News* before my recollections came flowing back. All the city work-vehicles and earth-moving equipment were pulled by mules and most of the delivery wagons around town were horse-drawn. There was another profession that has disappeared—the plowmen who drove a horse and wagon around town, doing odd-job plowing or harrowing or maybe operating a fresno to level up a front yard. They would unhitch their horse or mule, leave the wagon sitting in the street, put a plow (usually a Georgia stock) in its place, and set to work with a great deal of clanking, slapping of harness, and talk to the animals. The freshly cut earth would peel away from the moldboard, the crushed winter grass would give off a sudden aromatic odor—or combine with the musk of the opened earth—and the heavy labor of man, plow, and beast would simply bring another kind of world into my back yard. It was something of a status symbol among young boys to have someone plowing at your home. My great-grandmother, those springs when she could afford the dollar or so, always had herself a garden plowed for turnips, Swiss chard, okra, black-eyed peas, field corn (for roasting ears), and tomatoes, which she would not allow to ripen but would pick green for chowchow. A second or third cousin, as we referred to all imprecise collateral kin, of my father's, an extremely fat man named Walter Flanagan, was the last of these plowmen I can recall in Abilene. For years he wore an old, brown felt hat with an immensely tall crown and a ragged brim which gave him instant identification with me. (He always called my father "Titten," which was a very early family nickname. My father would never admit how he came by it.)

Abilene is split almost equally by the T&P Railway running through it east and west. When I was a youngster this sectionalism of North Side and South Side was most pronounced, particularly as applied to the divided business sections. When a person wanted to get hold of some esoteric rural product or maybe pick up a pair of khaki pants or a secondhand shovel, he would go over on the South Side to shop. The South Side was the "country" part of town and contained most of the feed and grain stores, with their marvelous dusty, sweet smells, the wool and hide warehouses, the big farm-implement firms, the hock shops, whorehouses, hamburger and chili parlors, questionable medical services, and third-run picture shows where, on Saturday afternoons, the farm women would send their little kids down to the front to pee because they didn't want to be bothered getting up and taking them to the restrooms. There were a number of barbershops which catered to the farm and ranch trade and were from a dime to two-bits cheaper than their North Side competitors. When I was in high school if you showed up with a particularly atrocious barbering job—say a "white sidewall" that lifted your hair an inch or more above the ears—someone was sure to make the snobbish remark that "you must be getting your haircuts over on the South Side." I had to use a South Side barber for years because he actually cut hair for fifteen cents a head. I only left the South Side when haircuts in general went to thirty-five cents. (An Abilene barber of the North Side variety, got on the state board of licensing for barbers and forced all the shops in town to come up to the price in his establishment—which, in Texas, is why you have state boards and why you get on them, in case you are interested.) The South Side barbershops were the real thing. The biggest one, Mr. Nisbett's, next door to the Oddfellows Building on South Second, had three bath tubs in the rear for cowboys to use and was patronized by a very manly strain of customers. Waiting for a chair, you sat around on wooden benches with tall mirrors at their backs and hat and coat racks at the ends. The reading matter was *True Detective* and Western pulps. One of my landmarks of maturity was the day when the barber started to get a board to put over the chair arms so as to elevate me up to his scissors and the boss of the shop said to him: "That boy don't need the board. He's big enough to sit up in that chair like a man." Another landmark came a few years later when, at about age twelve or thirteen, I entered that same shop while my Uncle Stub was being worked on and addressed him, of course as "Uncle Stub." He waited until after I had finished getting my haircut and took me to one side. "Don't call me 'Uncle Stub' in here any more, A.C. I do a lot of trading with these men that hang out in here and it makes me sound older than I am to have a big thing like you call me 'Uncle.' From now on just call me 'Stub.' "

There were quite a few thousand people from all over Taylor and Jones counties who headed for the South Side as soon as they hitched their teams or got off the

Abilene & Southern train (that had its depot on the South Side). The North Side was just too sophisticated for these folks. Besides, over there the stores displayed women's underwear right out in the front windows. It made them uneasy.

PINE WAS the glory street of Abilene. The streetcar line came down it, the corner of Pine and North Second was the hub of the world, and it had traffic lights. You turned north off South First, crossed the T&P (unless a freight train was blocking the way, which, until an underpass was dug in 1936, was usually the case), and it reached thirty or so blocks in front of you. Most of the streets in Abilene were wide, because the town planners, for once, weren't greedy when it came to planning thoroughfares, but Pine was the widest of them all. And it was always congested—at least, inasmuch as congestion was a problem in that day and time. My most embarrassing moment behind the wheel of an automobile came at an early age (you could drive at age fourteen then in Texas), when my grandmother's new Nash, the only brand-new car anyone in my family had ever purchased, had a vapor lock just as the 5 p.m. traffic started behind me through the Pine Street underpass. Honking drivers were stacked up for three or four blocks, for while Pine was wide, the turnouts from the underpass were single-lane, and everyone leaving town seemed to be turning the same way I had been turning. Some Good Samaritan rescued me by pouring a cold Dr. Pepper over the fuel line where bad engineering had passed it too close to the hot engine-block. (A vapor lock forms when gasoline in the fuel line vaporizes and will not pass into the carburetor.) That Samaritan told me to clip clothespins to the fuel line to keep it from vapor-locking, but this didn't seem to work with that Nash, and the car continued to sputter to a halt with that same affliction at the most crucial traffic occasions.

North on Pine Street, Abilene's business section came to a halt at North Seventh. It had already thinned out considerably by North Fifth. This was where on alternate years, the marching soldiers in the Armistice Day parades used to turn. (Parades used two routes so as to please all the merchants.) Beyond North Seventh the street was spattered with residences. Turning east off Pine at North Seventh you descended the social and economic scale rapidly until by a block or two you had come to the northern end of a mixed Latin and Negro community. But this was an important road, used daily by more white persons than any other class, so it was kept sprinkled by the city water-wagon; then, with later progress, it was paved.

It goes east for four more blocks and comes to a long line of woven-wire fence and hedge. This is the south end of the old Abilene cemeteries, the City, the Masonic, and Cedar Hill. This corner, at the southwest, contains the forgotten dead whose demise came during the time when Abilene was attempting to survive its first year. One small tombstone is for a little girl named Abilene who had been born a few days before the town-lot sale in 1881 and, I suspect, was the first child born on the site.

The cemeteries (now owned by the city although still carrying the old names) stretch north for several blocks and contain shaded roadways and long lines of variously marked and memorialized graves. And having reached this place, the end of my journey is in sight.

THE OLD Masonic Cemetery used to be entered through a tall, iron gate with a pierced metal sign that stretched over the passageway. An open wooden shelter stood in the middle of a circle where buggies could pull up to let the women sit out of the sun or rain during a graveside service.

The Masonic and City cemeteries are old, as old as the town, and the headstones are curiously carved, many imposing in that way of magnificence no longer considered appropriate to mark the dead. Over some of the old plots there are big shade trees, live oaks, pecans, elms, and cottonwoods. Even in the summer-time it is cool and peaceful, the locusts and cicadas alone to sing and disturb the day, chirring loudly, then letting their sound fall away softly to an echo.

Merchant, Steffens, Lowden, Radford, Alexander, Pearre, Wooten, Minter, Sayles . . . the names call softly from gray stone to remember their history. The evidences of man.

On a shelf in my office, far away from West Texas but still lying where I emptied my pockets, are a dozen objects I had picked up from a day of walking over the land. Evidences.

A large piece of flint, as big as a man's open hand, shows the unmistakable signs of human endeavor; crudely chipped ridges, a roughly beveled forward edge, and a long, almost random grip which cleverly fits snugly up between the thumb and forefinger in that little saddle of the hand.

It is a brownish piece, with a heavy layer of patina over it, showing that skillful ancestor to be more ancient by several millennia than whoever it was that carefully chipped the little flint scraper that lies beside it. Of that scraper, there is little hesitation in assigning it to human use, for it is a triangle with razorish edges, the work of much more patience and technique than the crude, fearsome hammerhead.

Beside these flints are three square nails, one with precise sides from having spent its century or so in the heart of a wooden plank, the others rusted and pitted from lying atop the ground to feel the torch of God knows how many summers.

Two triangles of bottle glass, broken and softened by the white lime of countless rains, merciless suns, and turning years, one thick, tapering to a badly made thinner side (the flaw that broke it?), the other retaining a tiny jagged parapet as evidence it formed the bottom of a bottle.

And then an odd, bronze contrivance with a ceramic tip, alien to my eyes but obviously some artisan's craft, with words sunk into the rounded half-moon of yoke that rides a short, threaded pipe: BRAY'S LUTA.

What does all the junk and trash of my pocket mean? Evidence of what?

Nothing at all, or everything. The stuff of time and man in it. The hand-ax is from a remote, wordless age, made by a man who probably came to the land with the mammoths, hunting the black, hairy herds across the same acres I walked. The more carefully chipped and honed scraper, from some red man following the later buffalo, almost a part of our own time, in comparison to the hand-ax fellow.

And the bottle glass came with the white buffalo hunters who followed the herds so relentlessly that only a few winters and both hunter and hunted were gone, leaving mostly the broken shards to mark the places where their camps and sudden cities erected themselves, sold, bartered, and died in the space of a season.

The nails meant permanence. We know what hammer blows sunk these rough-cut steel pieces into the rawhide lumber, and we know they meant them to remain.

The piece of bronze pipework is civilization of a kind

we understand and define all civilization by, for this was light in a literal way, being part of the jet system of a carbide light, glowing, hissing, spewing brilliance to blind the rider who stumbled in out of the dark, standing sheepishly with a forearm over his eyes to protect them from the new nighttime sunlight.

And the whispers from the gray stones.

These objects are West Texas. Pieces of time. None of them is rare or historic or of much interest—even the stone hammer and the flint scraper are common. There are thousands of them scattered over the face of West Texas, not quite alike, of course, for they are the products of a thousand different hands, but common enough so that one takes them home and gives them to young sons or nephews instead of museums.

Chips of time, floating up from the ground, left by man to remind the earth that he once owned it. Never relinquishing his claim, the hand-ax there to witness, the flint scraper saying an Indian name we cannot pronounce but hear, the broken liquor bottles laughing through time, those nails that put up doors and walls and rafters to last forever, the brass with its white flame and its lettering. And the gravestones. Every one of the owners thought he would never part with what he owned, and what he had made; never thought that what he parted with might endure beyond even the memory of him.

What is time? Time is what you do with something. What is a place? A place is something you cannot scrub off your soul, something you cannot get rid of. Somewhere in the womb of time lies my father, my real father, the place where I began. I wonder in how many bloodstreams my blood was mixed and mingled, I wonder what part of my ancient father survives, physically, in me as a chip of time and place? Some portions of my body are from time before time. Microscopic science works every day with portions of things smaller than the part of me that was my first, my original father. Not many generations are needed to take us back to before time was.

But how unimportant the names appear when we are alive and see them only on a stone, or a chart; a branch from nothingness related by a line toward another name which culminates in the history of the world: ourselves.

THE LITTLE gravel road is shaded as I turn through another pair of gates marked Cedar Hill. I follow around the narrow drive and pass the landmarks one by one until I reach an even narrower lane.

And going down between the graves whose names and dates are sad reminders of inevitability, I come to the place. Standing alone, with the winter wind unceasing in its pull and toss, I look down on two mounds of red West Texas dirt, side by side, where the grass has not covered either memory or sorrow. And I know how my journey ends.

Afterword

THIRTY YEARS have passed since those months when I sat writing *A Personal Country*. I completed the manuscript one stormy night in April, 1968, while I was a Fellow at Frank Dobie's Paisano Ranch west of Austin. It was a doubly momentous night. Our four children were asleep in the two rear bedrooms of the rustic little farm house Dobie had used as his country retreat. Betty, my wife, was folding laundry in the large front bedroom we shared. (When you have four kids, you do laundry every day.)

I walked in, threw the manuscript on our bed, and, as casually as I could manage, announced, "There it is . . . finished." Then, like Leigh Hunt's Jenny, "jumping from the chair she sat in," Betty kissed me. It was a kiss of affection, of course—we had been married for eighteen years—but it was more than affection and love. It was a salute, it was a sword-tap on the shoulder that knighted me into the nobility of the pen: I was an author.

I said it was doubly momentous, that night. As I had walked from the little tack room I used as a scriptorium back to the house, I heard the soft but terrible whisper of a large caliber bullet passing over my head. But not even this could intrude on my euphoria, and I didn't mention it to Betty until we had had two glasses of congratulatory wine on the stone-paved front veranda of the house. I called the local game warden and told him the sound put me in mind of a 30-ought-six, and he agreed.

"But it wasn't anybody shootin' at you," he consoled me. "It was some ol' boy jack-lighting deer. I could probably go to the Circle Inn right now and put my hand on his shoulder. They'll deny it, but I'll warn 'em that if there's any more of it, I'm comin' after all of 'em." He paused and chuckled. "Your first book was damn near your last one, wasn't it?"

A Personal Country had been three years in the making. It was started, you might say, by accident. As Book Editor of *The Dallas Times-Herald* I had written a Sunday column about what I perceived as inevitable changes coming in Texas literature. The late Frank Dobie (I wrote) had been one of the worst things to happen to Texas writing, not because Dobie was a bad writer, but because his infectious style was so strong that an entire generation of Texas writers had tried to follow his lead and failed. It was something like the way Ernest Hemingway's style had done to writers in general.

The next day, at work, a man came up to see me at the *Times-Herald* office and told me he had been Dobie's editor at Little, Brown Publishers. His name was Angus Cameron and he was now with Alfred A. Knopf. He said he happened to be in Dallas and had read my column. I expected something of a blast from Editor Cameron, but instead he was both understanding and complimentary. We talked about Texas and Texas letters—he had visited Dobie at Paisano and had been editor for other Texas writers, including Tom Lea. He asked me if I had a book he might look at, but I said that unlike most newspapermen, I had no secret manuscript ready for his gaze. In that case, Angus told me, I should write one.

"How about a book on West Texas?" he asked. "A sort of guide book?" I replied, with uncertain enthusiasm, I would certainly like to try. I set to work writing about my home country, but mixing in too much ethereal philosophy. I wasn't sure how or where I was taking the whole thing, but I sent Angus about 10,000 words. Fortunately, Angus was the kind of editor who saw his job as helping the writer do his best rather than trying to assign the writer the editor's thoughts. He was patient, remarking now and then on changes he thought might help me say what I wanted to say.

Then, at the request of Maurice Carlson, who was putting together the first issue of the *Arlington Quarterly* at the University of Texas at Arlington, I submitted an essay on West Texas attitudes and mores called, "God and Man in West Texas." I mailed a carbon (ah, those old days!) to Angus and his answer came quickly: "This is exactly what I want. If you can do a book continuing this approach, this voice, I'll buy it!" With that impetus, it was not hard for me to pound my thirty-year-old Underwood into a writing machine rather than a mere typewriter. I took 35,000 manuscript words to Angus in New York, and in due course received half of the modest advance due from Knopf. (It is ironic that of those 35,000 words, fewer than 10,000 appeared in *A Personal Country* when it was published. I am happy to say, the excisions were mine, not at the demand of Angus.)

Writing the book, I had many adventures involving everything from ghosts to floods to skinning rattlesnakes with a native flint knife. I wrote the book in numerous locations: at my little garage office at my home on Stefani Drive in Dallas; then, when that house burned, I was given the shelter of a former maid's quarters by the late Frances Sanger Mossiker. In early summer of 1967, I took out the rear seats of my Volkswagen van, stuck in a typing table, the Underwood, a folding lawn chair, and an ice chest and toured West Texas, spending most of my time on the back roads and among the lost villages along the highways of my youth. The ghosts were encountered near the forgotten town of

Eolian, south of Breckenridge. The flood hit me one midnight when I was camping on the ranch of Marshall Jackson, at Tuscola. It was the worst lightning, rain and wind storm I ever encountered. My van began rocking dangerously, but this woke me in time for me to spot Marshall, looking for me in his pickup, to lead me out of the deepening waters to safer ground. Next morning, which was bright and cheery, I found exposed by the thunderstorm, the beautiful flint knife I later used to skin the rattlesnakes.

A Personal Country was my title, coming to me after praying over a couple of dozen others. At first Angus mused that everybody has a personal country, and I said, exactly, that's why I like it. He agreed, and wrote the dramatic jacket copy for the first edition. Artist Ancel Nunn did the illustrations and also painted the scene on the jacket of that first edition. The painting is of a lost school building in a sea of grass at Maryneal, a community south of Sweetwater. Knopf flopped the picture (reversed it) to fit the jacket. The original painting was owned by a retired banker at Plano who a few years later, refused a handsome offer for it.

A Personal Country was published in September, 1969 . My first copy arrived when my family and I were living at San Cristobal, a beautiful layout several miles west of Austin. I found the book in my Route 6 mailbox, and had parked the van up off the road to look over my treasure. A deputy sheriff, thinking I was a hippie (because of the Volkswagen van) pulled off the highway, came over to my where I was parked and asked, rather belligerently, "What do you think you're doin' here?"

"I'm reading this book," I said, displaying my shiny new treasure. "I wrote it."

Knowing that hippies were notorious writers of books, he wasn't persuaded. "You better move on. These people may not like you parkin' on their property."

I pointed to my house in the distance—a noticeable structure with three big stone arches—and stated (with quiet satisfaction), "That's my house," then to exact a bit more satisfaction, pointed and said, "And, incidentally, that's my mailbox."

In the years that have passed since *A Personal Country* appeared, I have written many other books of many kinds. I have even done the words for a set of operatic arias. But nothing will compare with my attachment, my "fatherhood," of that first book. As is often true of first books, I poured all my feelings and stories into it; consequently I have produced three other books, the germs of which are contained in *A Personal Country*. And, I trust, I am not through yet.

My own life has gone through significant changes in those same thirty years. Betty died a decade ago and I married Judy Dalton Hyland, a friend I met when she was visiting Betty after the house fire of 1967. I have undergone serious medical problems and drastic solutions—including a heart transplant and prolonged radiology. When Judy and I moved to Bell County in 1992 I discovered I was kin to a whole raft of interesting people who had lived or were living there—including my great-great-grandmother, Revenny Sutton Craighead, a fabled beauty who died six decades before I was born. Also, a few years back, I had Betty's body moved, with Bob and my son Eliot accompanying it, to the lovely family cemetery on Bob and Nancy Green's Shackelford County ranch. Judy and I will be buried there also, unless some unforeseen fate intervenes.

As for West Texas, yes, there have been many changes. Many military installations are closed, but the West Texas skies still throb with jets. The many little railroads are gone—no more Abilene & Southern, no more Roscoe, Snyder & Pacific—and the main roads have changed their names—no more Texas & Pacific, no more Santa Fe or Katy—but the long freight drags still cross West Texas up and down, east and west. The universities no longer play major league football, but have grown steadily and well. The oil business has fluctuated up and down, but the pump-jack is still the economic symbol for huge areas of the region. The cattle business has undergone great changes, too, but the cowboy on his horse, the rancher watching the skies for rain or freeze, the farmer who has gone from cotton to feed grains—they remain, and despite the television bowl in the side yard and the round-bale hay baler in the shed, they see life pretty much as their fathers and grandfathers did.

But mostly the years have not changed the people of West Texas. The heart is still good and first meetings tend to form instant friendships. You can still get help or advice from almost anyone when you are lost or in trouble. The "idea" of West Texas remains very much as it was, not just when this book was written, but as it has been since its beginning. And the vastness of the place, the overwhelming landscape, still has not been scraped and paved over. The sky is still there, high, like a blue tent covering the land. The horizons remain distant and magnetic.

And I have great hopes that *A Personal Country*, having been readable for thirty years, will remain so for at least thirty years more.

A. C. Greene
Salado, Texas

Index

ABOUT THE AUTHOR

A. C. Greene was born in 1923 in Abilene, Texas, and after service in WWII he graduated from Abilene Christian College. He served on the staff of the *Abilene Reporter-News*, ran his own bookstore and headed the journalism department at Hardin-Simmons University. He joined the Dallas *Times-Herald*, serving as book editor and editorial page editor before being awarded a Dobie-Paisano fellowship during which he wrote *A Personal Country*. He currently writes a column for *The Dallas Morning News* and has written more than 22 books to date.